Approaches and Implementation of Asian and European Official Development Assistance (ODA)

Similarities, specificities and convergences

Vincent ROLLET (ed.)

OUVRAGES PARUS DANS LA MÊME COLLECTION :

17. *Visions de l'Empire du Milieu au 18e siècle en France. Illustrations des Mémoires concernant les Chinois, 1776-1791*

16. *Transferts artistiques. Entre Orient et Occident du 17e au 21e siècle*

15. *Altérité rencontrée, perçue, représentée. Entre Orient et Occident du 18e au 21e siècle*

14. *La traduction entre Orient et Occident. Modalités, difficultés et enjeux*

13. *Entre Mer de Chine et Europe. Migration des savoirs, transfert des connaissances, transmission des sagesses du 17e au 21e siècle*

12. *Christianisme et Orient (17e-21e siècles)*

11. *Mondialisation et identité. Les débats autour de l'occidentalisation et de l'orientalisation, 19e-21e siècles*

10. *Entre puissance et coopération. Les relations diplomatiques Orient-Occident du 17e au 20e siècle*

9. *De l'Orient à l'Occident et retour. Perceptions et représentations de l'Autre dans la littérature et les guides de voyage*

8. *Images de la Chine à travers la presse francophone européenne de l'Entre-deux-guerres*

7. *La diplomatie belge et l'Extrême-Orient. Trois études de cas (1930-1970)*

6. *Passeurs de religions : entre Orient et Occident*

5. *Droits humains et valeurs asiatiques. Un dialogue possible ?*

4. *Perception et organisation de l'espace urbain. Une confrontation Orient-Occident*

3. *The Korean War : A eurasian perspective*

2. *Individu et communauté. Une confrontation Orient-Occident*

1. *La mort et l'au-delà. Une rencontre de l'Orient et de l'Occident*

RENCONTRES ORIENT-OCCIDENT

18

Approaches and Implementation of Asian and European Official Development Assistance (ODA)

Similarities, specificities and convergences

Vincent ROLLET (ed.)

Louvain-la-Neuve 2016

academia
L'Harmattan

Acknowledgments

This book benefitted from the support of the National Research Fund in Belgium (FNRS), the Faculty of Arts of the Catholic University of Louvain (UCL), the Ministry of Science and Technology in Taiwan (MOST) as well as of the Asian Educational Scientific & Culture Organization (AESCO).

It would not have been possible without the trust and full support of Emeritus Prof. Paul Servais (UCL), the participation of the contributors to the workshop entitled "Approaches and Implementation of Asian and European Official Development Assistance (ODA): Similarities, Specificities and Convergences" organized on February 6th, 2015 in Louvain-la-Neuve, as well as the assistance of M. Eric Lee who carefully proofread the whole text, and Mrs. Françoise Mirguet, who read over all the contributions and facilitated the layout of this volume. We thank all of them for their time and constructive contribution.

D/2016/4910/37 ISBN 978-2-8061-0295-9

Grand-Place 29

B- 1348 Louvain-la-Neuve

www.editions-academia.be

Contributors

Thierry AMOUGOU, Professor, Catholic University of Louvain, Belgium

Jean-Christophe DEFRAIGNE, Professor, Institute for European Studies, University of Saint-Louis, Brussels, Belgium

Mollie GLEIBERMAN, Professor, University of Antwerp, Belgium

Pooja JAIN-GREGOIRE, Research fellow, Cambridge University, the United Kingdom

Axel MARX, Deputy Director, Leuven Centre for Global Governance Studies, University of Leuven, Belgium

Nadia MOLENAERS, Professor, University of Antwerp, Belgium

Vincent ROLLET, Assistant Professor, Wenzao Ursuline University, and associated researcher, French Center for Research on Contemporary China (CEFC), Taiwan

Jadir SOARES, Research fellow, Leuven Centre for Global Governance Studies, University of Leuven, Belgium

Anna Katharina STAHL, Research fellow, EU-China Research Centre, College of Europe, Bruges, Belgium

Yumiko YAMAMOTO, Research fellow, Center for International Studies and Research (CERI), Sciences Po Paris, France

Content

Part 2.

Euro-Asian cooperation in ODA: achievements and challenges

Introduction

Vincent ROLLET

Official Development Assistance (ODA) materialized in the form of technical and financial assistance in various fields represents since the end of the World War II an essential component of the international involvement of governments and local collectivities toward development. "Bilateral" when assistance is directly provided to another country and "multilateral" when such assistance goes through international/global institutions, ODA had to adapt to the profound changes of what is also known as the "market of international aid".

Among these transformations, there is certainly the proliferation of aid actors. Indeed, since more than a decade, one observes the multiplication of providers of international assistance which have different profiles ("emerging countries", International Non-Governmental Organizations (INGO), multinational corporations, foundations, etc.) as well as specific priorities and modalities of intervention. Simultaneously, the multiplication of domains of assistance is also another specificity of the recent evolution of international aid. Thus, health, agriculture, education, environment, renewable energy, transportation as well as new technologies represent nowadays some of the numerous fields towards which ODA is flocking in a more or less coordinated way and in a sometimes competitive context.

Lastly, this last decade, international aid has been also characterized by the development of an international framework of reference for political and operational activities whose main objective is to improve the effectiveness of international assistance. Among the international agreements that define the normative framework of development aid one finds the MDGs (2000-2015), the Paris Declaration of Aid effectiveness (2005), the Accra Agenda for Action (2008), the Busan Partnership for Effective Development Cooperation (2011) and, since September 2015, the Sustainable Development Goals (SDGs).

While the above trends have questioned the role and limits of governmental agencies towards international aid, the influence of civil society and international non-governmental in aid policy-making and implementation, as well as the whole efficiency of the actual international aid regime, they have also invited the traditional providers of ODA to reconsider their role, their partnership and the nature of their assistance in a redesigned and rather complex international aid governance. Among these donors, European and Asian countries occupy an important place, notably because, the European Union and its 28 Member States represent the world's largest aid donor as they provide more than half of the ODA worldwide (EUR 52,8 billion in 2014, i.e. up 2,4% from 2013) (EU Delegation to the United Nations, 2015) and simultaneously, because the total volume of development cooperation from Asian providers (China, India, Japan, South Korea, Taiwan, Thailand, Indonesia) has progressively increasing confirming then the strong interest of Asia to support the global effort of poverty alleviation and to participate to the global aid governance (The Asia Foundation, 2014).

However, given the central position occupied by the European Union in the field of aid development and the increasing importance of Asian aid providers, three main questions deserve to have our attention: on the one hand, can we observe similarities between Asian and European ODA notably in terms of motivations, policy, budget, governance, nature and implementation? Simultaneously, to what extend Asian and European ODA are different and how to explain such specificities? Finally, based on such understanding, are there any possibilities of collaboration between Asian and European aid providers and, if it is the case, what might be the added value of such cooperation?

To provide and to debate answers to these main questions have motivated several Asian and European scholars to participate to an international workshop entitled "Approaches and Implementation of Asian and European Official Development Assistance (ODA): Similarities, Specificities and Convergences" organized on February 6th, 2015 in Louvain-la-Neuve. This book is the fruit of this unique academic exchange.

The first part of this volume, which is dedicated to the principles and markers of Asian and European ODA, starts with a fertile reflection proposed by Nadia Molenaers and Mollie Gleiberman on similarities and differences between donors as well as on aid evolution and effectiveness. N. Molenaers and M. Gleiberman notably emphasize how it is important to go beyond the recurrent dichotomies such as traditional/non-traditional donors or the DAC donors/ non-DAC donors[1] oppositions notably because the first distinction

[1] Development Assistance Committee (DAC) – donors sit inside the Economic Cooperation and Developments (OECD) and have pledged to implement recommendations adopted by OECD-DAC since its inception. Today, there are 29 DAC donors including 19 from the EU, the European Union and 2 from Asia (Japan and Korea).

opposes very heterogeneous groups while the second categorization contrasts groups of donors which are certainly different but – as the authors explained – "have a lot more in common than would be expected". In other terms, N. Molenaers and M. Gleiberman invite us not to oversimplify or to overstate differences between European and Asian donors. A bias that all contributors of this volume have been extremely careful to avoid. In this context, the authors recommend to study the origin of different aid approaches, notably the factors that drive the development of certain aid objectives and modalities and then suggest an analytical framework for such research agenda.

This reflection on aid comparison is then followed by three well-documented and innovative contributions about the development assistance policy and implementation of three specific Asian countries, namely Japan, South Korea and Taiwan.

In her study on Japan's aid development in Western Africa, Yumiko Yamamoto dresses a systematic study revealing particularities and motivations of Japanese aid policy in a region considered as "serious" aid partner since 1989. In her assessment of Japan's ODA management in West Africa – in terms of ODA amount, organizational system, type of aid, delivery system and destination – she identifies specificities of Japan's aid implementation as well as similarities and important differences with other donors in the region. When it comes to Japan's aid motivation, Y. Yamamoto argues that – as it is the case for other donors Japan's development assistance in Western Africa is driven by political and economic/commercial dynamics. Indeed, Y. Yamamoto argues that through its aid to Western Africa, Japan actually seeks, on the one hand, to increase the number of its allies in the region supporting its request for a seat at UN Security Council. On the other hand, since the 1990s and the continuing political instability in the Middle East, to have an access to natural resources in some Western African countries known as Nigeria (oil), Ghana (minerals) and Senegal (aquaculture).

Next comes an analysis of Taiwan's aid development policy and implementation by Vincent Rollet. The author proposes to appreciate its evolution in view of Taiwan's domestic politics, notably since 2008 and the election of President Ma Ying-jeou (re-elected in 2012) who has promised to make the foreign aid mechanism more professional and more effective. Then, taking into account such evolution and the particular status of Taiwan within the international community, V. Rollet focuses on the main specificities of Taiwanese development assistance, examines its main challenges and proposes a comparison with European donors. Interestingly, while one of the most notable specificities of Taiwan's ODA is certainly its strong dependence on Taiwan-China relations and the good will of Beijing, the study also reveals how Taiwan shares numerous similarities with several European donors.

In the last chapter of the first part of this book, Jean-Christophe Defraigne proposes to answer the following question: "Is European aid so different?" To this end, he presents a long-term comparison of European, Japanese and Chinese aid programmes. Echoing precedent contributors, J.C Defraigne argues that while there is a great heterogeneity of aid policy between various EU Members States, the behavior of the largest European donors is not fundamentally different from China or Japan. Thus, while European and Asian donors have their own rhetoric and ideological framework to legitimize their aid policies, ODA from European and Asian donors are increasingly linked to business interests and often benefit directly to their national firms. Furthermore, if European and Asian donors impose political conditionality to recipient countries – even if the nature of these latter are not the same –, they are also lenient to corruption and authoritarian practices in recipient countries when it suits them. Finally, J.C. Defraigne claims that ODA from Europe, Japan and China share another common similarity of not being designed to strengthen the development capacities of recipient countries.

The second part of the book is dedicated to a phenomenon that has been less studied by scholars so far, namely the interaction between European and Asian donors and the potentials for Euro-Asian cooperation in ODA.

Thus, in her contribution, Anna Katharina Stahl explores the opportunities and challenges for the cooperation between the EU and China in the field of development in Africa. Thus, after appreciating the China's growing role as a donor in Africa and then the EU's development cooperation with China, A.K. Stahl shows how the EU's development cooperation has actually evolved in response to China's growing role as a (re)emerging donor in Africa and simultaneously how Brussels played an important role to integrate China into international development frameworks. Nevertheless, she argues that while there were initial positive signs in the context of post-2015 development agenda negotiations, the establishment of a new EU-China development cooperation in Africa still faces numerous challenges.

Continuing the theme of Asian-European aid cooperation, Pooja Jain-Grégoire focuses then on EU-India development partnership in Africa, notably by examining its potential in Senegal. In order to appreciate whether there are incentives for the EU and India to cooperate, P. Jain-Grégoire explores first the motivations to cooperate that exist between India and Senegal where she conducted fieldwork in 2010, 2011 and 2012. These motivations behind the Indo-Senegalese cooperation notably include the mutual support of each other's rights within the international community as well as common development challenges. This is within the framework of such south-south cooperation, that P. Jain-Grégoire explores the impediments and possibilities for the EU and India to cooperate with African countries.

For the last case study of this second part on Asia-Europe partnership in the domain of development, Axel Marx and Jadir Soares assess the opportunities of collaboration between Korea and the European Union. After analyzing Korean development cooperation policies and comparing them with other donors, most notably the European Union, the authors argue that there are several opportunities for EU and South Korea collaboration. Indeed, according to A. Marx and J. Soares, trilateral cooperation could be promoted when South Korea and the EU are both assisting the same county in similar sectors such as agriculture or education. However, they also identify possible obstacles for cooperation. Thus, cooperation seems much more difficult in a domain such as human rights where the EU and South Korea – although both human rights defenders – do not share the same approach regarding the promotion of such rights through ODA.

Finally, in the concluding chapter of this book, Thierry Amougou underlines that confronted to a similar international conjuncture effect, Asian and European ODA remain different in many aspects but also share similarities which lead to convergences and potential cooperation as several authors have argued in this book. However, stressing that ODA is too often appreciated for its role as geopolitical, political or economic instrument, T. Amougou also reminds us the importance to think about the very purpose of ODA, its tangible impact in terms of development and its support for a truly sustainable development.

If covering all the issues related to approaches and implementation of Asian and European ODA in a single volume amounts to squaring a circle, this collective book has to be considered rather as the result of a rare attempt to invite experts on Asian and European development aid to share their point of views on such topic and as an opportunity for these scholars to meet and to think about further collective research which might be beneficial to the future evolution of Asian and European ODA and for development itself notably in the context of the 2030 Agenda for Sustainable Development Goals (SDGs).

Bibliography

EU DELEGATION TO THE UNITED NATIONS. (2015) *The EU remains the world's largest aid donor in 2014*, 8 April. <http://eu-un.europa.eu/articles/en/article_16293_en.htm>.

THE ASIA FOUNDATION (2014) *The Changing Aid Landscape in East Asia: The Rise of Non-DAC Providers*. May, Washington, 66 p.

Part 1.

Principles and markers of European and Asian ODA

The end of aid as we know it?

Reflections on the conceptualization of aid effectiveness

Nadia MOLENAERS & Mollie GLEIBERMAN

Introduction

For a long time now, the OECD/DAC has occupied a monopoly position with regards to setting out the aid effectiveness landmarks and goals. Particularly the last decades, in line with the 'governance turn of aid' (Knack, 2003), the DAC ideal of aid effectiveness did become increasingly normative and highly ambitious in terms of *what* aid should achieve and *how* it should be delivered. In terms of its level of ambitions/goals, aid has moved from micro to macro, from projects to policies, and from beneficiaries to citizens (Cornwall and Gaventa, 2000). This move thus put good governance as both a condition and an objective of aid (Santiso, 2001), with donors aspiring to bring a highly normative end-goal to these countries, namely the post-card version of Denmark (Fukuyama, 2010). The DAC is also quite ambitious in *how* it wants to do this. The Paris Declaration (2005) had set out a number of important aid delivery principles, such as harmonization and alignment, which ideally allow for maximum recipient country ownership. The aid modality that best fits these principles is general budget support while tied aid, projects and donor driven adversarial conditionalities were to be avoided (Koeberle et al., 2006).

On the opposite side of the spectrum are the rising economies and middle income countries like the BRICs whose approach to development assistance takes place outside or beyond the DAC-norms. Good governance is mostly not of concern for these donors as they preach non-interference norms in recipient domestic affairs. In terms of aid delivery, they prefer the use of projects, often with tied aid. Combined, this has led to some scholars labelling these new players as unambitious in their aid endeavors, driven by self-interest, and posing a threat to the (fragile) achievements of DAC donors and the international stability in the aid architecture.

Put bluntly, DAC donors have been found guilty of being too ambitious and too pushy, while the Non-DAC donors have been accused for not being ambitious enough in terms of bringing structural changes to lesser developed countries[1].

These documented differences between DAC and non-DAC however tend to neglect that there are also quite some similarities between these donors, and these form the entry point of this paper in order to rethink the conceptualization and practices regarding aid effectiveness.

The main contribution of this paper is that drawing on the different approaches of DAC and non-DAC donors, we come up with a reconceptualization of aid effectiveness. 'Reaching Denmark', we argue, is just one and very particular (normative) aid goal which (in theory) brings together different dimensions namely a high level of ambition and the use of specific aid modalities (policy, program support). If we allow for some variation on these dimensions (high ambitions, modest ambitions – project modalities, policy/program support), and if we introduce the idea of dynamic evolutions and changes over time, the concept of aid effectiveness can escape the rigid and overtly ambitious Denmark connotations and it can become broader and more diversified. We furthermore argue that this variety of aid effectiveness conceptualizations is also more appropriate since contexts matters. Fragile states need a different approach than middle-income countries. But context, we propose, is not just about recipient characteristics. It is also about donor characteristics and donor-landscapes in a given country. Context must thus be seen as a multidimensional set of factors which drive aid choices (both goals and modalities).

Finally, rather than juxtaposing donors in how different their approaches to aid are, we propose that a more interesting research venue lies in understanding how these different approaches come about. Looking into the drivers of aid choices is an understudied field of research, for both DAC and non-DAC donors. In terms of effectiveness, rather than expecting all interventions to contribute to 'Denmark', it is more valuable to discern impact at a more disaggregated level, adapted to the goal and the level of intervention.

---

[1] It is possible to reflect upon aid effectiveness in terms of how effective it is in satisfying donor-interests, or in massaging, soothing international relations. In this paper however we mostly stick to the idea of thinking about aid in terms of promoting or supporting structural change in less developed countries.

1. DAC versus non-DAC: Diverging norms, converging practices?

1.1. Non-DAC norms versus DAC norms: the differences

Lumping diverse donors together as "non-traditional" or "non- DAC" is unfortunate because of course these are very heterogeneous groups. We argue nonetheless that the term DAC donor (DD) and *non-DAC donor* (NDD) are the most accurate starting point forms for our discussion, since they capture the relevant common denominator of the countries to which they refers. It is important to stress that the label NDDs does not imply a shared identity, but merely reflects donor positioning vis-à-vis DAC-norms, which are consensus-based values, frameworks and standards (Manning, 2006; Kim & Lightfoot, 2011) to which DAC donors commit (in theory at least). Walz & Ramachandran (2011) show that the NDDs actually can be organized in three different groups in terms of how they position themselves vis-a-vis these DAC norms. A first group of NDDs pattern their development cooperation after DAC norms, and, in many instances, aim to join the DAC[2]. Second, the Arab model, comprising a multiplicity of long-established institutions and actors. And third, a Southern model of NDDs that have coalesced around a re-emergent third-worldist perspective emphasizing Southern[3] solidarity.

Particularly the latter group purposefully seek to distance themselves from DAC donors by asserting Southern solidarity (Rowlands, 2008), making this group interesting for our endeavor. The *motivation* for Southern donors' development cooperation is rooted in the Bandung Conference of 1955, which brought together Asian and African leaders and resulted in the adoption of *Five Principles for Peaceful Co-existence*: mutual respect for sovereignty and territorial integrity, mutual non-interference in the domestic affairs of another country, mutual non-aggression, promotion of mutual benefit and co-operation, and peaceful co-existence (de Bruyn, 2013). The principles of non-interference and mutual benefit are especially important, and form the cornerstone of contemporary Southern development initiatives (Mawdsley, 2012); these are also the main source of friction with the DAC regarding the potential destabilizing effect of NDDs on aid architecture. South-South Cooperation (SSC) has emerged as the

---

2 Indeed, it is notable that many donors that fell into this category when Walz and Ramachandran proposed it (2011) have since become full-fledged members of the dac: South Korea joined in 2010, and the Czech Republic, Iceland, Poland, Slovak Republic, and Slovenia joined in 2013. (Source: OECD dac members, retrieved from <http://www.oecd.org/dac/dacmembers.htm> on 23 March 2015).

3 As used here, "Southern" refers not to geographical regions but as a metaphorical space affiliated with the third-worldism of the NAM and G77.

emblematic modality of Southern-led development, though a precise definition remains elusive and the term is often used to denote any type of exchange between two or more Southern countries.

Discursively, the Southern donors' emphasis on mutual assistance is reflected in a rejection of the DAC-idea of altruistic aid; rather, the focus is on cooperation (Mawdsley, 2011). Southern donors eschew the donor/recipient hierarchy, instead stressing partnerships and horizontal relationships (Rowlands, 2008; Walz and Ramachandran, 2011). Historically, SSC has been synonymous with the term Technical Cooperation among Developing Countries (TCDC), and Brazil, especially, retains TCDC's emphasis on technology transfer and knowledge-sharing as the rhetorical basis for development cooperation (Vaz and Inoue, 2007). Mutual assistance also implies that benefits flow to both partners, with China being particularly adamant about stressing the win-win quality of its development cooperation (Brautigam, 2009; Dehart, 2012; Herman, 2010; Mawdsley, 2010; Rowlands, 2008).

One very important DAC norm refers to the *definition of ODA*: it should carry a grant proportion as opposed to just concessional loans. The ODA definition also excludes commercial activity. ODA flows are also annually reported to the DAC. NDD flows contrast this as they often include a high amount of concessional loans and encompass commercial activity such as tied exports and investments (Kragelund, 2008). The lack of transparency and absence of shared monitoring and evaluation standards among many NDDs prevents the donor community from knowing the full extent of their activities and aid flows (Rowlands, 2008).

Another DAC norm refers to the reduction or *elimination of tied aid* and this is a deeply-held tenet of the DAC, which seeks to downplay benefits that donors may receive from participating in development activities (Brautigam, 2009). The prominent position of tied aid for Southern NDDs – generally under the banner of mutual assistance – violates this DAC principle.

The DAC has also been a keen follower of *aid effectiveness insights.* In the late 1990s and early 2000s, recognition of the *failure of many projects* (Dollar & Pritchett, 1998) and prompted the recommendation to shift away from project aid, focused on building *things,* and to move to program aid, focused on *building institutions* (Duffield, 2002; Killick, 2004; Kragelund, 2008). Not only was there a strong concern with regards to 'white elephant' projects, but more importantly, it was considered that projects are less apt to produce sustainable results at the aggregated level. Thus working on an improved policy environment, including an enabling environment for state building, civil society and markets, became the tenets for aid in the new millennium. But this implies a long term, predictable and sustained commitment and the use of aid modalities which do not undermine institutions. By contrast, Southern donors have typically taken a more *ad hoc* project approach, responding to recipient requests or specific goals of domestic firms (Chandy, 2011; Quadir, 2013). Chinese cooperation, especially, is seen as a undermining long-term stability and potentially re-introducing "white elephants" by promoting unsustainable investments in infrastructure and sectors such as mining and energy (Brautigam, 2009; Manning, 2006). Such actions may also create a race to exploit natural resources, turning LDCs into "the battleground in wars of scarcity for oil, gas, minerals and timber" (Ladd, 2010:6).

The aid effectiveness debate also heavily promoted the idea of *harmonization to decrease transaction costs*. The sheer increase in the number of donors acting in a recipient country is perceived as potentially increasing donor fragmentation and thereby leading to higher transaction costs. In the 2000s, DAC donors deliberately shifted from project to program aid as part of the effort to harmonize donor activity, which in turn was understood to combat donor fragmentation and reduce transaction costs (Killick, 2004). An influx of new donors may destabilize these efforts by requiring both donors and recipients to take on greater administrative burdens – whether as a result of efforts to coordinate and share information, or from donor competition and fragmentation (Dreher et al., 2013; Knack & Rahman, 2007; Kragelund, 2008).

Another tension between DAC and non-DAC relates to the *non-conditional nature* of Southern development cooperation, which stems from the principles of non-intervention and respect for sovereignty. While DAC donors and the major multilateral institutions have pulled back from the type of macroeconomic conditionalities prominent in the 1980s and 1990s (e.g. structural adjustment), new types of conditionalities (ex-post, results-oriented and negotiated), expressed in terms of good governance and accountability, have taken their place (Koeberle et al., 2005; Manning, 2006; Mawdsley, 2010; Woods, 2008; Walz and Ramachandran, 2011). Southern donors stress that their development cooperation has "no strings attached" which could offer recipient governments a way to circumvent DAC accountability and governance mechanisms (Dreher et al., 2013; Kragelund, 2011; Manning, 2006; Woods, 2008; Zimmerman and Smith, 2011).

Today, the DAC is still perceived as representing the state-of-the-art in development thinking. This development thinking has moved into high ambitions in terms of goals ("Denmark") and high expectations in terms of aid delivery principles (away from projects and into long term program/budget support). These highly ambitious DAC-norms are contrasted with more 'pragmatic' discourses and expectations of NDDs: no Denmark-like aspirations, ad hoc projects, non-interference. From this perspective the Southern donors are often seen as potentially destabilizing the fragile achievements of DAC donors, which include advances in reducing poverty, consensus-based norms for transparency and reporting standards, and, especially, gains in governance and institution-building (Manning, 2006). The most extreme version of this concern posits donors like Saudi Arabia, Venezuela and China as offering "rogue aid" that is "motivated by desire to further their own national interests, advance an ideological agenda, or sometimes line their own pockets" (Naìm, 2007:95).

1.2. Similarities between DAC and non-DAC donors

In spite of the huge differences described in the section above, we argue here that DAC and non-DAC practices have a lot more in common than would be expected.

In terms of *aid motivations*, a longstanding aid allocation research tradition has shown that DAC-donors are heavily driven by geopolitical agendas and economic self-interest (Brautigam, 2009; da Silva, 2008; Kragelund, 2011; Quadir, 2013; Six, 2009). There is thus a huge gap between discourse and practice. But NDDs too display this contradiction. Rowlands (2008) notes that NDD development assistance shows "the same sort of hierarchical roles and mixed motivations that characterize traditional donor-recipient relationships" (Rowlands, 2008: 6). Development assistance in general is better understood as a negotiation "embedded in, and to some extent constituted by, global political and economic circuits" (Whitfield and Fraser, 2009:34; Martens, 2005). This brings us to our first point of similarities: both DAC donors and NDDs are engaged in such negotiations, and aid always carries an element of donor-interest (Berthelemy, 2006). In terms of rethinking aid effectiveness, the real role donor interests may play must be taken into account because they will influence the level of ambition of a donor, but also how aid will be delivered. And more importantly, if the overarching rationale of aid is to massage and sooth (a certain set of) international relations (for trade, security or other interests), rather than boosting recipient domestic development processes, the question arises if aid can still be considered effective if it contributes more to the former goal than to the latter.

In terms of ODA and ODA reporting, the DAC's *definition of ODA may be outdated* in separating the humanitarian and commercial sectors because most donors recognize and agree that trade and investments are important drivers of economic growth. As such donors have been advocating for more financing for development since the 2002 Monterrey Consensus (Atwood, 2011; Chandy, 2011; Chin and Quadir, 2012). This is also visible once we start looking at how well DAC donors meet other DAC norms such as tied aid. Variations in the amount of tied aid are also prevalent among DAC donors. Whereas Norway, Australia and the UK have 0% tied aid, Greece has 61.29% *tied/partially tied aid*, the US has 44.68% tied/partially tied[4]. Thus, adherence to DAC norms is highly variable within member states. Brautigam (2009) writes that "[f]or many years, the US Agency for International Development's website boasted that US foreign assistance generated over $10 billion in exports of US goods and services, supporting about 200,000 jobs" (Brautigam, 2009:152). In terms of rethinking aid effectiveness, this reiterates the point made above that donor-interests matter in terms of what donors want to achieve and how the aid will be delivered.

Also with regards to practicing the policy recommendations which surfaced in the aid effectiveness debate, DAC donors vary strongly in their commitments. The shift away from projects actually never happened. In reality projects have remained the aid modality through which most aid volumes are disbursed. DAC donors have used budget support to some extent but even the most progressive donor has never fully turned to this aid modality (Faust et al., 2012) because of the fiduciary, political and accountability risks the instrument carries (Koeberle et al., 2006). These risks are of course larger in weak gover-nance contexts. In terms of effectiveness, Budget support has proved to be particularly effective in supporting public finance management reforms, but a crucial success factor resided in the political leadership (willingness, commitment) of the recipient country to start and continue a reform. Budget Support however is unable to buy such willingness and less even if the reforms reques-ted are political in nature. The DAC focus on program aid and budget support has also had some perverse effects; it led to overcrowding in social sectors, such as health and education, leaving a deficit of support for other sectors and infrastructure; it has also led to an increase in political conditionalities (Molenaers et al., 2014).

Killick (2004) argues that the switch to programs does not necessarily lead to lower transaction costs or greater harmonization, while Kragelund (2012) shows that program aid, such as budget support, frequently results in more donor control, not less. Thus the focus on programs comes with its own problems, while leaving a gap in financing for other types of development, such as infrastructure. Dreher et al. (2013) point out that the NDD projects fill these gaps. Kragelund recognizes that "no one can eat a stadium" (Kragelund, 2012:712) but goes on to remind us that infrastructure acts a source of legitimacy for institutions; projects, then, have a complementary role alongside programs. Finally, the concern about NDD inexperience as donors with scattered

---

[4] Source: <http://www.cgdev.org/initiative/commitment-development-index/index> and Commitment to Development Index 2013.

development systems overlooks NDDs' experience as *recipients*, in which they gained important insights about what does and does not work in given contexts (Dreher et al., 2013).

Harmonization efforts have also been limited in practice, plus the questionable desirability of such harmonization for recipients has been acknowledged. Chun et al. write that attempts to harmonize donor practices in a program in Guatemala did not streamline donor activity, but led instead to "strong competition among over 15 donor agencies for visibility and leadership in the donor harmonization process" (Chun et al., 2010:798). In other cases, donor harmonization has been perceived as donors 'ganging up' against the recipient government (Hazlewood, 1991:140). Killick (2004) describes efforts to harmonize donor activities in Uganda as leading to *increased* transaction costs due to the difficulty of coordination. On the other hand, looking at donor fragmentation from a recipient's perspective, Sato et al. (2011) find that the Cambodian government welcomes an increased number of donors despite the lack of harmonization, since more donors means more choices.

The use of *new-style conditionalities* (ex post, consensual, results-oriented) has also been problematic. Mounting evidence shows that conditionalities do not achieve their aim (Killick, 2004; Svensson, 2003), nor does it take into account the increased administrative costs associated with burdensome conditions. Rather than reducing or streamlining conditionalities, these new style conditionalities in combination with harmonization efforts have often intensified donor involvement in governance, potentially undermining recipients' ownership and capacity (Fraser and Whitfield, 2009; Killick, 2004; Kragelund, 2012) and increasing administrative burdens (Knack and Rahman, 2007).

At the same time, the policy advice and prescriptions for economic growth and democratic governance dispensed by DAC donors and institutions are increasingly questioned. Nancy Birdsall (2004) highlights the amnesia-fueled donor impatience regarding the length of time it takes a country to meet certain benchmarks[5], and many donors offer policy advice that excludes (or even prohibits) the methods used historically by Northern countries to amass wealth (Whitfield and Fraser, 2009). The rapid growth of East Asian economies that eschewed Washington Consensus policies has further deepened the tendency to "look East" for alternative models of growth (Amanor, 2013; Önis, 1991). The emergence of developmental states, with impressive growth spurs but poor

[5] She shows that despite being considered off-track for meeting the MDG in school enrollment, Burkina Faso is performing at a rate comparable to the US when the latter embarked on a similar undertaking.

track records in terms of democracy and human rights also question the Denmark model and delegitimize the many governance conditions imposed by traditional donors. Finally, the Financial Crisis of 2007-09 has seriously undermined the soundness of Northern prescriptions for economic growth (Chin and Quadir, 2012). The legitimacy crisis provoked by these issues formed the backdrop for the OECD's 4th High Level Forum on Aid Effectiveness in 2011, which promoted a *development effectiveness* agenda as an antidote to the shortcomings of the aid effectiveness paradigm (Esteves and Assunção, 2014; Eyben and Savage, 2012; Kim and Lee, 2013; Mawdsley et al., 2014).

The practices of NDD also diverge. In practice, the development cooperation of powerhouses like Brazil, India and China bears little similarity to SSC efforts between smaller, low income countries, e.g. SSC between Bhutan and Benin (PSC, 2005). Thus the Southern donors' affirmation of mutual assistance is laced with considerable asymmetry – particularly concerning development cooperation with LDCs (Ladd, 2010). Mutual assistance often translates into what the DAC refers to as tied aid; for benefits to flow in both directions, the Southern donors interpret trade and investment opportunities as types of mutual assistance (Walz and Ramachandran, 2011). Decoupling development from altruistic aid or charity enables Southern donors to blend state and private sector motives, and to position FDI and commercial activities as appropriate development modalities (Brautigam, 2009; Carmody, 2011; Chandy, 2011; Kragelund, 2008). Though such relationships may be asymmetrical, this does not preclude mutual benefits. China, Brazil and India see the African continent as an opportunity, and, unlike DAC donors, they tend to invest in much-desired "turn-key" projects and infrastructure (Brautigam, 2009; Chin and Quadir, 2012; Kragelund, 2008, 2012; Sato et al., 2011).

2. Mapping a diversified approach to aid effectiveness

The norms and practices discussed above allow us to distinguish a number of dimensions when thinking about aid effectiveness (see table 1 below). We have seen that donors differ in their perspectives on *what aid should do* (goals, level of ambitions) and *how it should be delivered* (intervention).

The DAC goal is closely related to the Denmark ideal and thus reflects a set of values and norms which could be labelled as Western and democratic. As such aid flows are assessed to the extent to which they contribute to this Denmark end-goal. Aid flows are expected to have an impact on policies and institutions, and this in turn should impact aggregate level indicators such as democratic governance, economic progress, investment, productivity, employment, etc… According to the DAC norms, these goals are best realized through long-term commitments and flexible aid using programme modalities, policy support, and instruments like General Budget Support.

The other extreme, we have seen, does not propel governance ambitions, but rather sticks to more delineated, pragmatic, short term goals. Such goals do not relate directly to policy change or reform but they aim, at best, to ensure (continuity of) service provision and/or gradually improving implementation /services at local or sector level.

In reality however the lines between both extremes are not always clear-cut. As such some caution should be taken not to oversimplify or overstate their differences. Some projects for example, even if *ad hoc* and short term may very well exceed any given programme in terms of size (i.e. large infrastructure projects) and impact. Some policy support or budget support operations are absolutely not long-term and they may carry project-like characteristics such as ring-fencing and having separate financial and administrative procedures[6].

Table 1: Aid effectiveness = level of ambition x level of intervention

High ambition	Focused institutional change limited policy change Increase investment, productivity, employment	Broad governance reforms 'Getting to Denmark'
Modest ambition	Delivering resources/services to beneficiaries/ non-governmental actors/ local government	Support (implementation) (sector) plans, Overcoming a crisis (economic, financial, political)
	Intervention project	**Intervention programme (SWAPs, SBS), policy based support (GBS, results based grants)**

[6] For example when the government of a country is not able to pay the salaries of the civil servants (including policy and army), donors may step in and pick up that bill for a limited time period. This may prevent both political and economic instability.

If we set out both dimensions in a two by two table, in theory, four different readings or interpretations of aid effectiveness surface where ambitions and levels of intervention meet. Since "Getting to Denmark" as proposed by the DAC envisages broad governance reforms in the political and economic sphere, this is probably the highest level of ambition one can imagine. One can also imagine that such ambitions cannot be realized through ring-fenced, stand-alone projects. Aid to reforms tends to require interventions at a higher level such as General Budget Support, or results-based grants as a form of ex-post conditionality. Projects however are a good modality to deliver services and resources to well specified groups of actors, and hence reach more modest ambitions which not necessarily touch upon policy or institutional issues.

Between both extremes however there are two other, more intermediate levels of aid effectiveness which are important to discern because they do manifest themselves in reality. In reality many donors have used program approaches and even budget support to goals that are a lot more modest than 'Denmark'. Sector wide approaches (SWAPs) have been used to gradually and slowly improve a specific sector strategy, general budget support has been used in a more 'ad hoc' manner to prevent the public sector from collapsing (also referred to as crisis budget support) (Chauvet and Collier, 2004). Results-based grants have been linked to all or nothing disbursement schemes which are tied in with specific indicators, giving this aid a more ad hoc character. In other words, not all 'higher level modalities' actually aim for the kind of deep reforms or larger policy shifts to which they in theory are often linked. In that same vein, project impact has not always remained limited to 'localized results', but as mentioned earlier are at times able to realize high level ambitions if these interventions are tied in with policy learning, or take the form of experiments to inform/change policies (e.g. Esther Dufloo's work on RCTs). Some larger infrastructure projects like dams have also enabled trade in energy and an increase in productivity. China's preference for large infrastructure projects which may (or may not) impact aggregate level indicators (employment, growth), also in part reflects their own development model. As such, societal models implicitly or explicitly form part of the aid choice algorithm in terms of picking goals and picking modalities.

The fact that modest ambitions however may have large impacts points at the importance of the time dimension and the need to think about aid effectiveness in dynamic ways since modest ambition may evolve into high ambitions, and vice versa, and aid modalities may evolve from projects into higher level modalities, depending on the context, evolutions and windows of opportunity that present themselves. This points at the importance of context, which matters greatly for aid effectiveness. The dollar report (Dollar & Levine, 1998) already stipulated that impact on the aggregate level needs an enabling environment. In other words, high ambition goals require a minimal level of recipient government commitment/leadership/willingness to pursue the set out objectives. Modest ambition goals however are intrinsically defined in more short term timeframes and with less demanding concerns with regards to recipient commitment and sustainability of the effects of the intervention.

3. Mapping the context factors that drive the preferences for certain aid goals and aid modalities

If the variety of aid goals and aid modalities is in reality already a fact, and if our reconceptualization of aid effectiveness (table 1) is actually nothing more than a more sophisticated visualization of 'what is already out there', then we need to look beyond old versus new donors, or DAC versus non-DAC. The relevant and interesting research question then becomes: What drives the variety of approaches to aid? Which elements drive the implicit or explicit preference for high or modest ambitions? And which factors drive preferences for certain aid modality choices?

We distinguish three groups of context factors which push certain preferences. First there is the recipient side, second the donor side and third, the composition of the donor landscape in a given recipient country (see table 2).

With regards to recipient characteristics levels of ownership and capacity have been put forward as crucial for the long term sustainability of development processes and thus for high ambition aid effectiveness. Less explicit attention has been given to the government capacity to deal with – what has been referred to in the EU literature as – veto-players (Börzel, 2003; Tsebelis, 1995). Capacity has been mostly captured as the technical know-how or expertise of a recipient government and much less with regards to the political capacity required from the ruling elites to deal with/outsmart/buy off resistance to reform (Khan, 2002). A very important element of course is the level of aid dependence of the recipient. This may influence the level of leverage donors have and thus they may adapt their aid goals and modalities accordingly. Geo-strategic importance of a country may also influence donor decisions with regards to aid goals and modalities. International security concerns, but also presence of natural resources may overshadow the aid agenda and lead donors to opt for aid goals and modalities which are suboptimal in terms of achieving development goals in the recipient country.

Table 2: Factors shaping donor decisions on aid goals and aid modalities

Recipient characteristics	Donor characteristics	Donor landscape
Ownership, willingness to reform/poverty reduction /development	*Size/weight / leverage*	*Number of donors, composition landscape*
Capacity to plan, implement, adapt and deal with veto-players	*Capacity/autonomy / institutional setting*	*Variety aid approaches/modalities*
Aid dependence *Geo-strategic value*	*Capacity to manage accountability pressures/veto-players*	*Relations: coordination, cooperation, division of labour, competition, conflict*
The art/history of preference alignment Political cost/benefit calculation of players		

Donor characteristics matter too. The size, the weight and the leverage of a given donor may be important elements which influence the preference for certain aid goals and certain aid modalities. The size relates to absolute aid volumes, but just as important is the relative weight a donor has (historical ties with recipient for example). Both together give some idea with regards to leverage a donor has in a given recipient country. Ideas about leverage do influence the levels of ambition a donor has (Del Biondo, 2011). Just to give an example: a relatively small donor like Belgium may have a relatively high weight in DRC due to the colonial ties, giving it a lot more leverage in policy dialogues with the government of DRC than would be expected when looking at absolute aid volumes alone. Belgium, in spite of its relative weight and high ambitions in DRC, has been mainly implementing projects, while avoiding higher level modalities. In order to understand this, it is important to look at a donor's capacity, autonomy and institutional setting (Molenaers et al., 2015). Capacity refers to expertise in the agency. Some agencies can draw on specific fields of expertise which make them more inclined to certain aid goals and modalities. Belgium for example has a strong project expertise, and particularly in the health sector. Other donors have specialized in water in sanitation, or gender… Autonomy refers to the space for autonomous decision making.

Integration in a ministry of foreign affairs or trade will impact the preferences and choices with regards to aid goals and modalities. The wider institutional setting, like implementing agencies or subcontractors tied in with the aid agency will also influence the aid choices regarding goals and modalities. The capacity to manage other stakeholders, like parliament, NGOs, enterprises, which may all (want to) have a stake in the aid business may lobby and pressure for certain choices. There too the capacity of the aid agency to manage these pressures and veto-players matter. The latter also implies that democratic donors tend to have less leeway for making autonomous decisions than donors where democratic accountability structures are weak or non-existent. A less democratic donor like China has a lot more freedom and policy space to take aid decisions without being 'bothered' by overtly critical parliamentarians and activist NGOs.

Thirdly, the donor landscape will also influence donor decisions regarding aid goals and modalities. The number of donors and the composition (number of multilaterals, presence of BRICs, presence of like-minded or not-likeminded bilaterals) influence important donor concerns like donor-visibility and leverage calculations. The aid approaches present in a given country context may also influence donor decisions on aid goals and instruments. Whether or not to use budget support for example may be dependent on whether or not the World Bank uses it. In the same vein if many donors use budget support, yet another donor using it may become invisible. In such a context, the use of projects may yield more visibility and more interaction possibilities with government. Or division of donors over sectors, regions, etc. may also influence how and where a donor deploys its aid envelope.

In conclusion, the large number of factors which may influence donor choices in terms of which goal aid should pursue, and how aid should be delivered, and the fact that this is a largely understudied domain, allows scholars to avoid a DAC versus non-DAC categorization of research, and instead forging links to undertake comparative research on the drivers of aid.

Concluding thoughts: back to the future?

If in theory and in practice, by and large four different approaches to aid effectiveness exist, this underscores the importance of aid effectiveness research at the disaggregated level. For too long now researchers have been trying to discern whether or not aid has impacted development/democracy or not. The scholarly debate is still not settled and rather than thinking that most of the debates can be traced back to methodological disputes, the truth of the matter is that aid is far too heterogeneous (in flows, in goals, in players, in modalities) to actually really be able to have a clear-cut one-directional impact (Denmark). Particularly now certain donors are supporting end-goals that may look more like China or South Korea rather than Denmark, there is a need to look into these flows, deconstruct them and assess them in relation to the envisaged goal rather than assuming all interventions aim for Denmark.

Added to this, an interesting research agenda unfolds itself when scholars, rather than emphasizing aid approach differences between (groups of) donors, would study how these different aid approaches come about and which factors drive the deployment of certain aid goals and modalities. For this we have presented a framework of contextual factors that matter for this aid decision.

Bibliography

AMANOR, K. (2013) South-South Cooperation in Africa: Historical, Geopolitical and Political Economy Dimensions of International Development. *IDS Bulletin*, 44.4.

ATWOOD, J. B. (2011) The Road to Busan from Aid to Global Development Cooperation, The 2011 Brookings Blum Roundtable Policy Briefs, Brookings, pp. 21-27.

BIRDSALL, N. (2004) Seven Deadly Sins: Reflections on Donor Failings. Center for Global Development, Working Paper No. 50, December.

BÖRZEL, T. (2003) *Shaping and Taking EU Policies: Member State Responses to Europeanization* (No. p0035). Queens University Belfast.

BRAUTIGAM, D. A. (2009) *The Dragon's Gift: The Real Story of China in Africa.* Oxford: Oxford University Press.

CARMODY, P. (2011) India and the 'Asian Drivers' in Africa. In E. MAWDSLEY & G. McCANN (eds), *India in Africa*, Oxford: Pambazuka Press, pp. 30-47.

CHANDY, L. (2011) Reframing Development Cooperation From Aid to Global Development Cooperation (The 2011 Brookings Blum Roundtable Policy Briefs), Brookings, pp. 4-12.

CHAUVET, L. and COLLIER, P. (2004) *Development effectiveness in fragile states: spillovers and turnarounds.* Centre for the Study of African Economies, Department of Economics, Oxford University.

CHIN, G. and QUADIR, F. (2012) Rising States: Rising Donors and the New Aid Regime. *Cambridge Review of International Affairs*, 25(4): 493-506.

CHUN, H.-M., MUNYI, E. N. and LEE, H. (2010) South Korea as an Emerging Donor: Challenges and Changes on its Entering OECD/DAC. *Journal of International Development*, 22, 788-802.

CORNWALL, A. and GAVENTA, J. (2000) From Users and Choosers to Makers and Shapers Repositioning Participation in Social Policy1. *IDS Bulletin*, 31(4): 50-62.

DA SILVA, K. (2008) Aid as Gift: An Initial Approach. *Mana*, 4(1): 141-171.

DE BRUYN, T. (2013) Adding New Spices to Development Cooperation: Brazil, India China and South Africa in Health, Agriculture and Food Security HIVA Working Paper. Leuven: HIVA KU Leuven.

DEHART, M. (2012) Remodeling the Global Development Landscape: the China Model and South-South cooperation in Latin America. *Third World Quarterly*, 33(7), 1359-1375.

DEL BIONDO, K. (2011) EU aid conditionality in ACP countries: Explaining inconsistency in EU sanctions practice. *Journal of Contemporary European Research*, 7(3): 380-395.

DOLLAR, D. and PRITCHETT, L. (1998) *Rethinking the Money and Ideas of Aid Assessing Aid: What Works, What Doesn't, and Why*. New York: Oxford University Press for World Bank, pp. 1-27.

DREHER, A., FUCHS, A. and NUNNENKAMP, P. (2013) New Donors. *International Interactions*, 39(3): 402-415.

DUFFIELD, M. (2002) Social Reconstruction and the Radicalization of Development: Aid as a Relation of Global Liberal Governance. *Development & Change*, 33(5): 1049-1071.

ESTEVES, P. and ASSUNÇÃO, M. (2014) South-South cooperation and the International Development Battlefield: Between the OECD and the UN. *Third World Quarterly*, 35(10): 1775-1790.

EYBEN, R. and SAVAGE, L. (2012) Emerging and Submerging Powers: Imagined Geographies in the New Development Partnership at the Busan Fourth High Level Forum. *Journal of Development Studies*, 49(4): 457-469.

FRASER, A. and WHITFIELD, L. (2009) Understanding Contemporary Aid Relationships. In L. WHITFIELD (ed.), *The Politics of Aid: African Strategies for Dealing with Donors*. Oxford: Oxford University Press.

HAZLEWOOD, A. (1991) Foreign Aid and Economic Development in Kenya. In U. LELE and I. NABI (eds), *Transitions in Development: The Role of Aid and Commercial Flows*. San Francisco: International Center for Economic Growth, pp. 125-150.

HERMAN, H. (2010) South-South Relations: Sino-African Engagement and Cooperation. *Poverty in Focus*, vol. 20: 7-9.

KHAN, M. H. (2002) State failure in developing countries and strategies of institutional reform. In ABCDE Conference Europe, June, Oslo.

KILLICK, T. (2004) Politics, Evidence and the New Aid Agenda. *Development Policy Review*, 22(1): 5-29.

KIM, E. M. and LEE, J. E. (2013) Busan and Beyond: South Korea and the Transition from Aid Effectiveness to Development Effectiveness. *Journal of International Development*, 25: 787-801.

KIM, S. and LIGHTFOOT, S. (2011) Does 'DAC-Ability' Really Matter? The emergence of non-DAC Donors: Introduction to Policy Arena. *Journal of International Development*, 23(5): 711.

KNACK, S. and RAHMAN, A. (2007) Donor Fragmentation and Bureaucratic Quality in Aid Recipients. *Journal of Development Economics*, 83: 176-197.

KOEBERLE, S., BEDOYA, H., SILARSZKY, P. and VERHEYEN, G. (eds) (2005) *Conditionality Revisited: Concepts, Experiences, and Lessons Learned.* Washington DC: World Bank.

KRAGELUND, P. (2012) The Revival of Non-Traditional State Actors' Interests in Africa: Does it Matter for Policy Autonomy? *Development Policy Review,* 30(6): 703-718.

KRAGELUND, P. (2011) Back to BASICS? The Rejuvenation of Non-traditional Donors' Development Cooperation with Africa. *Development and Change,* 42(2): 585-607.

KRAGELUND, P. (2008) The Return of Non-DAC Donors to Africa: New Prospects for African Development? *Development Policy Review,* 26(5): 555-584.

LADD, P. (2010) Between a Rock and a Hard Place: LDCs in a G-20 World *Poverty In Focus 20: South-South Cooperation – The Same Old Game or New Paradigm?*, International Policy Centre for Inclusive Growth, vol. 20.

MANNING, R. (2006) Will 'Emerging Donors' Change the Face of International Cooperation? *Development Policy Review,* 24(4): 371-385.

MARTENS, B. (2005) Why Do Aid Agencies Exist? *Development Policy Review,* 23(6): 643-663.

MAWDSLEY, E. (2012) *From Recipients to Donors: Emerging Powers and the Changing Development Landscape.* London: Zed.

MAWDSLEY, E. (2011) The Changing Geographies of Foreign Aid and Development Cooperation: Contributions from Gift Theory. *Transactions of the Institute of British Geographers*, NS 37: 256-272.

MAWDSLEY, E. (2010) Non-DAC donors and the changing landscape of foreign aid: the (in)significance of India's development cooperation with Kenya. *Journal of Eastern African Studies,* 4(2): 361-379.

MAWDSLEY, E., SAVAGE, L. and KIM, S.-M. (2014) A 'post-aid world'? Paradigm shift in foreign aid and development cooperation at the 2011 Busan High Level Forum. *The Geographical Journal,* 180(1): 27-38.

MOLENAERS, N., DELLEPIANE, S. and FAUST, J. (2015) Political Conditionality and Foreign Aid. *World Development*, November, vol. 75: 2-12.

NAÍM, M. (2007) Rogue Aid. *Foreign Policy,* March/April, (159): 95-96.

ÖNIS, Z. (1991) The Logic of the Developmental State. *Comparative Politics,* October, pp. 109-126.

PSC (2005) Regulations: Programme for South-South Cooperation on Sustainable Development between Benin, Bhutan and Costa Rica.

QUADIR, F. (2013) Rising Donors and the New Narrative of 'South-South' Cooperation: what prospects for changing the landscape of development assistance paradigms? *Third World Quarterly*, 34(2): 321-338.

ROWLANDS, D. (2008) *Emerging Donors in International Development Assistance: A Synthesis Report*: IDRC, Partnership & Business Development Division.

SANTISO, C. (2001) International Co-operation for Democracy and Good Governance: Moving Towards a Second Generation? *The European Journal of Development Research*, 13(1): 154-180.

SATO, J., SHIGA, H., KOBAYASHI, T. and KONDOH, H. (2011) 'Emerging Donors' From a Recipient Perspective: An Institutional Analysis of Foreign Aid in Cambodia. *World Development*, 39(12): 2091-2104.

SIX, C. (2009) The Rise of Postcolonial States as Donors: A Challenge to the Development Paradigm. *Third World Quarterly*, 30(6): 1103-1121.

SVENSSON, J. (2003) Why Conditional Aid Does Not Work and What Can Be Done About It? *Journal of Development Economics*, 70(2003): 381-402.

TSEBELIS, G. (1995) Decision making in political systems: Veto players in presidentialism, parliamentarism, multicameralism and multipartyism. *British journal of political science*, 25(03): 289-325.

VAZ, A. C. and INOUE, C. Y. A. (2007) *Emerging Donors in International Development Assistance: The Brazil Case*. IDRC Partnership & Business Development Division.

WALZ, J. and RAMACHANDRAN, V. (2011) *Brave New World: A Literature Review of Emerging Donors and the Changing Nature of Foreign Assistance*. Working Paper 273, November, Centre for Global Development.

WHITFIELD, L. and FRASER, A. (2009) Negotiating Aid. In L. WHITFIELD (ed.), *The Politics of Aid: African Strategies for Dealing with Donors*. Oxford: Oxford University Press, pp. 27-44.

WOODS, N. (2008) Whose Aid? Whose Influence? China, Emerging Donors and the Silent Revolution in Development Assistance. *International Affairs*, 84(6): 1205-1221.

ZIMMERMANN, F. and SMITH, K. (2011) More Actors, More Money, More Ideas for International Development Co-operation. *Journal of International Development*, 23(5): 722.

Japan's Development Aid to West Africa in the context of Globalization[1]

Yumiko YAMAMOTO

Introduction

A member of Development Aid Committee (DAC) since 1961 and of OECD since 1964, Japan began to provide the Official Development Aid (ODA) in 1954 as war reparation to Asian countries[2] (Brooks, 1985; Imamura, 2004). Since then, the major part of Japan's ODA was for a long time directing to Asia, and still nowadays, this tendency is strongly observed in Japan's aid distribution pattern, representing more than 50% of its total. Although two Japanese Foreign ministers conducted an official visit to Africa in the 1970's (in 1974 and 1979), until Japan starts to consider Africa as its "serious" aid partner, it took still 10 years after those visits. Japan's ODA to Africa started to increase around 1989 when Japan accessed to the top contributor in ODA amount among DAC countries.

Being promoted by the Tokyo International Conference on African Development (TICAD), Japan's ODA to Africa has been progressively increased and Africa became today its second important destination (Lehman, 2007). In 2007, for example, more than one third of Japan's aid was extended to African continent[3]. Until 2009 where South Korea adhered to DAC, Japan was the only non-western player of DAC officially recognized in international arena. How much

[1] This article is a developed version of the study conducted by the author between 2008 and 2011 as doctoral dissertation "Aide internationale au-delà des questions techniques : les politiques d'aide au développement à destination de l'Afrique de l'Ouest de la Chine, de l'Inde et du Japon (1997-2010)" at Sciences Po Paris and defended on 30 January 2012.

[2] An example of large scale project is the construction of high way Maharlika in Philippines in 1969 (USD 30 millions of ODA) (Takahashi, 1990).

[3] 38% of the total aid (OECD, 2007).

does Japan provide its aid to West Africa, a diverse and predominantly francophone region composed of 16 countries (Côte d'Ivoire, Benin, Burkina Faso, Guinea, Mali, Mauritania, Niger, Senegal, Gambia, Ghana, Togo, Sierra Leone, Nigeria, Liberia, Cape Verde, Guinea-Bissau)? What are their tools (aid modalities and management) and on which countries does Japan focus and why?

Based on quantitative data analysis and qualitative method of a semi-directed interview technique, this study investigates Japan's aid practice in West Africa, in particular on its six aspects (aid statistics, management, delivery system, diplomatic relations with West Africa, aid destination and motivation).

This article synthesizes, in the first section, the results of literature revues on Japan's ODA to West Africa before investigating how Japan's ODA to West Africa functions, giving a particular attention to the characteristics of aid statistics, organization system and aid management (second section). In the third section, the study examines the major drivers of Japan's aid diplomacy in West Africa (bilateral relations with West Africa, aid destination and motivation), in order to assess on what motivates Japan to aid West Africa. Lastly, at conclusion, the study includes observations on Japan's ODA to West Africa in comparison to China and India's aid.

1. Four domains of study on Japan's ODA but not concerning West Africa

In this study, we exploited the following data: First, the three groups of sources discussing on Japan's ODA (scholarly literature[4], publications of governmental agencies and of companies of Japan, of West Africa, of China and of India and interviews conducted in these countries). Precisely, we consulted 300 scholarly literatures and 48 publications of governmental agencies. We have taken 86 interviews with 73 actors (18 in China, 9 in Japan, 25 in India, 21 in Germany) of whom 34 high-ranked officials in governmental agencies, 5 industrials and 34 researchers. We conducted a field work of two months both in China and India between 2008 and 2009[5] and three fieldworks of two months in Japan between 2008 and 2010. In addition, we devoted two visiting research fellowships financed by DAAD in Germany for this study in 2008 and in 2009

[4] 85% of the literatures consulted in this study were in Japanese language and the rest was in French and English.

[5] In China, affiliation to the Department of Humanities and Development of China Agricultural University (Beijing) and in India, to the Centre for African studies of Jawaharlal-Nehru University (Delhi).

(Berlin and Bonn)[6] and for this reason, a part of our interviews was taken in Germany. Also, the observations of the author, made at Embassy of Japan in Senegal as Counsellor in charge of research on Japan's bilateral ODA to Senegal, Mali, Gambia and Guinea-Bissau for three years (2005-2008) contributed to set up the principal interrogations of Japan's ODA to West Africa.

Among the consulted scholarly literatures, we identified 60 studies discussing on Japan' ODA and those relate to one of the four following domains: (1) the role of Japan's ODA actors, (2) Japan's ODA as policy, (3) Japan's ODA in comparison with other ODA and (4) the related debate on Japan's ODA. First, Japan's ODA actors' role discusses on the institutions participating to Japanese ODA project management. Some studies are, for example, those of Igarashi (1990) and of Ohashi (2005) that treat the role of consultants cabinet in Japan's ODA, while the study of Gôtô (2005) analyses the weak presence of non-governmental organizations (NGO) in Japan's ODA and that of Igarashi (1990) on private companies.

Second, the study on Japan's ODA as policy examines how ODA functions and explains, for example, different types of Japanese aid. Among them, there are studies of Nishigaki (1999) and Watanabe (1991). The study of Matsui (1983), Nishigaki (1993) and Sumi (1990) discuss particularities of Japan's Grant aid including "project loan" and "non-project loan"[7]. Arase (1995), Fukushima (2000) and Matsui (1983) look at Japan's aid policy in historical perspective. Beside those studies, we note that some studies suggest a reform on Japan's ODA (Rix, 1993; Kohama, 1998; Sato and al., 2004; Bobrow and al., 1996; T. Yamamoto, 1978). Among those, contrary to what we usually consider, Bobrow and Boyer show that what Japan's aid is not only following what other donors do and Japan has certain originalities in its aid. But on the other hand, they criticize Japan's position of engaging in bilateral and multilateral aid but very reluctant in aiding through regional organizations.

As for the comparative study of Japan's ODA, besides of Orr (1993) and of Kato (2002), the study of Arase (2005) is very interesting, although the study is more than 10 years old. Indeed, it describes how Japan's ODA is different from others. Thus, compared to British ODA, the study points out that Japan has very little experience in working with developing countries, therefore it is lack-

---

[6] In Germany, affiliation to the German Institute for International and Security Affairs (Berlin) and to the German Development Institute (Bonn).

[7] "Project Loan" is designed to a specific project in Infrastructure, while "Non-project Loan" does not require being a specific project and can finance any project which could improve macroeconomic condition of the beneficiary country (Nishigaki, 1999:163-195).

ing the expertise in development issues, familiarities to local needs and capacities to understand cultures of developing countries. Compared to Swedish ODA which initiated the International standard of philosophy and practice of humanitarian aid, the study of Arase regrets that Japan has taken a great delay in introducing such principal in its ODA. Moreover, compared to Australia, financing projects of small dimension, Japan tends to finance large scale of projects and finance rarely sector-project which covers different projects within one domain (for example, an aid to education sector). Lastly, as for (4) the related debate on Japan's ODA, we would refer to the study of Tuman (2006), of Lancaster (2010) and of Yanagihara (1991) which discuss on the influence of public opinion and of external pressure to Japan's decision making within its ODA.

Those studies mentioned above discuss on Japan's ODA in general and do not observe it within a particular region of the world. There are some studies on Japan's aid to Africa published in recent years but one of the most recent one is the study of Suzuki (1989). The latter enumerates the characteristics of Japan's ODA to Sub-Saharan Africa (SSA) and underlines the lack of identifiable African policy in Japan's aid. Suzuki underlines three reasons for Japan to be attracted by SSA.

First, SSA possesses a significant number of UN member states that corresponds to one third of total. Secondly, SSA has a growing economic potential. Third, SSA could become the best trade partner for Japan and also possesses rich natural resources which are essential for Japan's economic growth. The study continues that, because of poverty, conflicts and repeated food crisis, a leading world economic power like Japan is expected to support Africa's economic growth. Some of his arguments are still relevant, but the study itself dates more than 20 years ago and since then, the situation surrounding Japan's ODA and one the ground in West Africa has seen a number of transformations. Among these transformations, one important transformation observed in the last decade is the increasing presence of emerging economies – in particular China and India – in African and without taking into account of such transformations, we would not be able to discuss on ODA in West Africa of 21st century. Moreover, Suzuki examines Africa as a whole, but as an analysis of Japan's ODA to West Africa, his study is insufficient. In addition, the study ignored examining institutional system, project management, aid statistics, destination and relations with beneficiary countries and focused only on the motivations of Japan in Africa.

In contrast with the number of studies on Japan's ODA in general and few to Africa, we identified that there is a lack of study on Japan's ODA to West Africa. This study thus attempts to dress the first systematic study, revealing the particularities of Japan's ODA policy in West Africa.

2. Japan's ODA management in West Africa

Although for historical reasons, Japanese ODA's major destination was Asia, how much does Japan extend its aid to West African countries today? Which organizations manage the Japanese aid to West Africa and how the aid is delivered to destination in practice?

2.1. Today's ODA figures: annual average of USD 428 million

In Japan's ODA, loan aid shares an important part (60% of total) (Table 1). But, this loan takes concessional form, thus its rate is lower and the reimbursement duration is longer than that of the market. In 2006, for example, average rate of the extended Japan's loan aid was 1.01% with maturity period of 34.2 years. Compared to other DAC members, Japan's ODA has been dominated by such loan aid: in 1995, the loan represented 28.4% in Japan's ODA, while it was 10.5% for USA, 6.4% for France, 5.6% for Germany and 12.2% for Italy. In 2002, Japan registered even higher proportion of Loan aid, 35% of total Japan's ODA (Arase, 2005).

Table 1. Budget of Japan's bilateral Aid by form (2007)

	USD Billion	Proportion in Total Bilateral Aid (%)
Grant	1.86	14.9%
Technical Cooperation	2.9	23%
Loan	7.8	62.1%

Source: MOFA, 2008

Contrary to this general tendency of Japan's ODA that shares the high proportion in loan aid, West Africa is an exceptional destination. Indeed, since most of aid beneficiary countries in West Africa are least developed countries, grant aid is the principal form used by Japan. For example, in 2007, Cape-Verde and Sierra Leone were the only countries of West Africa having received Japan's loan aid (Table 2).

Among Japanese ODA's four core domains in West Africa (water and health, infrastructure, education, food aid), in the domain of water and health, Japan has implemented an important number of projects against contagious diseases and malaria in Côte d'Ivoire, Burkina Faso, Guinea, Liberia, Nigeria, Sierra Leone, Mali, Ghana. In the domain of infrastructure, Japan financed construction projects of harbors and roads in Mali, Sierra Leone and Ghana. In the field of education, Japan built schools in Mali, Nigeria and Mauritania. And, Guinea-Bissau, Cape-Verde, Burkina Faso, Liberia, Mali, Mauritania, Nigeria, Ghana and Sierra Leone have benefited Japan's food aid.

Table 2. Japan's ODA projects in West Africa (2007)

Countries	Loan aid total (USD million)	Grant aid total (USD million)	Technical Cooperation (USD million)	Total aid in 2007 (USD million)
Benin	0	17.34	5.96	23.3
Burkina Faso	0	8.28	7.64	15.92
Cape-Verde	44.68	5.36	0.39	50.43
Côte d'Ivoire	0	2.18	0.53	2.71
Ghana	0	34.43	20.16	54,59
Gambia	0	0.1	0.57	0.67
Guinea	0	21.72	1.93	2.65
Guinea-Bissau	0	2.52	0.11	2.63
Liberia	0	6.8	0.37	7.17
Mali	0	26.36	1.78	28.14
Mauritania	0	12.59	2.66	15.25
Niger	0	5.09	11.02	16.11
Nigeria	0	29.94	3.04	32.98
Senegal	0	8.2	13.61	21.81
Sierra Leone	38.69	12.06	3.97	54.72
Togo	0	0	0.2	0.2

Source: Yamamoto (2015)

Concerning the scale of Japan's ODA projects, as it is observable in other regions of the world, most of them financed in West Africa in 2007 were "individual projects", not sector projects. Benin and Ghana were the only countries having received sector projects in West Africa.

To West Africa, in 2006, Japan provided in total USD 1.92 billion[8]. This amount includes USD 2.27 billion of grant aid, USD 73 million of technical cooperation and USD 428 million of debt. However, the year 2006 was an exception for Japan's ODA to West Africa, since Japan offered more than its habitual aid

[8] OECD statistics, <www.stats.oecd.org>.

amount due to the debt cancellation concluded with Nigeria. The average annual volume of Japan's ODA to this region was rather USD 444.32 million between 2000 and 2007[9].

In the year 2007, for example, the countries which received the most important amount of Japan's ODA in West Africa were Ghana (USD 54.59 million), Nigeria (USD 32.98 million), Mali (USD 28.14 million) and Senegal (USD 21.81 million) (Table 2).

2.2. Organizational system: "top-down", led by three core ministries

The management of Japan's ODA is often considered as very particular due to its complexity and diversity of actors. Japan's ODA to West Africa is not an exception. The decision making is top-down, exclusively centralized in Tokyo and, in total, 13 governmental administrations participate in the management of Japanese aid. Among them, Ministry of Foreign Affairs (MOFA), Ministry of Finances (MOF) and Ministry of Economy, Trade and Industry (METI) are the core policy makers, and the project implementation is directed by Japan International Cooperation Agency (JICA). Each of those central administrations has its own mission and vision for Japan's ODA and such situation creates conflict of interests among players and generates difficulties in terms of coordination (Ensign, 1992). Besides these 4 administrations, 9 other governmental administrations (Ministry of Environment, Ministry of Education, Ministry of Transport, Ministry of Justice, Ministry of Public affairs, Ministry of Internal affairs, National agency of Police, Ministry of Health, Work and Social Affairs, Ministry of Agriculture, Forest and Fishing) are minor actors of Japan's ODA, intervening only in technical cooperation (Beaudry-Somcynsky, 1999).

The grant aid and technical cooperation are administrated by MOFA's Economic Cooperation Service and JICA. MOFA is responsible for planning and global management of the grant aid, while JICA is in charge of arranging and dispatching experts (engineers, technicians, trainers, JOCV, consultants of infrastructure etc.). Loan aid is traditionally directed by a consensus of MOFA, MOF and METI and was managed by JBIC until 2008 when the responsibility was extended to JICA (JBIC, 2006a, 2006b). Contrary to the power given to these three main actors of Japan's ODA, Japanese Parliament is absent in the decision making in this domain. Its role is very limited and the Parliament is simply the place where the budget for a new project is requested. However, most of the time, projects have already been elaborated by bureaucrats based on the financial needs of each acting administration. Moreover, the role of Prime Minister towards Ja-

[9] Net payment: OECD statistics, <www.stats.oecd.org>.

pan's ODA to West Africa is rarely influential since West Africa has never received a particular attention of Japan's diplomacy.

The visions and objectives of three main actors of Japan's ODA are very different. MOFA sees Japan's ODA in the context of Japan's Foreign Policy and does never consider it separately from bilateral relation with aid beneficiary country. Therefore, for MOFA, ODA has to be used as a tool to enhance bilateral relation with recipient country. Also, MOFA considers the importance of respecting quality and quantity of its aid according to the DAC's objectives in order to improve Japan's image in international arena. While METI searches to promote international trade through ODA, MOF aims to control transparent tax utilization in Japan's ODA and often prefers to provide loans rather than grant aid (Figure 1).

Figure 1. Organizational system of loan aid

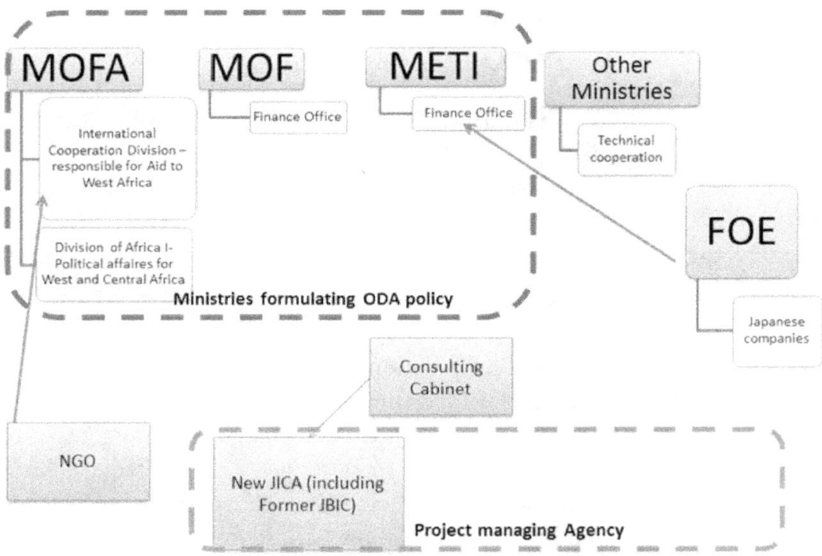

Source: Yamamoto (2015)

Besides these governmental agencies, Sōgō Shōsha (Japanese trading companies dealing a large variation of products and services) plays a key role in Japan's ODA to West Africa. They are in a better position to identify needs of West African governments and to formulate together with them an ODA proposal. The strength of such Japanese companies is to possess an office (even with only one staff sent from Japan) in West Africa, which allows them to be physically present and to search potential projects. Preparing an ODA project proposal allows them to include their competences and integrate their role within the project proposal. By doing this, they succeed in increasing their business chances, because when they obtain a call for tenders, they could become the principal supplier of the project (Katō, 2002).

Among such Sōgō Shōsha actively present in Senegal, the principal ones are Mitsubishi, Sumitomo Chemical, Kanematsu and Toda Construction Corporation. Their recent achievements include primary school construction in Mali and harbor construction in Guinea by Kanematsu and the rehabilitation of two maternity hospitals in the suburb of Dakar in 2008 by Mitsubishi[10].

Consulting agencies are often asked to intervene by JICA because of their engineering expertise. Three groups of consulting agencies are present in Japan's ODA: (1) agencies of independent consultants, (2) agencies financed by public funds and (3) subsidiaries of manufactures. The first group includes a company such as Nippon Koei, a largest consulting agency, active in Japan's ODA, with 1,550 employees. As an illustration, this company realized a construction project of wells to fight against Guinea warm in Niger in 2004 to 2006. The second group includes agencies of basic infrastructure where former government officials traditionally parachute to a high position at the end of their carrier. The Sanyô Consultants and the Hokkaidô Consultants are the examples of this group. Different from the first group, the latter group has the legal status of a foundation. Lastly, subsidiaries of manufactures are often directed by former employees of their parent company, such as Shin Nihon Gijutsu Consultants and the Dia consultant (Igarashi, 1990; Ohashi, 2005).

While it remains very marginal compared to these Japanese companies, Japanese NGOs also participate in Japan's ODA. Their presence is weak due to their financial constraint. Indeed, the total budget disposed by all the Japanese NGO (USD 226.8 million) does not even reach the budget of an international NGO like OXFAM (USD 1.2 billion) (Gotô, 2005). Although the first financial aid from the government to NGO started 25 years ago (in 1989) (Higuchi, 1991), the amount of governmental subvention is still very limited. Indeed, in 2007, such subvention concerned only USD 28 million remaining very symbolic amount (MOFA, 2007). The main reason of this limited support from the government is that the recognition and the acceptance by governmental agencies of the NGO's activities are rather recent. Before that, government officials' skepticism regarding NGO was strong. It took for NGO a long time to hold a first dialogue with government officials. As an example, Japanese NGO were

[10] Kanematsu: <www.kanematsu.co.jp/2010>, Mitsubishi: <www.mitsubishi.com/jp/ja>.

even not accepted to attend in the first two TICAD (in 1993 and 1998) (Committee on Japanese economic overseas cooperation, 2006).

2.3. Grants and loans: beside standard systems, some political projects

Most of the Japanese aid projects are taking one of the two delivery systems depending on the aid's nature (grant or loan). To go through the system, a project necessitates several years of time. For example, in Grant aid, since its budget is not available at MOFA, except "aid for associations and local communities", MOFA needs an agreement of MOF in order to provide such aid. In fact, among the 13 participating governmental agencies to Japan's ODA, MOF disposes the highest amount of budget that represents 60% of Japan's ODA total. MOFA follows it but reach only the half of the budget disposal of MOF (32%)[11].

Figure 2. Delivery system of Grand aid

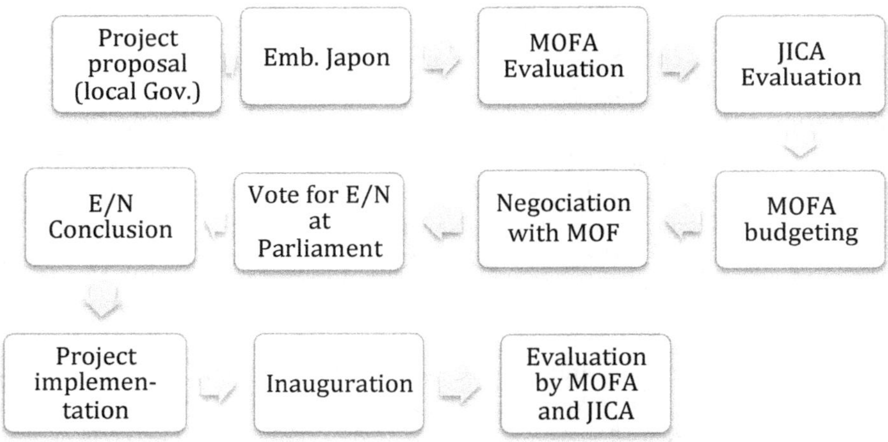

Source: Yamamoto (2015)

As to Loan aid, a consensus of three ministries (MOFA, MOF, METI) is necessary, which makes decision making processes even longer and complex. In order that a project emerges, Japanese consultant companies and Japanese Sōgō Shōsha search a potential project in West Africa and prepare a project proposal to be presented by a relevant ministry of the beneficiary country to the nearest Japanese Embassy. The first evaluation takes place at the Embassy before being

11 MOFA-International Cooperation Bureau (2008).

forward to MOFA in Tokyo. Once the project is considered as viable in Tokyo, MOFA fixes project budget before presenting to MOF in order to obtain their agreement. It is only after this agreement that the project is voted for *Échange des notes* (E/N) at Japanese Parliament before the project is signed by both countries (Figure 2).

This is the general delivery system of Grant aid in West Africa. The delivery system of Loan aid is different from this. After feasibility report is approved by Japanese Embassy, the project proposal is negotiated among MOFA, MOF and METI. It is only when the project is considered potential project, an official mission is sent to the requesting country to evaluate the key elements discussed in the earlier pilot meeting (MOFA, MOF, METI). Once the project is considered feasible, E/N is signed and JICA concludes the loan contract with the beneficiary country (Figure 3).

Figure 3. Delivery system of loan aid

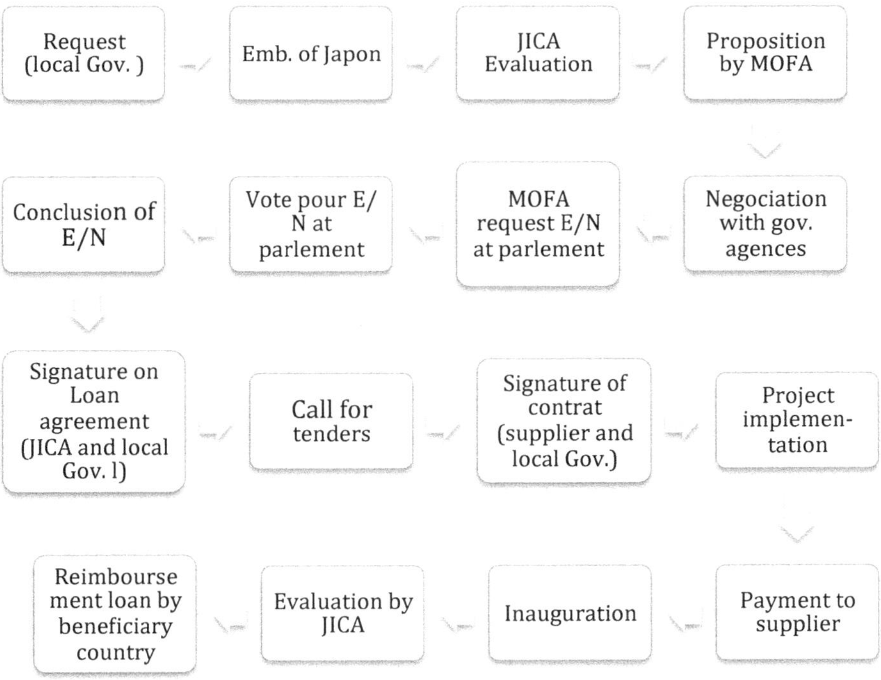

Source : Yamamoto (2015)

When a supplier is selected by the call for tenders, the beneficiary country buys the material which will be then directly paid by Japan to the supplier through a bank account created at the name of the beneficiary country. By this system of creating a bank account in Japanese Bank in Japan for the aid beneficiary country, Japan keeps its control over their fund designed for the project. Average time to form a project proposal is estimated as long as 1-2 years. To this, it is necessary to add 2-3 years of obtaining the budget (Watanabe, 1991). That means that the delivery of a loan project necessitates at least 3 years which represent the average duration of a diplomatic position in a country. Therefore, unfortunately it is very rare for Japanese diplomats to see the end of the loan project that they validated the proposal.

Beside these general delivery systems of Japan's ODA, we have noted an unofficial delivery system practiced in West Africa for political projects. It happens usually in the case where the request comes from former President or Ministers who are still politically influential within the region. And, for such projects, the request is not examined at Japanese Embassy. That means that whether the project proposal is feasible or not, it does not matter. Such proposal is forwarded directly to Economic Cooperation Service of MOFA in Tokyo to obtain a financial aid. In the region where Japanese Embassy in Dakar was in charge of Senegal, Mali, Mauritania, Guinea-Bissau, Gambia in 2006, such "political" projects were making almost one fourth of total Japanese projects[12]. Is it a lot or few?

When we asked this question, we opened the archive of aid financed by the same Embassy and we were surprised to note that in the 1990's, such "political" projects were proportionally even higher. However, by the strengthened control of Japanese MOF which sends each year auditors to Japanese Embassies selected randomly, such practice is decreasing and becoming only a tool of last resort.

3. The drivers of Japan's aid diplomacy in West Africa

West Africa is a particular region with 313 million inhabitants of ethnic and culture diversity. Except Liberia, all the countries have lived the colonial time under the administration of France, Great-Britain, Portugal of Germany. After the decolonization of West African countries between the 1950's and the 1970's, except Senegal and Cape-Verde, all of them suffered from a number of *coups d'états* and civil wars. Therefore, the political stability has always been an important issue for this region. However, West Africa possesses very rich natural resources, especially in the South and West coast, that attract more and more countries of high dependency to exported resources.

[12] Confidential official documents of Japanese Embassy in Dakar (accessed in 2005-2007).

How is Japanese bilateral relation with West African countries characterized? What are its particularities? To which countries Japan's ODA is extended most and why? Also, what are the motivations behind Japan's ODA in West Africa?

3.1. Bilateral diplomatic relation with West African countries: little attention given by Japan's diplomacy

Since Japan concluded its first diplomatic relations with West Africa in Ghana in 1957, Japan's ODA to West Africa reached annually USD 232.29 million in average until 2006[13]. Although the Japanese contribution to West Africa is not negligible, Japan remains still reluctant to reinforce its bilateral relations with West African countries. That is explained by the number of official missions conducted by Japanese Prime minister to the region. The first official visit of Japanese Prime minister dates back to 2001, with the visit of Prime Minister Mori Yoshiro to Nigeria. This visit gave an opportunity to Japan to address in Africa for the first time in its history Japan's African policy. It was followed by the second mission led by Prime Minister Koizumi Junichiro in 2006 to Ghana. In Ghana, the main mission was to inaugurate the Noguchi Memorial Institute for Medical Research[14] in Accra. However, by combining his visit to Ethiopia, this mission allowed Japan to address on Japan's engagements for African development at the headquarters of African Union in Addis-Ababa. More recently, Prime Minister Abe Shinzo conducted an official visit to Côte d'Ivoire in January 2014, being accompanied by 33 Japanese enterprises, associations and universities delegates. The visit to Abidjan was motivated by its highest economic potential of West Africa but also because the city of Abidjan had expected the return of African Development Bank in the near future from Tunis[15].

Before these visits to West Africa, Japan sent, for the first time, its Foreign ministers Kimura Toshio in 1974 in Nigeria and Sonoda Sunao in 1979 in Nigeria and Côte d'Ivoire. However, these visits did not show strong intention to establish a long term relation with West African countries but as a part of Japan's oil diplomacy, aimed toward the diversification of new sources of oil in West Africa in a context of the oil crisis of the 1970's. Until 2010, the number of official missions sent to West Africa by Japan was only 71 and, besides those

---

[13] Japan's ODA delivered between 1969 and 2006 to 16 countries of West Africa.

[14] Noguchi Hideo, Japanese doctor specialise in research on Yellow fever. He died from Yellow fever during his visit to Accra for his research. The research institute was established in 1979 by Japan's ODA to commemorate his contribution to the medical research.

[15] The African Development Bank was established in 1965 in Abidjan in Côte d'Ivoire. But the political instability of the country transferred its mission to Tunis in 2003. Since then, its headquarters had been based in Tunis before its return to Abidjan in 2014.

of Prime ministers and Foreign ministers, the other official visits from Japan were mainly conducted by high officials of Japanese Foreign office and by Japanese Parliament members (Table 3).

The presence of Japanese nationals in West Africa is also limited. The country that has most Japanese residents in the region is Ghana (331, October 2009), followed by Senegal (187, October 2008) and Nigeria (126, October 2008). Yet, most of these residents are people working on Japan's ODA (government officials, staffs of enterprises and of NGO) and their family. The countries to which Japan extended most aid in West Africa (based on the aid total between 1969 and 2006) are those countries which has an important presence of Japanese residents (USD 2,232 million to Nigeria, USD 1,714 to Ghana and USD 1,004 to Senegal).

Although until 2006, Japan had only four embassies in West Africa (Accra (Ghana), Conakry (Guinea), Abuja (Nigeria) and Dakar (Senegal), by opening a new Embassy in Benin, Burkina Faso, Côte d'Ivoire, Mali and Mauritania between 2007 and 2010, Japan is now present in nine countries in West Africa (Map 1). Since, traditionally Japan's ODA in West Africa has been formed around Japanese institutions (Japanese embassy, JICA, Japanese enterprises), the increased Japanese presence in West Africa might modify the destination pattern of Japan's ODA in West Africa in the future.

Map 1. Japan's presence in West Africa (2010)

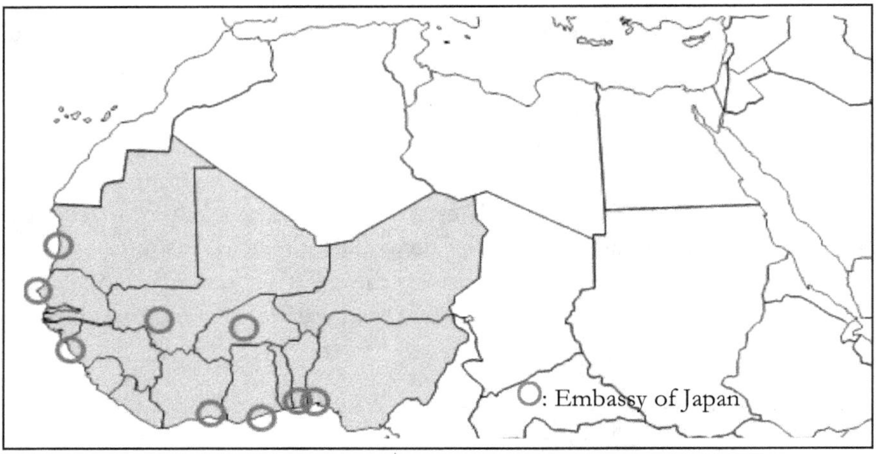

Source: author

Table 3. Japan's Diplomatic Relations with West African countries

Countries	Opening year of diplomatic relations	Number of Japanese residents	Permanent resident Mission: In West Africa	Permanent resident Mission: In Japan	Official Visits to West Africa: Visit of PM	Official Visits to West Africa: Other official visits	Japanese Aid between 1969 and 2006 (US$ million)
Liberia	1961	5 (June 2010)	1973-2004 at Monrovia	since 1969 at Tokyo	-	Jan. 72(Amb.), July 81(SEAE), April 04(Amb.), Jan. 06(SEAE), July 06(P), Nov. 06(Amb.)	107.37
Mali	1960	25 (Oct. 2008)	Since 2008 at Bamako	1993-2002 at Tokyo	-	98(Amb.), Oct. 99, Jan.02, Jan.04(P), May 04(Amb.), Aug 04, June 05, June 07(P)	471.56
Mauritania	1960	9 (April 2010)	Since Dec. 2008 at Nouakchott	Since July 1989 at Tokyo	-	Aug 04(P), Aug 06, April 07(SEAE)	459.53
Niger	1960	106 (Oct. 2008)	-	-	-	Feb 97, July 06(P), Feb 08(SEAE)	479.1
Nigeria	1960	126(Oct. 2008)	since 2002 at Abuja	at Tokyo	Jan. 2001	Nov. 74(Minister of FA), Feb. 78(Special envoy of PM), July 79(Minister of FA), April 84, Nov. 88(Special envoy of PM), Dec. 05(P)	2,232.47
Senegal	1960	187 (Oct. 2008)	since 1962 at Dakar	since 1975 at Tokyo	-	April 00(Minister of Education), sept. 00(SEA), Feb. 01, Jan. 02(Mission of PM), May 04(Director of JICA), Aug 04(P), Jan. 05(SEAE), Jul 06(P), Aug 06(SEAE)	1,004.17
Sierra Leone	1961	18 (oct.2004)	-	-	-	Jan. 05, June 06(Amb.), July 06(P), August 07(SEAE)	139.24
Togo	1960	1 (March 2009)	-	-	-	March 85, July 06(P)	173.28

Countries	Opening year of diplomatic relations	Number of Japanese residents	Permanent resident Mission		Official Visits to West Africa		Japanese Aid between 1969 and 2006 (US$ million)
			In West Africa	In Japan	Visit of PM	Other official visits	
Benin	1960	78 (Oct. 2009)	since 2010 at Cotonou	since 2002 at Tokyo	-	Dec. 2000(P), Jan. 2004(SEAE), sept. Dec. 2004(P), July 2006(P), July 2007(SEAE)	267.33
Burkina Faso	1960	97 (Oct. 2008)	since 2009 at Ouagadougou	1962-1967, Oct. 1994-	-	1982, 2001(P), Jan. 2004(SEAE), July 2006 (P), Dec. 2007(SEAE)	248.22
Cape-Verde	1975	2 (Oct. 2009)	-	-	-	Aug 2006(Minister of Justice)	103.86
Côte d'Ivoire	1960	55 (Oct. 2009)	1964-April 2004, sept. 2007- at Abidjan	since 1969 at Tokyo	-	July 1979(Minister of FA), 1981(SEAE), Oct. 1987(SEAE), April 1993(Royal family members), July 1999(Director of JICA), Jan. 2004(SEAE)	547.08
Ghana	1957	331 (Oct. 2009)	since 1959 at Accra	since 1960 at Tokyo	May 2006	Before 1987(Minister of FA), Aug 88, July 91, Feb. 92(P), May 993(Royal family members), Aug 93(P), May 99(Counselor of Minister of FA), Jan. 01(Secretary of PM), Aug 0(Minister of FA), June 04(SEAE), Dec. 05(P), April 08, sept. 08(SEAE), March 10(princess et prince)	1,714.03
Gambia	1965	6 (Oct. 2009)	-	till 1998 at Tokyo	-	May 05, June-July 06(Amb.)	108.02
Guinea	1958	42 (Oct. 2009)	1976 at Conakry	1972-	-	May 95(P), Aug 99(SEA), Aug, sept. 04(P), Dec. 04(Amb.), Feb. 05(SEAE), June 05(P)	465.73
Guinea-Bissau	1973	2 (Oct. 2008)	-	-	-	-	73.99

Source : Yamamoto (forthcoming)

3.2. ODA *destination in West Africa: few regional economic powers*

Figure 4. Japanese Aid destination in West Africa (2000-2007)

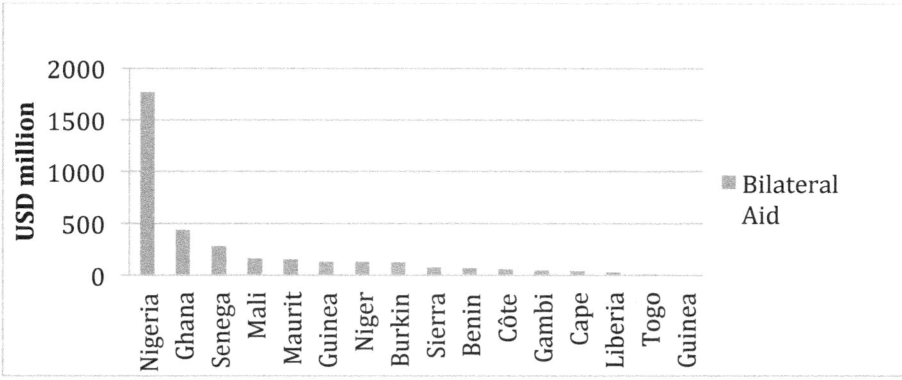

Source : Yamamoto (forthcoming)

We observed that there is a particular pattern in Japan's aid distribution in West Africa. Indeed, aid does not go to every country of West Africa in the same volume but goes principally to few regional economic powers, namely Nigeria, Ghana and Senegal (figure 4). The illustration 4 shows how much aid in total was delivered by Japan to 16 West African countries between 2000 and 2007 and that Nigeria received an outstanding high amount of Japanese ODA compared to 15 other countries. However, as we mentioned earlier, this significant gap between Nigeria and others comes from the debt cancellation of USD 18 billion agreed for Nigeria in 2005. Without counting this debt cancellation amount, the three "key countries" (Nigeria, Ghana and Senegal) received similar amount of ODA from Japan, reaching USD 3-4 million in total between 2000 and 2007.

3.3. Aid motivation: first political, then economical

What are the main factors that motivate Japan's ODA to West Africa? While three dimensions of such motivation (political, economic/commercial and ideological) are observable, we note that the highest importance has been given to the political dimension. Indeed, to obtain a permanent seat at UN Security Council is an objective that motivates Japan since long time. Japan is eager to take political support from any country, including those from West Africa, in order to succeed in such goal.

In 2005, Japan proposed a reform of UN Security Council in cooperation with Germany, Brazil and India that are the candidates for a permanent seat. Their main target was to convince the member countries of African Union but their proposal could not obtain enough support as much as that of two third of 192 countries at the UN's General Assembly.

Japan believes that a political support can be obtained only after having many years of donor-beneficiary relations supported by Japan's ODA (Yamamoto, forthcoming). Therefore, Japan does not hesitate to influence the decision of West African countries by providing them a small grant aid (around 75 000 euros) when they have to vote at the General Assembly[16].

Moreover, Japan uses its ODA in order to obtain fishing rights and natural resources exploitation contracts in West Africa (economic and commercial motivation). Japanese fishing companies which conduct their activities in the coast of West African benefit from such aid and Japanese Ministry of Agriculture, Forests and Fishing (MAFF) supports using ODA in that domain. This explains why in Senegal and Mauritania, a number of Japanese achievements related to fishing activities, especially fish market and pirogue constructions are observed.

As for economic and commercial motivations, another action we observed is the use of Japanese ODA for the negotiation of natural resources exploitation project. Japan has very limited oil reserve, principally located at offshore areas of western coastline of Japan, while oil is the essential resource for Japanese industrial development (U.S. Energy Information Administration, 2015). Therefore, its oil consumption is completely depending to the imported oil, traditionally from Middle East. However, due to the instable political situation of oil producers of Middle East, it is crucial for Japan to have several alternatives source of oil. West Africa possesses a rich oil reserve in the Gulf of Guinea, especially in Nigeria that produced 2,356 millions of barrels in 2007. These economic and commercial motivations to extend Japanese aid in West Africa are strongly supported by METI and *Keidanren* (Japanese Federation of Economic organizations – FOE).

The last dimension observed in this study concerns the ideology of Japan's ODA. Indeed, Japan seeks to expand an Asian model of development in West Africa, based on construction of basic infrastructures and the support of initiatives for local economic and social development. Japan believes that the economic growth experienced by Asian countries in the last decade is largely due to the support of Japan's ODA that helped to strengthen basic infrastructures and to encourage local people's will to rapid economic growth and to life quality improvement (Orr, 1993). Japan expects to achieve the same conse-

---

16 A large scale of Grant aid is difficult to offer in such situation, since MOFA needs a budget approval of MOF and also for the large scale grant aid, the aiding reasons have to be well-founded.

quence in West Africa, and by doing this, Japan aims to highlight a development way of a "non-western industrial nation" in the western-dominated power competition like ODA.

Conclusion

This study investigated the motivation of Japan's ODA in West Africa. It underlines that Japan's aid is strongly driven by political and economic/commercial motivations. Politically, Japan aims to increase the number of its allies in West Africa, in order to seat at UN Security Council. Economically, Nigeria, Ghana and Senegal are the most attractive countries for Japan's ODA in West Africa, because of their rich natural resources (oil reserve in Nigeria, mineral reserve in Ghana and aquaculture in Senegal). The study discussed also the strategic aspects of Japanese ODA in West Africa. In fact, in 1989, as "the N°1 donor", Japan showed its intention to improve quality of its aid in order to respond to the needs of developing countries, but the ODA Charter of 2003 declared priority sectors and preferential regions of Japan's ODA. The Japanese position shown by the Charter explains very well that Japan choose what it wants to provide. What the beneficiary country think is secondary. Although it is not surprising that ODA is used as a national strategy by a donor since ODA is a political, diplomatic and economic instrument, the new statement of a country like Japan which had been usually neutral and rather hiding the strategic parts of its ODA in its official statements gave an impression of turning point to the new phase of its ODA.

Compared to Chinese and Indian aid to West Africa, Japan's ODA shown the several differences. Historically, Japan has 10 years longer experience than China and India in the domain of aid: Japan begins its ODA in 1954, while China and India in 1964. Statistically, while the reliable Chinese aid figures are unfortunately absent, in 2009, Japan's ODA volume to West Africa (USD 444.32 million in average)[17] was only slightly higher than that of India (USD 386.96 million)[18]. However, we have to note that this Indian volume includes only Lines of credits and Grant aid, and technical cooperation are excluded since these figures are not published to public. Yet, considering the limited India's Grant Aid activities' size, it is less probable that the India's Aid volume goes far

---

[17] Annual amount between 2000 and 2007.

[18] Interview in Delhi (4 December 2009).

higher than that of Japan. Thus, we estimate that the total amount of India's aid to West Africa on that year would limit between USD 387 and 400 million[19].

Also, these three donors' aid destination pattern is different. China provides its aid to all the countries which have diplomatic relations with PRC, and currently Burkina Faso and Gambia are the only ones outside of China's diplomatic ground in West Africa[20]. Japan and India focuses to a small number of countries. Indeed, India's aid goes particularly to actual and former Commonwealth countries (Ghana, Nigeria, Gambia), while Japan's ODA looks at economic and political powers of the region (Ghana, Senegal, Nigeria).

Moreover, China is most physically present in West Africa, possessing its embassy in 14 countries, while Japan in 10 and India in 7 countries. The frequency of official visits to the region until today distinguishes also China, as Chinese officials made 101 official visits, against 71 for Japan and 31 for India.

Lastly, an official frame of dialogue with Africa was initiated firstly by Japan in 1993 with TICAD and followed by China in 2000 with Forum on China-Africa Cooperation (FOCAC) and India in 2008 with India-Africa Forum. Until 2014, the frequency of organization of such forum in China and India was more intense (every 3 years) than that of Japan's TICAD (every 5 years). But because Japan has been observing China and India as its competitors in Africa, Japan revised the frequency of TICAD organization in 2014. Thus, starting from 2016, TICAD will be taken place every 3 years.

Strategically speaking, for China, not having a diplomatic relation with Taiwan is a condition to benefit Chinese aid. In the last decade, under such condition, China succeeded to establish new diplomatic relations with 4 countries (Liberia in 1993, Nigeria in 1996, Guinea-Bissau in 1998, Senegal in 2005). By offering aid, China also promotes integration of Chinese companies' activities in West Africa. For India, as it is for Japan, obtaining a seat at UNSC represents an important objective. But this dimension is secondary in Indian aid compared to its economic and commercial objective. In fact, inside of Indian Foreign Office which directs Indian aid, three different interests coexist: MAE's West African Division searches to seat at UNSC, while Division of Investment and Trade Promotion (ITP) promotes to mobilize maximum of budget for aid projects in order to bring economic and commercial benefits back to India. MAE's technical cooperation Division seeks traditionally to contribute to development of

---

[19] Estimation of 2009.

[20] Although Gambia has cut its diplomatic tie with Taiwan in November 2013, China has not yet reopened its diplomatic relations with Gambia.

human resource in West Africa. In conclusion, three Asian donors share certain traditions and geographical proximity, their aid is different both in practices and in strategies.

Bibliography

ARASE, D. (2005) *Japan's foreign aid: old continuities and new directions.* London; New York: Routledge.

BEAUDRY-SOMCYNSKY, M. et al. (1999) Japan's System of Official development Assistance – Profiles for Partnership n°1, Ottawa: International development Research Center.

BOBROW et al. (1996) Bilateral and multilateral foreign aid: Japan's approach in comparative perspective. *Review of International political Economy*, 3: 1.

BROOKS, W.L. et al. (1985) Japan's Foreign Economic Assistance. *Asian Survey*, 3 vol., n°25.

COMMITTEE ON JAPANESE ECONOMIC OVERSEAS COOPERATION (2006) *Kaigai Keizai Kyoryoku ni kansuru Kentoukai Houkokusho* [« Committee's report on Japanese economic overseas cooperation meeting »], Ministry of Internal affairs (Japan), 28, February.

ENSIGN, M. (1992) The structure and implementation of Japanese Bilateral Assistance (Chapter 2). In M. ENSIGN, *Doing Good Or Doing Well?: Japan's Foreign Aid Program.* Columbia University Press, pp. 27-46.

FUKUSHIMA, A. (2000) Official Development Assistance (ODA) as a Japanese foreign policy tool (Chapter 9). In T. INOGUCHI, *Japanese foreign policy today.* New York: St. Martin's Press, pp. 152-173.

GOTŌ, K. (2005) *Nihon no Kokusaikaihatu Kyôryoku vol.4* [« Japanese ODA vol. 4 »]. Tokyo: Nihon Hyôronsha.

HIROKI, S. (2007) Wagakuni ODA Jitushitaisei no Hensen to Jidai no Yousei [Transformation of Japan's ODA system and adaptation to the changing external demand]. *MOFA monthly research review*, n° 2.

IGARASHI, (1990) *Nihon no ODA to Kokusai chitujo* [Japan's ODA and International order], Tokyo: Nihon Kokusaimondai Kenkyûjo.

IMAMURA, M. (2004) A Note on the Beginning of ODA in Japan (1945-1963-4). *Gunma University Social Information research paper*, n°11, pp. 241-265.

JBIC (2006a) *JBIC Kokusai Kinyō Gyōmu ni tuite* [JBIC's international financing activities], 18 january.

JBIC (2006b) *JBIC Kokusai Kyōryoku Ginkou* [Japan Bank of International Cooperation], 18 january.

JICA (2006) *Dokuritu Gyōsei Hōjin Kokusaikyōryoku Kikō* [Japan International Cooperation Agency], 18 January.

KATŌ, K. (2002) Development cooperation policies in Japan and Germany after the war (Chapter 4), K. KATÔ *The Web of Power. Japanese and German Development Cooperation.* Oxford: Lexiton Books.

KOHAMA, (1998) *ODA no keizai Gaku* [Economics of Official Development Aid]. Tokyo: Nihon Hyōronsha.

LANCASTER, C. (2010) Japan's ODA: *Naiatsu and Gaiatsu*/Domestic sources and transnational influences (Chapter 1). In D. LEHNY and K. WARREN, *Japanese Aid and the Construction of Global Development.* London; New York: Routledge.

LEHMAN, H. (2007) Japan's National Economic Identity and African development – An analysis of the Tokyo International Conference on African Development, Research Paper n. 2007/61, UNU-WIDER, October.

MATSUI, K. (1983) *Keizai Kyôryoku: Towareru Nihon no Keizai Gaikô* [Economic Cooperation: Japanese Economic Cooperation Diplomacy in question]. Tokyo: Yûrinkaku.

MOFA, *Japan's ODA White Paper 2001, 2002, 2003, 2004, 2005, 2006, 2007, 2008.*

–, <www.mofa.go.jp> (accessed between 2007 and 2009).

MOFA-Economic Cooperation Bureau (1999) *Japan's Assistance to Africa*, April.

–, *Japan's Official Development Assistance Charter* (2003), 29 August.

MOFA-International Cooperation Bureau (2008) *Japan's International Cooperation.*

NISHIGAKI, A. (1999) *The economics of development assistance: Japan's ODA in a symbiotic world.* Tokyo: LTCB International Library Foundation.

OBAYASHI, M., TICAD (2004) Un processus favorable au développement de l'Afrique? *Afrique contemporaine*, hiver.

OECD, OECD Credit Reporting System, <www.oecd.org> (accessed between 2007 and 2010).

OECD-DAC (2003 et 2010) *Peer Review Japan.*

OHASHI (2005) "ONG no Kokusaikyoryoku", [International cooperation by NGO] in Gotō, *Nihon no Kokusai kaihatu kyōryoku* [Japan's international development cooperation]. Tokyo: Nihon Hyoron sha.

ORR et al. (1993) *Japan's foreign aid : power and policy in a new era.* Boulder: Westview Press.

ORR, R.M. (1994) Japanese foreign aid in a new global era. *SAIS Review.*

RIX, A. (1993) Chapiter 1 « The philosophy of Japan's foreign aid », Japan's Foreign Aid challenges – Policy reform and aid leadership. London: Routledge, pp. 12-44.

SATO, M. (2005) « Japanese aid diplomacy in Africa: an historical analysis ». *Ritsumeikan Annual Review of International Studies*, 4: 67-85.

SATO, M. et al. (2004) La diplomatie japonaise de l'aide et l'Afrique. *Afrique contemporaine*, n° 212(4).

SUMI (1990) *Kirawareru Enjo – Segin Nihon no Enjo to Narmada Dam* [Disliked aid – the World Bank and Japan's aid and Narmada Dam]. Tokyo : Chikushi Shobō.

SUZUKI, N. *Nihon no Keizai Kyôryoku: Tojôkoku Keizai hatuten no Shitenkara* [« Japanese Economic Cooperation: perspective of developping countries's Economic growth »]. IDE, Tokyo, 1989.

TAKAHASHI, A. (1990) *Japan's ODA to the Philippines*. July, pp. 1-26.

TUMAN. J. (2006) The role of mercantilism, humanitarianism, and 'gaiatsu' in Japan's ODA programme in Asia. *International Relations of the Asia-Pacific*, 6 (1): 61-80.

U.S. ENERGY INFORMATION ADMINISTRATION (2015) *International Energy Data and Analysis*. January.

YAMAMOTO. K. (1995) International Trends in Development Assistance and Japan. *Journal of Development assistance*, n°1, July.

YAMAMOTO (1978) *Tsuyoshi, Nihon no Keizai Enjo* [Japan's Economic Development Aid]. Tokyo: Sanshōdō.

YAMAMOTO, Yumiko, *Politique d'aide au développement de la Chine, de l'Inde et du Japon en Afrique de l'Ouest*. Paris : Les Indes Savantes, forthcoming.

YANAGIHARA, T. (1991) An overview of Japan's foreign aid. *Shafignel, Yen for development*.

WATANABE et al. (1991) *Nihonno ODA wo dôsuruka* [« what to do with Japan's ODA »]. Tokyo: NHK Books.

Recent evolution, persistent challenges and future direction of Taiwan's ODA and its comparison with European aid

Vincent ROLLET

Introduction

Taiwan has experienced rapid progress on multiple indices of economic and human development over the past century, resulting in its recognition as one of the "four Asian tigers" and being among an elite group of "high-income economies. With this rapid development, Taiwan has progressively transformed from aid recipient to donor. Taiwan's first ODA initiatives can be traced back in 1959, when Taiwan with the US support sent its first agricultural mission to Vietnam followed in 1961 by a programme of agricultural cooperation with several African countries (*Operation Vanguard*) with the objective of improving local production of vegetables and fruits. At that time, Taiwan was still a recipient country of the US aid which provides its economic and military support to the island until 1965.

While representing "China" at the UN since the inception of the international organization in 1945, the government of the Republic of China established in Taiwan since 1949 had to face the growing pressure exerted by the PRC on the international community in order to take the China seat at the UN. In this context, ODA was seen by Taiwan as well as by China as an instrument to convince developing countries of their right and legitimacy to represent "China" at the UN and in all the UN agencies. Such instrumentalization of ODA did not stop with the replacement of the ROC by the PRC at the UN in 1971 as the only lawful representation of China to the UN. The reverse is the case. Indeed, this "dollar diplomacy" using ODA as an instrument of persuasion continued then until the beginning of the 21st century. Obviously, such diplomatic battle have influenced the nature, the amount, the geographic distribution, the modalities as well as the impact of Taiwanese ODA over the period. However, since his first election in March 2008, President Ma Ying-jeou (Kuomintang KMT) has put in place policies aimed at improving ties between Taipei and Beijing as well as elevating Taiwan's "international standing" under what he has called a "flexible diplomacy". In this context, it might be asked how such new policy framework has influenced Taiwan's ODA? And then by extension, how this Taiwan's ODA today is similar or different from ODA provided by European countries?

To answer these questions, after a short overview of the academic literature on Taiwan's aid and the content of Ma's flexible diplomacy, this contribution proposes to examine the recent evolution of Taiwan's ODA (nature, governance, policy, implementation...) under Ma presidency, its challenges and its future, and to compare this aid to European ODA.

1. Literature review and political contextualization

1.1. Overview of the academic literature on Taiwan's aid

A number of academic articles have contributed to a better understanding of Taiwan's ODA. Thus, in the 1990's, articles underlined the role played by foreign aid in the Taiwan's Southward policy (Lin, 1995), examined ODA as an instrument of Taiwan's foreign policy (Lin, 1996) or aimed to provide information on Taiwan's aid and to evaluate its main challenges and prospects (Chan, 1997). Then simultaneously to a growing amount of Taiwan's aid under the presidency of Chen Shui-Bian (2000-2008) and a very competitive relationship between Taipei and Beijing, an increasing number of scholars have focused on Taiwan's international aid and notably highlights its instrumentalization for strategic purposes (international recognition and natural resources) in different parts of the world and its social and political consequences (Kondoh, 2012; Navejas, 2007; Tubilewicz, 2004; Tubilewicz, 2007) as well as its main motivations or the role played by NGOs (Lin 2003). In this context an academic/political debate emerged about the necessity of increasing Taiwan's aid and the impact of the aid race for diplomatic competition between Taipei and Beijing in diplomatic and developmental terms (Guilloux, 2009; Tubilewicz and Guilloux, 2011).

Since the presidency of Ma Ying-jeou (2008-2016), it seems however that given the slowdown of Taiwan's aid, fewer articles have focused on Taiwan's ODA. Those who examine Taiwanese ODA conclude that strategic considerations remains an important factor of Taiwan's ODA (Tubilewicz, 2012), that contests and rivalries among Taiwan's political parties and government agencies form the objectives, policies and processes of Taipei's foreign aid-giving (Tubilewicz, 2015) or that certain continuity with past practices might be observed notably in terms of aid governance (Atkinson, 2014).

While few articles aimed at comparing the past Taiwan's ODA with the aid provided by other donors (Dreher, and al., 2010), to the best of our knowledge, no comparative study have been conducted to compare the recent evolution of Taiwanese aid with the aid delivered by European donors. Based on the analysis of numerous official documents (reports, brochures, policy papers), newspaper and academic articles, as well as several recent interviews with Taiwanese officials, this contribution aims to make a modest contribution to such comparison.

1.2. 'Flexible diplomacy' as a new framework for Taiwan's ODA

While in the past, Taiwan and China have frequently used ODA to lure potential diplomatic allies to switch their diplomatic recognition making aid assistance the instrument of their checkbook competition, in 2008, the new President Ma Ying-jeou decided that given the economic power of China, Taiwan could no longer play such game which had become unaffordable for the country which knew a comparatively inferior economic growth and some economic challenges. In this context, he developed his 'flexible diplomacy' whose main purpose is to ease the tension between Taipei and Beijing (*rapprochement*) as well as to elevate Taiwan's "international standing". This new policy framework rests on three main dimensions.

First, the acceptation by Taiwan of what has been called the '1992 Consensus' which was signed in 1992 between Taiwan and China in HK, which then reached an understanding that there was only one China but with different interpretation of what the concept 'One China' entailed. For China, "One China" means the PRC, and for Ma, "One China" indicates the ROC. Then, a 'diplomatic truce' was proposed. Indeed, under this diplomatic truce, Taiwan proposes to cease aggressive campaign to win over diplomatic partner with foreign aid and hope that Beijing would do the same. Finally, a pragmatic approach towards expanding Taiwan's international space which replaces Taiwan's former request to seek full membership in the UN by asking 'meaningful participation' in UN specialized agencies (notably WHA, WHO).

2. Volume, governance and nature of Taiwan's ODA

2.1. A decreasing volume of Taiwan's ODA

Today Taiwan's Official Development Assistance (ODA) is believed to be both low in absolute and relative terms. In 2013, Taiwan's foreign aid funding – including both bilateral and multilateral aid – was approximately USD 272 million (MOFA, 2014:4). In terms of ODA/GNI ratio, the Taiwanese ODA represents 0.054% of its GNI, very far from the goal of 0.7% set by the UN and from the average ODA/GNI ratio of DAC countries (0.3%) while Taiwan ranks 4th in terms of total GNI between Japan and Germany. More revealing is perhaps the evolution of Taiwan's ODA this last decade in terms of volume as well as ODA/GNI ratio. Indeed, while from 2004 to 2007, Taiwan ODA progressively increased from 421 million USD to 514 million USD, it starts to quickly decrease starting from in 2008 to reach 272 million USD in 2013. ODA/GNI ratio followed the same trends as it plunged from 0.14% in 2004 – already not very high – to 0.054% in 2013 (Figure 1).

Figure 1: Evolution of Taiwan's ODA volume and ODA/GNI ratio (2004-2013)

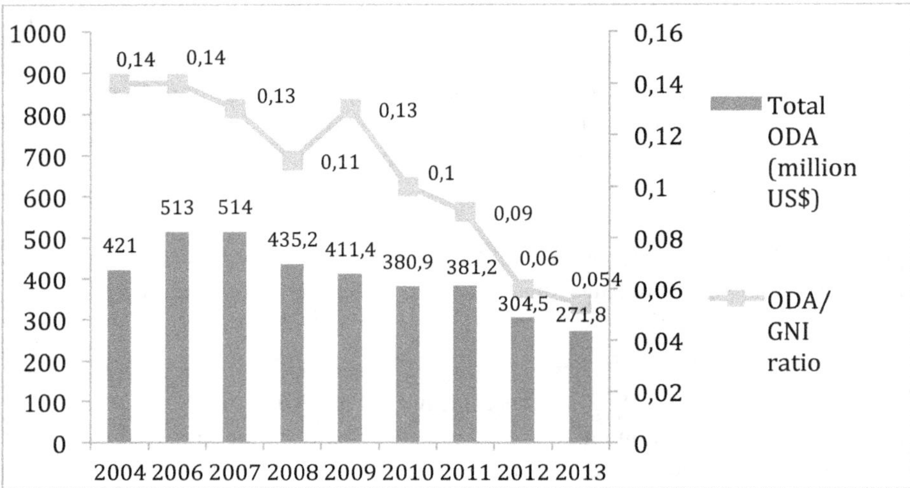

Source: Figures collected by the author in governmental reports as well as press articles (for 2004/2006); OECD, Development finance reporting of countries beyond the DAC, Paris, <http://www.oecd.org/development/stats/non-dac-reporting.htm>.

While such decrease has been explained by the Taiwanese authorities as a direct consequence of the global economic downturn as well as a consequence of the central government budget cuts, many observers and aid implementers have also seen a direct consequence of the 'diplomatic truce' proposed by President Ma (Interview, 2015). Indeed, while the volume of money dedicated to Taiwan ODA was dictated by the competition with China, the end of such 'dollar diplomacy' has had a direct repercussion on the total amount of Taiwanese ODA as Taiwan agreed not to compete with China anymore. As a specific illustration of such decrease, Taiwan aid to Haiti in 2011 (12 million USD) (China Post, 2013) deeply contrasts with Taiwan's aid to Indonesia following the tsunami in 2004 (120 million USD - 6% of the total international aid) and was minuscule (0.5% of the whole international aid) compared with what DAC countries have provided at that time (Reliefweb, 2005).

In terms of comparison, ranked 26th by the International Monetary Fund (IMF) in terms of GDP in 2013, Taiwan with its total volume of ODA reaching USD 272 million is situated between Greece (USD 310 million) and the Czech Republic (USD 210 million) while these two European countries are respectively ranked 44th and 51st in terms of GDP. Now, if we compare Taiwan's ODA total amount with the total volume ODA provided by countries with similar GDP, Taiwan is far to reach the total volume of ODA provided by Belgium (USD 2.3 billion), Norway (USD 5.5 billion) or Austria (USD 1.2 billion). Actually, Taiwan is more comparable to Poland which ranked 23rd in terms of GDP and provided a total amount of ODA around USD 487 million in 2013 when the country joined the OECD Development Assistance Committee[1]. Finally, if we consider the net decrease of Taiwan ODA since 2008, such trend has been also observed in several donors in Europe such as Portugal, Italy, Greece and Spain.

2.2. Governance of Taiwan's ODA

In charge of foreign policy to which ODA is an important part (around one-third of its budget), the Taiwan's Ministry of Foreign Affairs (MOFA) is certainly the main actor of Taiwan's ODA as it plans, coordinate foreign assistance and disburses the largest part of Taiwan ODA. Under its auspices, the ICDF (International Cooperation and Development Fund) created in 1996 received its main income from the MOFA – 10-15% of MOFA's aid budget – and has the responsibility to conduct ODA projects. Remaining MOFA's aid budget is either directly distributed by the MOFA or in coordination with other governmental and non-governmental organizations. In addition, Eximbank – fully owned by the Government of Taiwan – supports ODA projects by providing the services of an export-import bank: export and import credits and guarantees, overseas investment credits, overseas construction credits and guarantees, relending facilities and major public construction credits and guarantees.

The role and control of MOFA on Taiwanese ODA is then central and became even important under Ma presidency. Indeed, in the past, the need to explore alternative ways to provide ODA in the context of "diplomatic competition" with China, offered a greater role to other Ministries such as the Ministry of Health (MoH) or the Council of Agriculture (CoA). They had then more autonomy to develop their own international development programs which were then approved for financing by the MOFA. It is in such context that the MoH started its internationalization in 2002 with the establishment of a Bureau of International Affairs followed by the creation of three posts of "health attaché"

---

[1] OECD Statistics: Available at: <http://stats.oecd.org/Index.aspx?datasetcode=TABLE5>.

in Washington, in Brussels and Lilongwe (Malawi). At that time, it also planned and developed – with the financial support of MOFA – its own health and development projects such as the establishment of "health Centers" in the South Pacific or the opening of a clinic to treat HIV patients in Mzuzu (Malawi). However, recent interviews with officials from the MoH as well as from the MOFA show that since 2010, MOFA took back the control of the majority of Ministries' development programs notably by involving the ICDF in most projects in order to ensure that "diplomatic truce" was respected in the field (Interview, 2015a).

Similar remarks might be made about the cooperation between Taiwanese NGOs, the MOFA and ministries in delivering ODA which has then been less prominent under Ma's flexible diplomacy. As a consequence, very small part (0.6%) of Taiwan's ODA has been channeled to and through civil society organizations. A percentage much lower than in the Netherland (34%), Belgium (24%) or Austria and Germany (10%) but closer to the level of ODA dedicated to NGOs by France (1%)[2].

Although the Taiwanese experience of foreign aid can be tracked back to 1959, before Ma's election, international aid and development were omitted from its core public sector policy discourse as no single document outlined Taiwanese aid policies. The change occurred under Ma when in 2009 the MOFA published the *White Paper on Foreign Aid Policy: Partnerships for Progress and Sustainable Development* (MOFA Taiwan, 2009). In May 2010, the Legislative Yuan passed the *International Cooperation and Development Act* (hereafter ICD Act) (MOFA Taiwan, 2010), which since then serves as Taiwan's legal basis for international cooperation and development affairs. Completing this Act, six sets of regulations, have been also approved by the Legislative Yuan in order to solidify the legal foundation for the provision of foreign aid by Taiwan. The overall objective of these documents was to build the foundation of a scientific and professional management model of Taiwan's ODA, emphasizing pre-evaluation, mid-term supervision, and post-review of project effectiveness. If in terms of coordination, vision and coherence, such documents were certainly needed, in the context of the 'diplomatic truce', the publication of such policy papers can be also interpreted as a way used by Ma to demonstrate to China its good will and to show how transparent was its policy. In other terms that within the framework of its flexible diplomacy and the "diplomatic truce" Taiwan's international cooperation had no hidden agenda.

---

[2] OECD, Statistic from the Development cooperation report 2015. Available at: <http://www.oecd.org/dac/dacmembers.htm>.

In the 2010, six main objectives of Taiwanese aid have been listed (article 5) and as it was underlined that their order may suggest that the promotion of diplomatic relations, the enhancement of friendly relations with non-allied countries and the cooperation with international organizations remain the most important goals while improving welfare of the people of the recipient countries, to ensure human security, to safeguard universal values and to fulfill international obligation and responsibilities comes afterward (Atkinson, 2014:423; MOFA Taiwan, 2010).

In terms of alignment with global aid architecture and norms, presented as a "policy anchor", the 2009 White paper on Foreign Aid Policy calls to follow the spirit of the Paris Declaration on Aid Effectiveness drawn up by the OECD in 2005 as a means of establishing a professional and accountable aid model. It also highlights the importance of the Millennium Development Goals (MDGs) to which it proposes to align Taiwan ODA (MOFA Taiwan, 2009). The 2010 International Cooperation and Development Act was presented as being drawn on the Paris Declaration and identifies Taiwan with OECD best practices. Furthermore, MOFA also used the UN Millennium Development Goals (MDGs) blueprint to select five development goals as the fulcrum of its international cooperation: eradicating extreme poverty and hunger, achieving universal primary education, combating HIV/AIDS, malaria, and other diseases, ensuring environmental sustainability, and developing a global partnership for development (MOFA Taiwan, 2010). Efforts by Taiwan to align with the global aid architecture and its norms seems then real at least in terms of its declaratory commitment to OECD rules and MDGs. However, if such declarations intend to avoid to be just "a little more than window dressing" (Atkinson, 2014:419), many aspects of Taiwan ODA still need tremendous efforts and above all political will to be into line with the global aid regime starting with the level of transparency of Taiwanese ODA.

The level of transparency has rather improved since President Ma. Before Ma Ying-jeou, apart from the occasional report by Ministry of Foreign Affairs, Taiwan (MOFA) which never broke amounts down into individual projects or recipient countries, little was publicly known about the financial flows of Taiwan's ODA. Such situation was then explained by Taiwan's lack of membership to any international database, notably the OECD Development Assistance Committee (DAC) Creditor Reporting System (CRS) but above all, by the 'dollar diplomacy' with China which refrained officials to publish exact amount of development assistance by fear that recipients start a bidding competition and demand for more aid if such information were turned public. The few cases of publication of this amount were very criticized and seen as a threat to national security. At that time, officials also asked: Can Taiwan afford to disclose all its aid commitments when China did not? (China Post, 2005).

In 2009, in reference with the ICD Act which promised more transparency of aid flows, MOFA built the Taiwan ODA Database in order to collect information on international cooperation and development from all ministries. In addition, alike Estonia, Hungary or Latvia, Taiwan has voluntarily provided updates to the OECD while they still not belong to the DAC CRS. Since 2010, MOFA has also submitted its International Cooperation and Development Report every year to the Executive Yuan and forwarded it to the Legislative Yuan for reference. Here again, this willingness for more transparency is a direct consequence of Ma's "diplomatic truce". Indeed, the reason behind this move is that if the main reason of non-disclosure of Taiwan's ODA was in the past the threat of a 'bidding war' with China, with the détente in the Cross Strait, the end of the "dollar diplomacy" and the respect by China and Taiwan of the "diplomatic truce" there is no more reason to hide such information.

But does it mean that Taiwan's ODA is more transparent today? First, it is undeniable that there has been improvement in terms of transparency. Indeed, total amount of ODA and ODA/GNI ratio is published annually in the International Cooperation and Development Report, Taiwan's ODA amount and ratio by sectors are also published annually and total amount of all the development projects supervised and implemented by ICDF are publicly published on the ICDF website. However, this transparency has limits. Actually, Taiwan ODA Database is still not publicly accessible, the distribution concerning the large amount of ODA not allocated to ICDF is still very opaque, and there is no information on the modalities of allocation (technical assistance, loans, grants) of the total amount of Taiwan ODA. Furthermore, for each aid project supported by ICDF and MOFA, there is no public details concerning the allocation of money and many projects implemented by other ministries than MOFA are not well documented in terms of budget. Finally, there is no public information on the exact amount delivered to bilateral and multilateral channels.

In this regard, the 2009 White paper has been criticized for not being able to remove secrecy around Taiwan ODA and to strengthen timely, transparent and comprehensive budget reports to the legislature and citizens as it is suggested in the Paris Declaration (Atkinson, 2014:419). It was indeed unable to call for accountability mechanism to frame Taiwan ODA as it is urged in the Paris Declaration and rather confirmed the total control of MOFA about aid expenditure and decisions. Like the 2009 White Paper, the Act has been also criticized for not being able to make Taiwan ODA transparent notably by failing to set rules with which the Legislative Yuan could control the autonomy of the executive in the domain of ODA (Atkinson, 2014:422). In order not to facilitate transparency, the Act has even opened the possibility of arranging a classified budget for projects that involve national secrets (article 14). So, while it is fair to say that the transparency of Taiwan's ODA has reached a level never attained before, it has to be admitted that it is still opaque to the public and would need more efforts and political will to reach the level of transparency called by the Paris Declaration (2005), the Accra Declaration (2008) and the standards enacted by OECD for DAC countries' reports.

However, the problem of aid transparency is also an issue that concerns European donors. Indeed, while a group of European donors – Sweden, the UK, Denmark and the Netherland – continue to lead the way in aid transparency, and although other donors such as France, Germany or Spain have made considerable improvements to the quality of information published, some European donors – Belgium or Italy – are still off track from meeting their commitment to transparency (EU Transparency Review, 2015).

2.3. *Nature and modalities of Taiwan's* ODA

An assessment of Taiwan's ODA by sectors reveals that in 2013 more than half of Taiwan's foreign aid (56.87%) goes toward improving the social infrastructure (general education, scholarship, healthcare, water supply and sanitation, government and civil society) of recipient countries, followed by the support of their economic infrastructure (transportation and storage, information and telecommunication, energy) (15.23%) and development of specific sectors like tourism, mining, forestry, fisheries (14.23%) (MOFA Taiwan, 2014). The strong focus on improving social infrastructure is a trend that has lasted for a decade even if it was more balanced with support to economic infrastructure under the past presidency. While such focus on supporting social infrastructure is not a characteristic of European donors which in general allocate around one third of their ODA to such area, here Taiwan is however very similar to the UK, Ireland, Luxembourg and Slovenia which dedicated around half of their bilateral ODA to social infrastructures and services in 2013[3].

Furthermore, a distinction between bilateral ODA and multilateral ODA shows that Taiwan ODA has been so far mainly provided though bilateral channels (Figure 2). Thus, in 2013, 85.3% of Taiwan's ODA has been delivered through bilateral channels. Such situation might be explained by its exclusion from the majority of international organizations providing development aid including UN agencies but also by a lack of visibility when Taiwan financial support is pooled

[3] OECD, Statistic from the Development cooperation report 2015. Available at: <http://www.oecd.org/dac/dacmembers.htm>.

in a multilateral budget. This last point is notably the reason why Taiwan stopped its support to Global Fund against HIV/AIDS, Malaria and Tuberculosis in early 2000's after two grants of 1 million USD each.

While the percentage of bilateral ODA compared with multilateral ODA provided by European donors has not reached such level, alike Taiwan, for some European donors, bilateral ODA remains relatively important as it represents more than 70% of their whole ODA. It is notably the case of Switzerland (79%), Norway (78%), Denmark (75%), Germany (71%) and Luxembourg (70%).

Figure 2: Bi-/multilateral distribution of Taiwan's ODA (2007-2013)

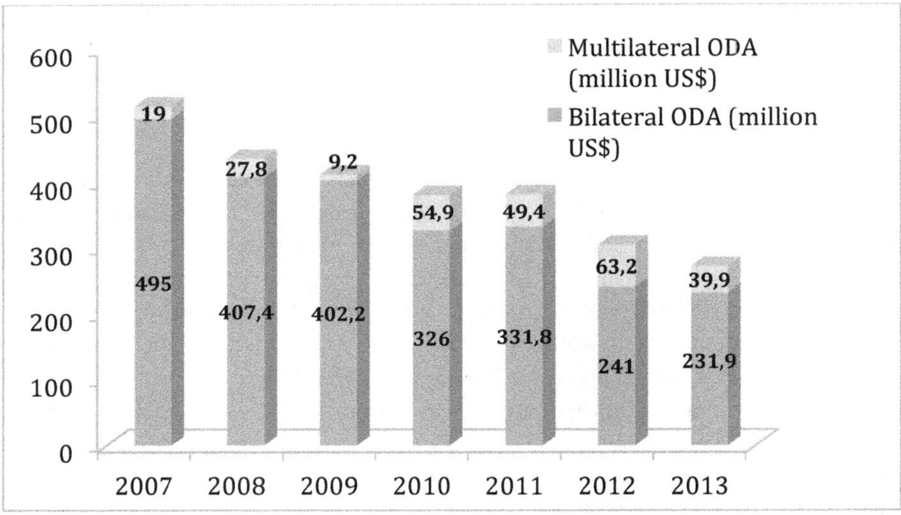

Source: OECD, Development finance reporting of countries beyond the DAC, Paris, <http://www.oecd.org/development/stats/non-dac-reporting.htm>.

Concerning Taiwan's ODA modalities, according to the 2010 Act the following methods may be used for international cooperation and development affairs: technical assistance, investments, loans; financial donations; gifts in kind; dispatch of personnel; development strategy consultations as well as "other feasible methods" which is a rather undefined method which may strangely open assistance to any kind of modalities. Nevertheless, in 2013, the largest share of expenditures of ICDF aid programs was given over to technical assistance (bilateral), and then projects funded by lending followed by grants and investments (Table 1).

Table 1. Evolution of the allocation of the total expenditures of ICDF project

	2008	2009	2010	2011	2012	2013
Total expenditures associated with all Taiwan ICDF projects (NT$ billion)	2.45	1.96	2.04	2.63	1.95	1.87
Technical assistance	65%	83%	76%	53%	64.6%	72,3%
Lending	**23%**	**4%**	**6%**	**35%**	**24.9%**	**13.5%**
Grants	3%	6%	4%	10%	3.5%	4.5%
Investments	9%	7%	14%	2%	5%	9.7%

Source: Taiwan ICDF Annual Reports since 2008.

Technical assistance represents for Taiwan ICDF the main method of channeling ODA to a recipient country over the recent years. Among the most numerous projects falling into the category of technical assistance are agricultural projects such as aquaculture project, eggs production project, banana production project, horticulture project, livestock project, agro-tourism, etc. Here, one interesting and revealing trend in Taiwan's ODA modalities is the evolution of loans. Indeed, in 2009, the first year of Ma's presidency, loans drastically decreased. This might be explained by the past bad experiences notably with Malawi that decided in January 2008 to terminate its 42-year-old diplomatic relations with Taiwan to recognize PRC. While in this country reimbursement was until then done on time, after this decision the loan were only partially repaid. In 2009-2010, Ma was still finalizing his "diplomatic truce' with China, and then at that time his government preferred not to lend money as a too high level to avoid any risk of non-reimbursement. This explained the decline of the ODA channeled through loans at that time which was then explained by the Taiwanese authorities as a will to conform to international call made by some institutions for reducing the share of loans within ODA in reference notably to the Paris Declaration. But after the launch by President Ma of a new flexible diplomacy framework, ODA assistance through loans increased revealing that Taiwan considered then that in the context of the diplomatic truce, it was not risky to lend money to allied countries as China won't try to lure them.

However, the percentage represented by loans in the share of aid expenditures of ICDF might be lower than presented as it is not certain that all loans meet with the definition of OECD to be qualified as ODA, namely that the loan ensures a minimum 25% grant element for LDCs. Indeed, assessment of ODA between 2000 and 2008 revealed that many loans provided by Taiwan with in general a repayment period of up to 25 years did not contain such grant element (Tubilewicz and Guilloux, 2011:330). Nevertheless, if loans do not represent the principal modalities of Taiwan's ODA, Taiwanese authorities considers it as an effective instrument for development and a tool to help improving incentive for fiscal discipline in the recipient country. Thus, as of December 31, 2013, the Taiwan ICDF was committed to 83 lending projects, for which commitments amounted to approximately USD 650 million. Such loans are provided for economic development project which offer returns on investments like the loan (AU$20.2 million) provided by Taiwan to Kiribati in November 2014 to support the upgrade of the Bonriki International Airport and then to complete a grant provided by the World Bank in 2011. Simultaneously, loans are also provided for social infrastructure projects (schools, hospitals) with a pay-back horizon more distant.

In term of comparison, the rather low level of Taiwanese bilateral ODA payments which take the form of loans in 2013 (13.5%) is more comparable to Italy (18.6%) or Spain (15.1%) than to France (55%) or Germany (30.3%) (Euractiv, 2014).

3. Implementation of Taiwan's ODA: many challenges ahead

3.1. The priority to diplomatic allies and an access to multilateral channel still limited

Like before 2009, Taiwan's ODA is provided to its 22 "diplomatic allies" (except Vatican) which are all considered as developing countries by OECD. Taiwanese aid assistance also goes to what is considered by MOFA as "friendly countries" which refers to countries that do not have formal diplomatic ties with Taiwan – and then recognized rather PRC –, but are willing to cooperate with Taiwan to achieve mutual economic development or to enhance substantial bilateral relations (Bahrain, Saudi Arabia, Hungary, Poland, Slovakia, Bulgaria, Latvia…). Interestingly, the number of countries which received ODA from ICDF has lightly decreased (Figure 3).

Indeed, while in the context of the 'diplomatic competition' with China, Taiwan had explored opportunities to provide bilaterally its ODA in order to convinced them to recognize Taiwan as a State, within the framework of Ma's "diplomatic truce" such exploration has been largely stopped and the major parts of ODA is provided to non-allied countries which already received aid assistance under former President Chen. The decrease of the general amount of ODA is certainly also a factor of such decline. So, in terms of geographic distribution, the lion's share of ODA channeled by ICDF goes to diplomatic allies. As an illustration, in terms of health ODA, an allied country such as Burkina Faso has been supported by Taiwan to build a hospital and received the daily assistance of a permanent medical mission while a non-allied country such as Kenya received episodically some medical donations and welcomed short-term medical mission.

Figure 3. Countries receiving ODA from Taiwan ICDF (2003-2014)

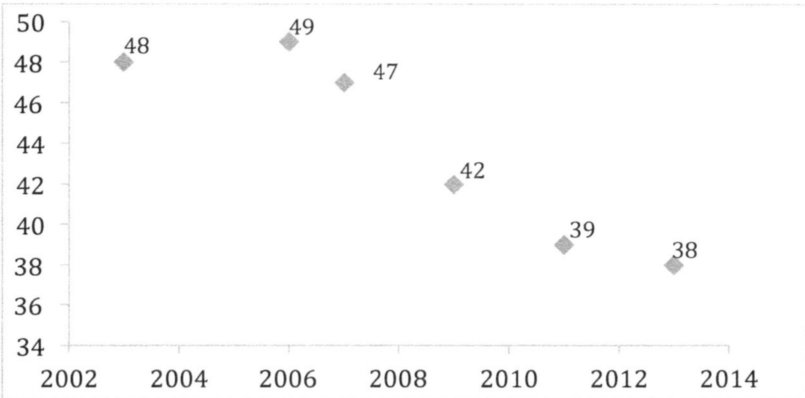

Source: Taiwan ICDF Annual Reports since 2003

One interesting difference with the previous period is the evolution of the nature of ODA provided to China. Indeed, the official aid provided to China by Taiwan might be tracked back to 1988, since then assistance was mainly done through donations (from quasi-governmental institutions). However, since Ma's election, the government as well as local government has not only provided financial donation but has also sent teams to provide technical assistance and humanitarian aid in China. It was notably the case after the Sichuan Earthquake in May 2008 where for the first time, rescue team from Taiwan City Government and Taiwan Red Cross flew in a direct flight from Taipei to Chengdu to provide assistance (Taiwan Review, 2008).

While in the past, Taiwan had limited success in supporting international organizations involved in development assistance (Global Fund, UNICEF, APEC, ERBD…), such situation seems to continue under Ma. In such context, "limited" continues to be the adjective that qualifies the best the Taiwan's multilateral ODA. In other terms, no clear breakthrough has been made in terms of providing ODA at the multilateral level since Ma is in power. Most of the multilateral ODA is flowed through channels which were opened previously by the Chen government. And as an illustration, even if Ma succeed in securing the observer status for Taiwan at the WHA in 2009, this did not convince WHO to accept a recent donation from Taiwan to support regional fight against avian flu in developing countries (Interview, 2015).

3.2. *Tied and unstable aid*

The provision of Taiwanese ODA in diplomatic country is still very dependent of the diplomatic recognition of Taiwan. Experience shows that when a recipient country of Taiwanese ODA decides to switch its diplomatic recognition for China, Taiwan immediately stops its ODA towards this country. Under Chen Shui-bian, the last case was Malawi in January 2008 (Rollet, 2008; Taipei Times, 2008). As an illustration, the program of treatment, counseling, monitoring and support of HIV patient in Mzuzu was immediately stopped and the Taiwanese team went back to Taiwan or was dispatched in another African ally. Consequences of such sudden move for the health of the patients would have been catastrophic if an INGO hasn't taken over the project (Interview, 2015b).

The influence of the Taiwan's international status on ODA reveals how a consequent part of Taiwanese ODA is indeed tied as it is provided "in exchange of" the recognition of its status of State. More recently, despite Ma's "diplomatic truce", Gambia suddenly decided to break with Taiwan in 2013, Taiwan also decided to immediately stop its aid to this African country. Such situation might continue in the future. In this context, diplomatic recognition still represents an important factor for ODA sustainability in diplomatic allies and for ODA in general since the biggest share of ODA goes to diplomatic allies.

However, tying aid to specific conditionality is not reserved to Taiwan, as European donors are also doing the same albeit to a lesser extent. Thus, in 2013, the European donors that have tied an important share of their ODA are Greece (97.3%), Slovak Republic (84.8%), Czech Republic (60%) and Austria (55.8%). The only European donors that provide an ODA fully untied are the UK, Ireland and Norway[4].

3.3. *Limited evaluation of Taiwan's ODA effectiveness on development*

First, in terms of securing the number of diplomatic allies, it seems that the use of ODA was not as successful as expected between 2000 and 2008 as Taiwan lost six of its allies during that period. On the other hand, one may also argue that without its ODA Taiwan should have lost even more allies. In terms of development effectiveness, it is very challenging to draw conclusions about the period 2000-2008, as it exist very few accessible evaluation reports of Taiwan ODA developmental impact in recipient countries.

Concerning effectiveness of Taiwan's oda since 2009, access to official evaluation of Taiwanese aid effectiveness in terms of developmental impact is still

---

[4] OECD, Statistic from the Development cooperation report 2015. Available at: <http://www.oecd.org/dac/dacmembers.htm>.

very limited. However scientific articles and officials interviews inform us about the level of effectiveness of Taiwanese oda in certain fields of oda. Thus, in terms of positive externalities, many articles underlined the significance of "technical upgrading" provided by Taiwan oda notably in the domain of health and agriculture by improving the access to health for people in developing countries and remote areas, protect people from diseases such as malaria (Sao Tome) or by ameliorating local agricultural practices and upgrading local standards of living. However, limited and negative externalities have also been mentioned. Thus, Taiwan's oda in the domain of agriculture has been sometimes criticized for its limited effects and beneficiaries (Marshall Islands, Gambia) (Chien, Yang and Wu, 2010:1200). Recently, recognizing that aid programs focusing on building "Taiwan farms" in Latin American or Caribbean countries have limited effects and beneficiaries, with production value falling short of 0.1 percent of those countries' annual agricultural production, the Taiwan icdf secretary-general Tao Wen-lung (陶文隆) acknowledged that some aid programs had been closed because of inefficiency or obsolescence (Taipei Times, 2013). Furthermore, it has been also said that Taiwan's oda does not always benefit to locals. Indeed, there was critics that significant portion of large business benefiting from Taiwanese funds are owned by Taiwanese-native residents. It is notably the case in Marshall Islands (Chien, Yang and Wu, 2010:1201). Finally, Taiwan's oda has also sometimes disrupted local markets. Early 2009, 500,000 pounds of rice were sent as food aid from Taiwan to relieve a local disaster caused by several floods in 2008. The rice was offered for free to the locals. But, this contribution destroyed the market for local rice sellers making the aid more problematic than positive for local residents.

However, since 2014, it seems that efforts from ICDF have been made to develop a better evaluation of their effectiveness in the light of the Paris Declaration. Such move has been clearly evoked in what it is called the 'Taiwan ICDF Vision 2022' and in MOFA's plan to reform the monitoring of Taiwan's ODA effectiveness but implementation is still being awaited.

3.4. *Future of Taiwan's* ODA

In the evolution of the instrumentalization of Taiwan's ODA in its bidding battle with China since Ma took the power in 2009, it seems first that Taiwan is serious about not raising ODA for competition with China and that China did not try to lure Taiwan's diplomatic allies with promise of more substantial aid. Indeed, if we take the diplomatic withdraw of Gambia in 2013 which could be interpreted – in the first sight – as a failure of Ma's "diplomatic truce" it has been largely recognized that China was not behind such move. Actually, it was a direct consequence of the Taiwanese refusal to provide secretly to the Gambian president an additional financial aid. Furthermore, after this episode, China did not recognized Gambia which is then today the only significant example of a country without diplomatic ties to either Taiwan *or* China.

However, behind this tacit acceptation of Ma's "truce diplomacy", Beijing is actually targeting the Taiwanese presidency in 2016. The Chinese position tells us how China really wants the Ma's administration to succeed. Whatever China is satisfied or not with the rapprochement/unification policy of Ma (often considered as too slow by China), China realized that the opposition and pro-independence party (DPP) will be the big winner if the truce is taken away under Ma. For the next presidential election, it will give the evidence to Taiwan's voters that Ma's rapprochement with the mainland has not brought the benefits he promised. So it is clearly a way to keep KMT in power in Taiwan which is keener to unify with China.

Another important point is that by trying to 'normalize' the deliverance of its ODA by asking notably to more accountability to the leaders in recipient countries, Taiwan could dissatisfied more diplomatic allies which did not get use to such imposed requirements from Taiwan in the past. It is thus known that Taiwan's insistence that Solomon Islands Prime Minister holds account for $1.5 million in development funding finally ended in his replacement as prime minister, not in a break with Taiwan. But then the new prime minister of Solomon Island met with Chinese official. Rumors of diplomatic break in Taiwan were numerous, but never confirmed. It is possible to think that China has convinced Solomon Islands not to withdraw diplomatic recognition of Taiwan now as it won't be able to recognize it (Islands Business, 2013).

One of the most influential element of the future of Taiwan's ODA is certainly the continuity or not of the "diplomatic truce" with Beijing. However, Taiwan's ODA won't increase massively and if the "diplomatic truce" disappeared, the new president and its administration would have to find alternatives that will have to take into account three important prerequisites, namely the protection of the number of allies, the containment of aid spending and the international reputation as an ODA donor which improved under Ma presidency (Atckinson, 2014:419).

Conclusion

Under President Ma Ying-jeou's flexible diplomacy, Taiwan's ODA has known some evolutions. First, a net decrease of its amount and the end of its instrumentalization against China are both linked and a direct consequence of a tacit agreement on a "diplomatic truce" between Taipei and Beijing. Then, a long-waited policy framework was finally designed in order to make ODA more effective and more professional but eventually also under the domination of the

MOFA. However, this framework did not succeed in bringing Taiwan's aid more into the line of the global aid architecture, norms and standards as the improvement of aid transparency, the accountability of the Executive, the untying of aid or the acceptation of debt relief remain unsolved challenges for Taiwanese ODA. Such challenges highlight how the continuity with past practices remains a dominant characteristic of Taiwan's ODA today. After the recent presidential election (16th January 2016), the debate is now open about the future of Taiwan's ODA and in general Taiwan's foreign policy. Nevertheless, one of the main determinants of the evolution of Taiwan's aid will be the continuity or not of the "diplomatic truce".

Finally, in terms of comparison with European aid, it must be acknowledged that Taiwanese and European ODA share more commonalities that it might be expected. Thus, Taiwan is very similar to Poland in terms of ODA/GDP ratio, to France for its small part of ODA channeled through civil society organizations, to Estonia, Hungary or Latvia for voluntarily providing updates to the OECD while they do not belong to the DAC, and to Belgium and Italy in terms of lack of ODA transparency. Simultaneously, Taiwan also shares similarities with Switzerland, Norway and Denmark who also mainly provide their ODA through bilateral mechanisms, with Italy and Spain for its low level of bilateral ODA payments taking the form of loans, or with Greece, the Slovak Republic and the Czech Republic for tying its aid to specific conditionality. Nonetheless, such similarities and others raise the question of the convergence between Taiwanese and European ODA and by extension of the possibility for Taiwan to be involved in trilateral cooperation with a European donor.

Bibliography

ATKINSON, J. (2014) Aid in Taiwan's foreign policy: putting Ma Ying-jeou's aid reforms in historical perspective. *The Pacific Review*, 27(3): 409-431.

BUSINESS INSIDER (2014) China To Lift Aid To Pacific, Sees Cooperation With Taiwan Allies, 13 November.

CHAN, G. (1997) Taiwan as an Emerging Foreign Aid Donor: Developments, Problems, and Prospects. *Pacific Affairs*, 70 (1): 37-56.

CHIEN, S.-S., YANG, T.-P. and WU, Y.-C. (2010) Taiwan's Foreign Aid and Technical Assistance in the Marshall Islands. *Asian Survey*, 50(6): 1184-1204.

CHINA POST (2005) Official decline to reveal aid to Senegal, 8 November.

CHINA POST (2013) Taiwan to stick with foreign aid projects despite funding cut, 16 January.

DREHER, A. and al. (2010) Are 'New' Donors Different? Comparing the Allocation of Bilateral Aid between Non DAC and DAC Donor Countries. Retrieved from: <https://pedl.byu.edu/Documents/Are%20New%20Donors%20Different.pdf>.

EU TRANSPARENCY REVIEW (2015) Available at: <http://roadto2015.org/eu-review>.

EURACTIV (2014) Growing Share of European development aid disguised as loans, 12 December.

GUILLOUX, A. (2009) *Taiwan, Humanitarian and Global Governance.* London: Routledge.

INTERVIEW (2015) Interview with an official from the Taiwan Ministry of Health and Welfare (MOHW), Taipei, 21 January.

ISLANDS BUSINESS (2013) China vs Taiwan gets hotter in the Solomons, April. <http://www.islandsbusiness.com/2013/4/pacific-update/china-vs-taiwan-gets-hotter-in-the-solomons/>.

KONDOH, H. (2012) Taiwan's Foreign Aid: Seeking Statehood. In H.S. KIM and D. M. POTTER (eds), *Foreign Aid Competition in Northeast Asia.* Boulder: Lynne Rienner.

LENGAUER, S. (2011) China's foreign aid policy: Motive and method. *The Bulletin of the Centre for East-West Cultural and Economic Studies*, 9(2), September.

LIN, J.-L. (2003) NGOs Diplomacy. A strategic thinking from 'Taiwan Experience'. *Review of Global Politics*, 2, April: 1-23.

LIN, T.-C. (1995) The ROC's Foreign Aid and the Southward Policy. *Issues & Studies*, 31(10): 1-20.

LIN, T.-C. (1996) Taiwan's Foreign Aid: Instrument and Foreign Policy. *New Zealand Journal of East Asian Studies*, 4(1): 58-80.

MOFA OF PEOPLE'S REPUBLIC OF CHINA (2015) *China's position paper on the Post-2015 Development Agenda.* Beijing, 13 May.

MOFA (TAIWAN) (2009) *White Paper on Foreign Aid Policy: Partnerships for Progress and Sustainable Development.* Taipei, May.

MOFA (TAIWAN) (2010) *International Cooperation and Development Act.* Taipei, June.

MOFA (TAIWAN) (2014) *International Cooperation and Development Report 2013.* Taipei, 29 April.

NAVEJAS, F.J. (2007) International relations among Tom Thumbs : Taiwan as provider of aid Central America. *Tercera Epoca*, N.1, June : 91-141.

OECD (2008) *Development Cooperation of the Republic of Korea.* DAC Special Issue. August, Paris. From: <http://www.oecd.org/dac/peer-reviews/42347329.pdf>.

OECD (2014) *Development Cooperation Report 2014. Mobilizing ressources for sustainable development.* OECD Publishing, Paris.

RELIEFWEB (2005) Taiwan extends helping hands to tsunami victims, 7 January. <http://reliefweb.int/report/indonesia/taiwan-extends-helping-hand-tsunami-victims>

ROLLET, V. (2008) Unsung victims of dollar diplomacy. *Taipei Times*, 17 January: 8.

ROLLET, V. (2015) Taiwanese and Chinese health diplomacies in the South Pacific. What identity and security dimensions?, Paper presented at the Conference "L'Océanie convoitée", CNRS, 14-15 September 2015, Paris.

STATE COUNCIL OF THE PRC (2014) China's Foreign Aid. *Xinhuanet*, Beijing, 10 July.

TAIPEI TIMES (2008) Malawi, Taiwan end 42-year relations, 15 January.

TAIPEI TIMES (2010) Haiti debt payment suspended, 29 may.

TAIPEI TIMES (2013) MOFA rejects most allies'aid project, 17 December.

TAIPEI TIMES (2008) Coming to the Humanitarian Force, 1st August.

THE GUARDIAN (2010) UK urges Haiti creditors to cancel debts, 19 January.

THE GUARDIAN (2011) China publishes first report on foreign aid policy, 28 April.

TUBILEWICZ, C. (2004) Taiwan's 'Macedonian project' 1999-2001. *The China Quarterly*, 179: 782-803.

TUBILEWICZ, C. (2007) *Taiwan and Post-communist Europe: Shopping for Allies*. London and New York : Routledge.

TUBILEWICZ, C. and GUILLOUX, A. (2011) Does size matter? Foreign aid in Taiwan's diplomatic strategy, 2000-8. *Australian Journal of International Affairs*, 65(3): 322-339.

TUBILEWICZ, C. (2012) The politics of compassion: examining a divided China's humanitarian assistance to Haiti. *International Relations of the Asia-Pacific*, 12(3): 449-481.

TUBILEWICZ, C. (2015) State transformation and the domestic politics of foreign aid in Taiwan. *The Pacific Review*, November.

Is European aid so different?

A long term comparison of European, Japanese and Chinese aid programmes

Jean-Christophe DEFRAIGNE

Introduction

The purpose of this chapter is to take a long term perspective to analyze the quantitative and qualitative changes of Europe ODA both at the European Union's level and at the member state's level. Focusing notably on the ACP and African economies, it will highlight the differences between the supranational and national aid policies in Europe and compare them with the two major aid providers from Asia: Japan and China.

Comparing official development aid flows between different donors has always been a difficult task. Development Assistance Committee of the OECD provides a common methodology to assess these flows for its 29 member states that include the EU, Japan and South Korea. Other donor countries from Asia also report their development aid programmes to the OECD such Thailand and Taiwan. Finally, the OECD provides estimates of other important donors, notably China and India (OECD, 2015). Nevertheless, the OECD has its own specific changes of methodology which do not necessarily correspond to those of non-DAC members.

Analyzing the European aid flows is also more complex because of the EU supranational policies and institutions that coexist with the development programmes of the individual EU member states. The total amount of flows from EU member states is more important than those originating from EU institutions (see graph 1 below) so one need to look at both these channels of aid coming from Europe. This chapter will provide a long-term analysis that looks into European aid programmes since the decolonization processes in Africa and Asia. It will show that beyond rhetorical differences, the behaviour of the largest European donors is not fundamentally different from China or Japan. It will also show that there is a high degree of heterogeneity of aid policies between the various EU Member states, notably between those who used to be colonial powers and the others.

1. The origins of European official aid

After the reconstruction of Europe and the decolonization process from 1945 to the early 1960s, the bulk of European aid programs, both national and supranational were designed to maintain existing trade and business links between the former European colonial powers and their colonies. Official aid from non-colonial European countries was strictly limited. Most of the European aid was directed to Africa, the Middle-East and Asia.

In 1957, the negotiations of the Treaty of Rome that would establish the EEC and the Common Market had to address the colonial question. It was already obvious that the European colonial empires were disintegrating fast. European colonies in East Asia gained their independence in the 1950s. In the six founding state, Luxemburg had never any colonies while Germany had lost all colonial possession outside Europe in 1918. The Netherlands gave up their main colonial possession of Indonesia in 1949 after a three-year long and bloody conflict (De Koninck, 2005). The humiliating defeat of Dien Bien Phu in 1954 provoked a brutal reassessment of the colonial question by the French government (Fontaine, 1983). By the time of the Messina negotiation, the French government had to take account the fact that some of its colonies would become independent entities after the creation of the EEC and would therefore find themselves outside the Common Market, facing its common external tariff. The French government had to secure market access to the EEC for the French companies that had invested in the raw materials and agricultural export industries of the colonies.

The French negotiators helped by the Belgians imposed their colonial agenda upon Germany as a last minute condition to join the Common Market (Holland, 2002:26). This led to the adoption of extra fourth part was included in the Treaty of Rome to enable four Member States: France, Belgium, Italy and the Netherlands to maintain their privileged colonial links (the UK would be added in 1973) (Mayall, 2005:296).

As many formers colonies became formally independent in the early 1960s, another agreement was reached that gave these countries a privileged access to the Common Market compared to the GATT's most favored nation status and even to Latin American developing countries. The Yaoundé convention was ratified in 1963 and created a reciprocal free trade agreement that maintained the historical economic links of the colonial times European firms that had been historical traders and investors in the African colonies.

The French government also negotiated hard to insure that EEC member states, most importantly Germany, would share the financial burden of the infrastructure development of their former colonies (Englebert, 2013). The French government obtained in 1958 the creation of a European Development Fund financed mainly by France and Germany (40% each of the $581 millions) (Jovanovic 2013:681). They also secured the possibility to use some of the European Investment Bank (EIB) for development projects in the former colonies (Jovanovic, 2013:681). These steps would generate a two-level development aid policy framework, one at the EEC (later EU) level and one at the Member state level. The provisions of the Treaty of Rome show without any ambiguity the colonial heritage in the first stages of the EEC development policy. The EDF and the EIB generated an incomplete but nevertheless significant EEC wide mutualisation of financial resources that funded development projects outside the EEC. However, the management of the EDF was more intergovernmental that supranational and in many instances a given member state could ensure that the funds it brought to the EDF would be used by its former colonies (Matthews, 2007).

Graph 1. ODA flows 1960-2013 (OECD, 2015)

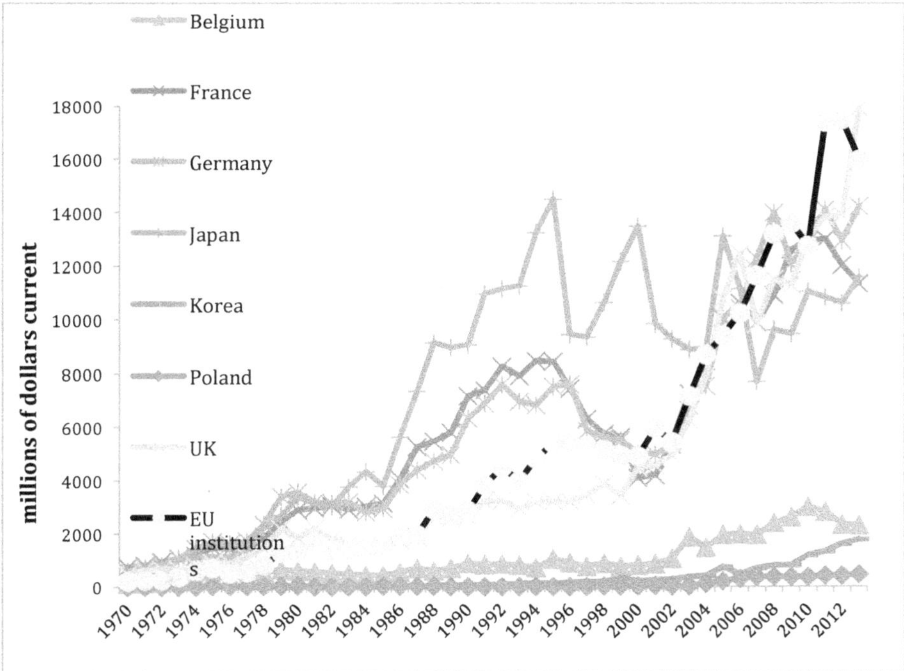

At the EEC member-state level, development policies were even more linked with the colonial past.

Bilateral aid flows between individual member states and their former colonies were always more important than the EEC aid flows (Matthews, 2007: 503; OECD, 2015). Bilateral aid flows from an EEC member state to a former colony were often tied aid to specific project carried out by firms from the EEC member state donor or projects that would facilitate the activities of the donor country's firms operating in the developing country (Barton, 2015). The former colonies of Europe have always been the main recipient of European aid except if one considers the transition period of the Eastern European economies toward capitalism and EU membership in the 1990s.

2. The origin of Asian official aid

The colonial experience clearly differentiated the European aid programmes from their Asian counterparts. Among Asian countries, only Japan has experienced in the 20th century the role of a significant colonizing power comparable as some Western European nations. Albeit one could claim that the Chinese Empire had established a regional tributary system for centuries but it progressively collapsed as Western penetration and colonization in East Asia grew deeper between the 17th and the 19th century. After the humiliating defeats of the Opium Wars and the war against Japan, the Chinese Empire lost its influence and imploded in the early 20th century. In the first half of the 20th century, large parts of China would find themselves under the rule of industrialized colonial powers.

Japan is the only Asian country who bears some similarities with Western European powers. Once it industrialized its economy and modernized its military capacity in the late 19th century, Japan engaged in a colonization process in East Asia by defeating China and imposing itself as the leading regional power. As a latecomer, Japan's colonial links were only regional and not as global as Western European powers. There were relatively short-lived. Japan took control of Taiwan in 1895 and of Korea in 1905. Its expansion in China started in the 1930s and in the rest of Asia Pacific in 1940. Only Korea and Taiwan were transformed in depth as they became a integrate part of the Japanese Empire for decades (Defraigne, 2005). Nevertheless, the Japanese occupation wanted to integrate much further the region for the purpose of developing their national industry and Japanese zaibatsu were strongly supported by the state in their regional expansion (Yamamura, 1997:27; Petri, 1993:39). The Japanese colonization and occupation of East Asia generated important FDI flows and increased considerably the level of economic interdependency between the colonizing power and the region. The crimes and repression of the Japanese military government across the region which generated more than 25 million casualties in less than two decade were strongly resented by indigenous populations, a situation not so different from the indigenous that experienced the brutal Western colonization process (Margolin, 2007; Ferro, 2003).

The major difference was that Japan was military defeated in 1945 and economically weakened by the chaotic effects of the defeat. Japan was a pariah nation isolated from the international community well into the 1950s, with a strictly limited sovereignty under the occupation of US forces until 1952. It was forced to relinquish its colonies. Thanks to the geopolitical situation of the Cold War and the active support of the US, Japan eventually joined international institutions like the UN and the GATT in the mid-1950s and began to resume international trade and investment with its former colonies (Komiya, 1988; Yoshihara, 1988). The European powers co-opted the governments of many of their colonies in Africa and Asia apart from those who were governed by political forces that openly opposed the former colonies, favouring non alignment (like Egypt or Algeria) or a rapprochement with USSR (like Angola or Vietnam) (Cooper, 2008; Schmidt, 2013). This was clearly different from Japan who had no influence on the formation of the new governments of its former colonies or the territories it once occupied in East Asia. The post-war Japanese governments and business had to overcome the deep hostility generated by the war crimes of the imperial military governments among the population of East Asia. In this context, Japanese ODA was used in the 1960s as a tool of soft power to build an image of a peaceful economy wishing to contribute to the prosperity of its neighbours and marking a clear break from its military imperialist past. In the 1960s and 1970s, Japanese ODA was mostly directed to East Asian countries that benefited from 90% of the flows (Hook, 1992:18). Japan became progressively the principal donor in the region. In the early 1990's, China got more than 50% of its aid from Japan, Thailand 60%, the Philippines and Indonesia more than 65%, Malaysia 80.6% (Yamamura, 1997:131). Despite a common position of colonizing powers, the first Japanese aid programmes were therefore developed in a quite different context than those of European former colonial powers and of the EEC.

As for the rest Asia, their development level was extremely low in the 1950s to be significant aid donor. There were more in a position of recipient. South Korea's GDP per capita was similar to that of Senegal, not to mention less advanced economies across East Asia.

The People Republic of China was an exception due to its political specificities. The revolutionary and nationalist character of its government made it a fierce opponent of the economic hegemony of the industrialized capitalist economies that were considered as imperialist powers. After the rupture with Soviet Union in 1960, the PRC engaged into an ideological competition with the USSR for the leadership of the anti-imperialist camp, notably in the developing countries. This generated a paradoxical situation of a developing economy with very a low level of GDP per capita providing aid programmes to other developing countries. Chinese aid flows were marginal compared to Western donors but proved to be significant for some countries, notably in the LDC of East Asia (e.g. Cambodia, North Korea, Burma) and in Sub-Saharan Africa (Zambia, Tanzania). Some authors even claim that Chinese development aid was more important in Africa than USSR during the 1960s and 1970s (Shin, 2014) although the lack of reliable and comparable statistics from both donors make it difficult to be very affirmative. Chinese aid was considerably constrained by its weak development level and domestic priorities, especially after the disaster of the Great Leap Forward. Most of the aid was ideologically rather than economically driven. There were nevertheless projects that pursued both objectives such as the TAZARA railway between Zambia, Tanzania and the Indian Ocean that also improved the access to key raw materials like copper (Fejtö, 1978; Cabestan, 2010; Shambaugh, 2013). Despite its financial limitations, Chinese aid was significant in medicine and public health (containing tropical diseases) (Shambaugh, 2013: 202). China developed better relations with the US after 1971 and normalized its relations with the USSR in the early 1980s. By the late 1970s with the coming to power of Deng Xiao Ping and the launch of economic reforms in China, the PRC's aid programmes were significantly scaled down as the priority was given to domestic economic reform rather than on a revolutionary foreign policy. Chinese aid programmes were thereafter limited until the 2000s.

3. Interested aid: the links between aid and business

3.1. The European case

During the decades that followed the independence, former colonial powers belonging to the EEC developed important tied aid programs to maintain their influence and protect the investments of their national firms in the former colonies. The development project to modernize the infrastructure in transport, utilities, telecom in the French African states also benefited French firms that were key actors in these industries such as Bouygues (building and telecom) or Bolloré (harbour facilities). Aid to develop infrastructure was also useful for the local subsidiaries of European companies producing commodities (Unilever, Lesieur), mining (Lonhro, Société Générale de Belgique) and energy product (Elf, Areva, BP) (Verschaeve, 2000; Braeckman, 1997; Englebert, 2013).

During the 1970s, many developing states nationalized the production of some of their commodities but the international distribution and transport networks continued to be controlled by European groups. Large infrastructure works carried out by European MNEs continued to be in part financed by tied aid programmes from European member states (Englebert, 2013). Many of these projects were not specifically adapted to the needs and capacities of the African economies. Indigenous human capital was not developed enough to operate some of the plants, power stations, telecom centres or hospital built by European firms. The size of the production units built by these large-scale project were often too big for the limited size of the domestic economy and did not allow them to operate at the minimum efficiency scale which undermined seriously their efficiency. This phenomenon continued to generate reliance of foreign experts or in the worst cases, led to the closure of these new facilities soon after their commissioning. Numerous examples of the so-called "white elephants" projects that were in part financed by European bilateral tied aid programmes can be found in many developing countries and notably in Africa (Englebert, 2013; Braeckman, 1997; Brunel, 2004). The lack of transparency of the aid programmes of the EEC member states in the 1960s to the 1990s that had been colonial powers is pointed out by various authors that have emphasized the economic motives behind many donations or soft loans (Englebert, 2013; Verschaeve, 2000; Cooper, 2008; Moyo, 2009).

The debt crisis of the 1980s and 1990s generated a lost decade in terms of economic development and the weakening of many developing states in Africa (Chad, Mali, Somalia, Sierra Leone, Rwanda, Congo) (George, 1990; Englebert, 2013). For the ACP countries that received the bulk of European aid, the tools designed by the EEC like Sysmin and Stabex proved insufficient to compensate the fall of commodity price (Holland, 2002:37). "White elephants" projects became notorious and generated a disillusion on the effect of aid programmes (Moyo, 2010; Moghalu, 2014). With the end of the Cold War, the financial support of pro-Western corrupted regimes and failed states in the developing world was serious questioned. These evolutions provoked three major changes in the EU aid policy.

Firstly, given the success of some East Asian newly industrialized economies (the Asian Tigers and China that were praised in the famous report by the World Bank on the "East Asian miracle") that had witnessed a major development thanks to the export of manufactured goods and the relative failure of most ACP to catch up with the industrialized countries, the EU Commission and many EU member states advocated that trade was more important than aid. As a result, OECD and EU ODA flows declined in real terms from 1990 to 2002 (Hugon, 2009:50; Moyo, 2010:25; Nixson, 2007:332). The DG in charge of Development (DEVCO) had to operate with a global framework designed by the DG Trade to try to help the insertion of developing countries in the world trading system and to facilitate trade with the EU. The European institutions in charge of aid tried to avoid the reproduction of "white elephants" projects and embezzlement by indigenous political elites. As aid flows declined, European aid became more horizontal and focused poverty alleviation, access to social services and education, gender equality and microcredit (Moyo, 2010). By 2005, 22% of EU supranational aid programme were directed to infrastructure projects and production activities against 45% for the social sector (Matthews, 2007: 510). Nevertheless, this evolution was not similar for all member states, notably for France. Furthermore, in the 2000, a significant share of ODA flows from the EU took the form of "budget support" that is contribution to the national budget of the recipient countries (Englebert, 2013:253). This means that it has become more complicated to precisely determine the share of ODA linked with tied aid programmes that could benefit to EU firms operating in the developing countries.

Second, the end of the Cold War and waning support to openly dictatorial state by public opinion and economists generated the adoption of the principle of political conditionality to receive EU aid to make sure that aid would be used effectively and to generate a leverage to induce democratic reforms (Englebert, 2013).

Thirdly, the EU and the former colonial powers of Europe started to consider their former colonies are relatively less important from an economic perspective, even marginal in many instance. From the 1970s to the 2000s, the share of the ACP group in the total EU trade and investment flows continued to shrink. The share of trade with Africa in the total trade flow of the EU fell by 50% between 1970 and 2008 (Hugon, 2009:46). European MNEs concentrated on emerging economies rather than the ACP. In 2004, Africa received only 2% of the world FDI flows, mostly directed to South Africa and North Africa.

The collapse of the Berlin Wall, the withdrawal of Soviet forces in Eastern Europe and the transition of the Eastern European economies towards capitalism put the ACP in the back of the picture. The priority in the 1990s until the enlargement of 2004 was to help these countries to shift to a market-led economy and to insert themselves in the Western European economy. The most advanced Eastern European economies received substantial financial aid (PHARE, ISPA, SAPARD) to adapt to the *acquis communautaire* (the EU legislation and the set of administrative procedures necessary to function within the EU) and to modernize their economy. The aid programs in Eastern Europe in the 1990s were also submitted to political conditionality (Berend, 2009). In the Eastern European case, aid programmes were closely linked with the interests of Western European business (Defraigne, 2013). Aid programs help to develop the EU institutional framework and the infrastructure that enabled Western firms to invest massively in Eastern Europe with market-seeking FDI and efficiency-seeking FDI (relocate labour-intensive activities to Eastern Europe to benefit from a cheap and flexible labour force and from lower corporate taxes). It smoothened the reorganisation of the regional division of labour organized by Western European MNEs (and to a lesser extent by non European MNEs, mostly from the US, Japan and South Korea) (Defraigne, 2013).

These various changes brought a new approach to EU-ACP relations that affected the EU aid programmes. Once WTO and some of their important members criticized the former Lomé system for its non consistency with WTO rules, the EU commission built a new framework to replace Lomé and define the new EU-ACP relations for 2000-2020 that became known as the Cotonou agreement (Holland, 2002). Cotonou was clearly focusing on trade more than aid and aimed at creating EPAs that were consistent with WTO rules (Crawley, 2006). It also considered that it was better to divide the ACP countries into 6 separate groups of countries (4 Africans, 1 Caribbean and 1 Pacific). The European Commission wanted these 6 groups to engage faster into economic regional integration within each group. The underlying economic analysis behind this demand for greater regional integration was that the size of the domestic economy was to attract MNEs to generate efficiency-seeking and market-seeking FDI as in East Asia. The narrowness of the domestic economy and the absence of common technical standards prevent to operate efficiently transport, energy and telecom infrastructure which had experienced significant increase of economies of scale since the 1980s. In the eyes of the economists of the European Commission, national economies of the ACP were too small to develop manufacturing activities and even keep their competitiveness in the trade of their traditional commodities due to inefficient infrastructure (Defraigne, 2015). Given that numerous infrastructure industries were built and operated by EU-based MNEs, this also allowed these firms to operate more efficiently. The EU them provided some aid programmes to encourage regional integration in the ACP. The six groups were based on existing regional integration processes.

The deepening existing regional integration schemes and the creation of interregional EPAs within the Cotonou agreement framework was a long and enduring process. In the 2010s, the EU also added a seventh region (Eastern-Southern Africa) and there were still two regions (Central Africa and Eastern-Southern Africa) who had not signed their agreement in June 2015 and only two had been fully ratified and effective (with Caricom and the East African Community) (European Commission, 2015). These seven intraregional agreements are not fully effective before at least a decade and the implementation schemes are not very precise. Fear of loss of specific rents by local government and business elites (loss of custom duties, loss of protection given by technical barriers to trade) as well as the insufficient development of existing integrated transport infrastructure at the regional level explain in part these slow progresses.

These elements show that ODA from the EEC-EU and from some of its member states also benefited to their national firms and were in part linked to business interests, in the ACP as in Eastern Europe. Various authors have questioned the effectiveness of the political and good governance conditionality since the 1990s (Englebert, 2013; Moyo, 2010; Barkan, 2009). The case of aid programmes given by EU member states or the EU to Rwanda in the 1990s and 2000s, to Eastern European countries or to Ben Ali's Tunisia as late as 2010 highlighted the leniency of the European donors to corruption and authoritarian practices. Recent analyses of Belgium and France development policies and political connections with some African economies have showed the pursuit of opaque and peculiar practices. In France, one should recall the affairs of the "valises" of Omar Bongo and Sassous-Nguesso and the dismissal of Bockel[1] in charge of development policies of the French government that had pleaded for the end of the *françafrique* by prime minister Fillon in 2008 (Harel, 2011:41; Englebert, 2013:337). In Belgium, this opacity and overlapping interests between trade and development policies with business can be seen with the nexus of the Michel family, Pierre Chevalier (state secretary for trade), Étienne Davignon and George Forrest, a prominent Belgian businessman operating in the RDC[2] as well as the scandal of the former minister Kubla involved in a bribery case in the RDC in 2015 (Sénat de Belgique, 2003; Ayad, 2006; Corporate Europe observatory, 2007). Doval has shown that for the West African region, 53% of EU Development contracts over 2 million euro went to EU firms between 2007 and 2012, a percentage more than twice the share of the EU in the world economy, suggesting a bias in favour the donor countries (Doval, 2015).

---

[1] French Minister of State with responsibility for Cooperation and Francophonie.

[2] In 2007 Charles Michel was appointed Belgian Minister of Development Cooperation at the age of 28 while his father Louis Michel was the European Commissioner for Development and Humanitarian Aid. George Forrest, one of the most active Belgian businessman investor of Congo had been nominated special adviser to the Belgian government by Pierre Chevalier and Louis Michel in 2000. Pierre Chevallier was the vice-president of George Forrest International (GFI). Louis Michel became the president of the scientific committee of the Foundation George Arthur Forrest, the foundation is located in Wavre whose mayor had been Charles Michel. In 2007 Louis Michel also came under the scrutinity of many NGOs because of the important EU aid projects to develop infrastructure in Africa, notably in the former Belgian colonies and Michel's ties with former commissioner Davignon who was an adviser to Suez, a French MNEs applying for infrastructure procurements in Africa (Corporate Europe observatory 2007).

Despite the post-Cold War rhetoric of international institutions and EU donors claiming to impose a strong conditionality linking aid with good governance and avoiding new white elephant projects, it seems that ties between EU aid and business are still important and conditionality remain a relatively flexible concept.

3.2. The Japanese case

Compared to the European case, the Japanese aid system is more openly linked with Japanese business and economic interests (Lincoln, 1992:28). Japan's Official Development Assistance (ODA) Charter adopted in 1992 and which has been the reference policy document of Japanese aid for two decades mentions that "as nations deepen their interdependence, Japan, which enjoys the benefits of international trade and is heavily dependent on the outside world for resources, energy and food, will proactively contribute to the stability and development of developing countries through its ODA. This correlates closely with assuring Japan's security and prosperity and promoting the welfare of its people. In particular, it is essential that Japan make efforts to enhance economic partnership and vitalize exchange with other Asian countries with which it has particularly close relations" (MOFA, 2015). Japanese aid agencies are understaffed and rely on the private sector, notably on large trading companies to get extra help to fulfil their missions (Yamamura, 1997:125). The trading companies and large keiretsu master the functioning of Japanese ODA better than the development agencies of the recipient countries themselves and can provide them with information on how to apply for Japanese ODA (Yamamura, 1997:126). This close relation between Japanese business and aid programmes can be traced back decades.

After 1985, Japanese ODA flows experienced a dramatic increase (see graph 1 *supra*). Due the massive appreciation of the yen after the Plaza accord of 1985, the rising Japanese wages and trade frictions with Western economies, the competitiveness of Japanese firms deteriorated. To respond to this challenge, the Japanese government and the *keidaren* (the Japanese private sector business organisation) began to encourage the relocation of labour intensive activities towards neighbouring economies who benefited from lower wages, a cheaper currency and had less trade tensions with the US and Europe. The powerful MITI ministry designed a "Project for Comprehensive Co-operation Asian Industrialization" also named "New Aid Plan". MITI, JETRO, *keidaren* and the Japanese Institute for Developing Economies collaborated closely together to use aid as a facilitator of the regionalization of the production process of Japanese firms that relocated labor-intensive activities abroad (Doner, 1993: 188).

Japanese firms often chose to relocate their labor-intensive activities in already developed areas of East Asia, not in the poorest and most remote region (such as Laos or Myanmar). Japanese aid schemes came to help the Japanese investors by providing transport, energy or building infrastructures to transform specific East Asian regions or cities into export platforms used by Japanese firms. This is why the Japanese ODA of the 1980s and 1990s did not prioritise Asia's least developed regions. For example, the poorest regions of Thailand received little Japanese ODA compared to the Bangkok area (Doner, 1993:233). During this period, most of the Japanese aid was tied and often took the form of loans for large infrastructure projects built by Japanese enterprises (Lincoln, 1992: 28, Yamamura, 1997:127).

As in the European case, Japanese aid programmes have been characterized by their strong links with national business interests. The bulk of Japanese ODA has helped to restructure the Japanese industry in the 1980s and 1990s by facilitating the regionalization of the production process of Japanese MNEs across East Asia. This is quite similar to the European aid programmes in central and Eastern Europe in the 1990s where PHARE, ISPA and SAPARD help to integrate these transition economies to the EU single market and to facilitate FDI from Western European MNEs. Given the limited degree of industrialization of many East Asian economies in the 1980s (apart from South Korea, Singapore, Hong-Kong and Taiwan) compared to Eastern Europe (which had experienced a state-led industrialization since the 1950s), the Japanese aid programmes and the big wave of efficiency-seeking FDI of the 1980s and 1990s proved a decisive catalyst to the development of the export manufacturing sector in East Asia. One could reasonably consider that the impact of Japanese ODA in East Asia must have been greater than Western European and EU ODA, most certainly in the case of the ACP recipients which did not benefit from substantial efficiency-seeking FDI flows.

3.3. The Chinese case

The experience of Chinese ODA is much more difficult to assess in quantitative terms. The PRC's accountancy rules and definitions of aid are not consistent with those of the OECD DAC (Belligoli, 2010; Zhang, 2010 & Wang, 2007). Furthermore Chinese data are aggregated by regions and country level data are not available on a systematic basis (Shin, 2014:148). Only in 2011 did China publish its first White Paper on Foreign Aid which contains systematic official data (Shambaugh, 2013). Despite these limitations, all sources available show that Chinese ODA flows began to increase rapidly in the 2000s. China has become one of the ten most important donors of the 2010s (ranked 6th by some estimates in 2012 (Kitano, 2014:17). Nevertheless, it remains a modest donor compared to the EU and even to Japan (OECD, 2015 & Barton, 2015) (see graph. 2 below). China is still a developing country with a GDP per capita at

PPP only one third of the EU one. Most of the aid flows go to Africa (45,7% in 2011) and Asia (32.8%) (Shambaugh, 2013).

Graph 2. Official Development Aid (2009-2012)

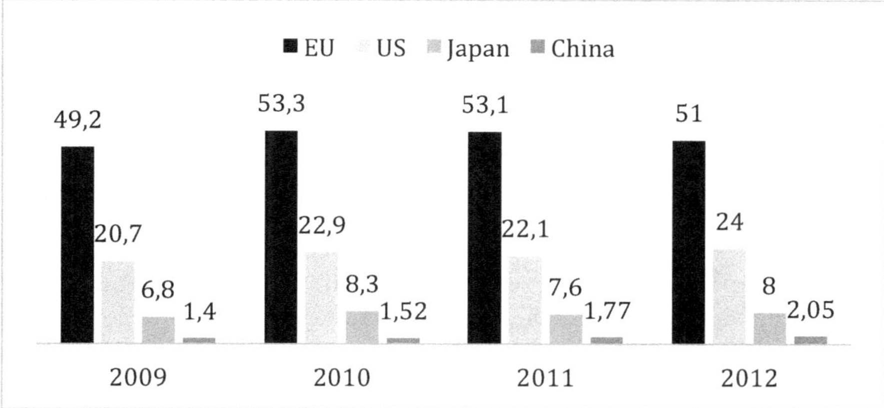

Sources: Eurostat, 2015; Kitano, 2014; own calculations. Chinese ODA are based on Kitano's estimates

From anecdotic evidence and qualitative studies, China ODA schemes resemble the Japanese experience as the economic objectives are put forward stated and aid schemes are often linked to the development of infrastructure (Shin, 2014: 152). Nevertheless, due to the structure and the development of the Chinese economy, Chinese ODA is more often linked to resource-seeking than efficiency-seeking investments. Unlike Japan, the relative stagnation of the low Chinese wages from the 1980s to the 2000s combined with the pegging of the Chinese currency to the dollar explains why most-labor intensive activities remain in China. Since 2010, wages increases and the appreciation of the real exchange rate have begun to generate some relocation of labor-intensive activities from China to Asian countries such as Vietnam or Bangladesh (Defraigne, 2015). Some Chinese firms have also relocated to least developed countries (LDCs) such as Ethiopia and Cambodia to benefit from the preferential trade regime of these countries (such as EU's Everything-But-Arms which provides a duty-free access to the EU market). These phenomenon is relatively recent and is still in an infancy-stages. Chinese ODA can facilitate these efficiency-seeking FDI but their focus remains on resource-seeking FDI. The weight of the manufacturing sector in the Chinese economy is one of the highest in the world and the extremely fast growth of these last three decades have made China increasingly dependent on overseas sources of raw materials. Resources access has become one of the highest priorities of Chinese diplomacy in the 2000s (Economy,

2014). ODA is seen as a facilitator to the access of key materials and commodities from the developing world by developing extraction and transport infrastructure. ODA from China is also used as a mean to facilitate the overseas development of Chinese MNEs in the infancy stage that provide services in the utilities industries such as Sinohydro or Huawei (Belligoli, 2010; Brautigam, 2009).

The Chinese aid policy, like those of the EU and other donors, has a specific rhetoric and ideological framework to legitimize their policies. In the case of China, it is still based on Zhou En Lai's "Eight principles for China's aid to foreign countries"[3] stated during his visit in Ghana in 1964 and on the "Five Principles of Peaceful Coexistence" of the 1954 Bandung Conference[4] (Belligoli, 2010). China has often been criticized for the lack of political conditionality of its aid programs which could undermine the efforts of the World Bank, the IMF and other donors, notably the EU who claim to promote good governance

[3] (1). The Chinese Government always bases itself on the principle of equality and mutual benefit in providing aid to other countries. It never regards such aid as a kind of unilateral alms but as something mutual.

(2). In providing aid to other countries, the Chinese Government strictly respects the sovereignty of the recipient countries, and never attaches any conditions or asks for any privileges.

(3). China provides economic aid in the form of interest-free or low-interest loans and extends the time limit for repayment when necessary so as to lighten the burden of the recipient countries as far as possible.

(4). In providing aid to other countries, the purpose of the Chinese Government is not to make the recipient countries dependent on China but to help them embark step by step on the road of self-reliance and independent economic development.

(5). The Chinese Government tries its best to help the recipient countries build projects which require less investment while yielding quicker results, so that the recipient governments may increase their income and accumulate capital.

(6). The Chinese Government provides the best-quality equipment and material of its own manufacture at international market prices. If the equipment and material provided by the Chinese Government are not up to the agreed specifications and quality, the Chinese Government undertakes to replace them.

(7). In providing any technical assistance, the Chinese Government will see to it that the personnel of the recipient country fully master such technique.

(8). The experts dispatched by China to help in construction in the recipient countries will have the same standard of living as the experts of the recipient country. The Chinese experts are not allowed to make any special demands or enjoy any special amenities.

[4] The Five Principles are:

(1). Mutual respect for sovereignty and territorial integrity

(2). Mutual non-aggression

(3). Non-interference in each other's internal affairs

(4). Equality and mutual benefit

(5). Peaceful coexistence

and the fight against corruption and human right abuses. The EU attempts to make China accept the concept of conditionality adopted by the Western donors but so far China has resisted to those demands (Alden, 2015). Chinese ODA is considered to be supporting corrupt and authoritarian regimes as in the case of Sudan or Myanmar or to take advantage of weak states by imposing asymmetric bargains in which Chinese stakeholders take the lion's share as in the case of the Democratic Republic of Congo with the so-called "deal of the century" in 2007 (Shin, 2014:293).

These criticisms are funded for many authors but China's behavior is not so different than other donors. China adopts a different political conditionality than the one adopted by the IMF, World Bank or the EU. Chinese authorities claim that governments are politically sovereign and will not interfere in their domestic politics. The type of political conditionality imposed by China focuses on international relations aspects. China has used ODA to promote its "one China policy" and isolate further Taiwan or to gain influence among LDCs and small developing countries (notably in the Pacific). The Chinese government provides some of its aid to countries which have tense relations with the Western countries. Because China is a newcomer in terms of securing access to overseas' sources of key raw materials compared to Western Powers and even Japan, it also develops ties with countries where Western penetration is more limited because of the hostile relations with the local governments (such as Iran, Sudan, North Korea, Myanmar or Zimbabwe).The way Western governments and media monitor human rights violations by Zimbabwe or Iran contrast sharply with the relative limited coverage of Equatorial Guinea or Gulf Emirates where Western oil companies have important investments. This sometimes conveys an image that China's aid supports dictatorships and promotes bad governance but it is also explained by the biased view of Western officials and media who fail to provide the same coverage of the aid flows received by pro-Western recipients in the developing world whose records on good governance and human rights are not fundamentally different. Furthermore, the PRC does not adopt a confrontational view on these aspects of its foreign policy and can be sensitive to the Western governments' pressures in some instances.

As in the case of EU and other Western countries and Western dominated IMF and World Bank, the Chinese rhetoric is also quite flexible in its enforcement according to China's own economic and geopolitical interests. However, Chinese aid is seen as quite efficient and sometimes more than the EU aid by many African actors (Barton, 2015). This could be explained by various factors, including the more direct and centralized control of aid project by the Chinese government; the experience of developing world working conditions by

Chinese firms that have developed similar project in the least developed regions of China and the simpler technology (compared to Western standards embodied in the Chinese infrastructure projects (Brautigam, 2009 & Moyo, 2009).

Conclusion

From the elements outlined in this chapter, one can claim that the EU, the Japanese and Chinese Aid programs are not designed to maximize the development capacities of the recipient countries but in part to serve specific national interests of the donor countries. ODA is regularly used as a trade or investment facilitator for national firms of the donor country in some European, Japanese or Chinese aid programs.

The most important difference between the EU, China or Japan probably lay in the specific state-enterprises relations that prevail in China. Most of the Chinese MNEs operating in the developing world are still directly or indirectly state-owned and all of them have a direct link between the Chinese Communist Party (Mc Gregor, 2010). This means that the political control of the CCP of the economic diplomacy is more centralized than in the EU member states and Japan. European and Japanese private firms engaged in development projects are far more autonomous from government interference than their Chinese counterparts. Companies like Total (and Elf before), Bouygues, Suez or GFI design their strategies without direct government scrutiny. In that sense, the relation between the business interests and the aid policies of the governments are different in the Chinese case where the approach is more top-down and closely directed by the leadership of the CCP. The Chinese development projects are part of a grand-national strategy to correspond to key national goals set by the CCP (McGregor, 2010; Huang, 2011). The EU member states seems to have a development aid strategy more influenced by national private firms lobbying on specific firms interest above the national interest of the donor country, not to mention the recipient country. As for the EU level programs, the lobbying of firms from member states is often more indirect (made through the representative of member states) but not always.

Bibliography

ALDEN, C., BARBER, L. (2015) EU-China-Africa and the challenges of African development. In J. WOUTERS, J.C. DEFRAIGNE and M. BURNAY, *China, the EU and the Developing World.* Cheltenham: Edward Elgar.

AYAD, C. (2006) Monsieur Forrest, une mine d'investissements. *Libération*, 13 septembre.

BARTON, B., de BELLEFROID, A. (2015) China and the European Union in Sub-Saharan Africa. In J. WOUTERS, J.-C. DEFRAIGNE and M. BURNAY, *China, the EU and the Developing World.* Cheltenham: Edward Elgar.

BELLIGOLI, S., DEFRAIGNE, J.-C. (2010) Ties Between Business and Aid Programs in Africa: a Comparative Analysis Between the European and Chinese Cases, EBHA annual conference 2010, 26-28 August.

BEREND, I. (2009) *From the Soviet Bloc to the European Union.* Cambridge University Press.

BERNARD, P., BEZAT, J.M. (2009) La France investit dans l'uranium du Congo. *Le Monde*, 28 March 2009.

BRAECKMAN, C. (1997) *Le Dinosaure.* Paris: Fayard.

BRAUTIGAM, D. (2009) *The Dragon's gift.* Oxford: Oxford University Press.

BRUNEL, S. (2004) *L'Afrique: un continent en réserve de développement.* Saint-Etienne: Bréal.

CABESTAN, J.P. (2010) *La politique internationale de la Chine.* Paris: Les Presses Sciences Po.

COOPER, F. (2008) *L'Afrique depuis 1940.* Paris: Payot.

CORPORATE EUROPE OBSERVATORY (2007) Chronology of the controversy about Davignon's conflict of interests, March 30th, Brussels.

CRAWLEY, A. (2006) Europe-Latin America (EU-LAC) relations: toward interregional coalition building. In H. HÄNGGI, R. ROLOFF and J. RÜLAND (eds), *Interregionalism and international relations.* Oxon: Routledge.

DEFRAIGNE, J.C. (2005) Commercial Integration. In DIETER, H. (ed.), *Report on East Asian Integration: Opportunities and Obstacles for Enhanced Economic Co-operation.* Paris: Notre Europe.

DEFRAIGNE, J.C. (2013) *Introduction à l'Economie Européenne.* Ouvertures Économiques, Brussels: De Boeck.

DEFRAIGNE, J.C. (2015) The historical links between China, Europe and the developing world. In J. WOUTERS, J.-C. DEFRAIGNE and M. BURNAY, *China, the EU and the Developing World.* Cheltenham: Edward Elgar.

DE KONINCK, R. (2005) *L'Asie du Sud-Est.* 2e édition, Paris: Armand Colin.

DONER, R.F. (1993) Japanese Foreign Direct Investment and the Creation of a Pacific Asian Region. In J. FRANKEL, M. KAHLER, *Regionalism and Rivalry: Japan and the United States in Pacific Asia.* NBER: University of Chicago Press.

DOVAL, V. (2015) The case of Senegal from Yaounde to Cotonou, Paper presented at the international conference "Africa, China and Europe: Challenges and opportunities generated by China's rise in Africa and its effects on African-European relations", Université Saint-Louis, 11 may, Brussels.

ENGLEBERT, P., DUNN K. (2013) *Inside African Politics*. London: Lynne Riener.

EUROPEAN COMMISSION (2015) Overview of EPA Negotiations, updated May. European Commission, DG Trade, Brussels.

FEJTÖ, F. (1978) *Chine-URSS: de l'alliance au conflit*. Paris: Seuil.

FERRO, M. (2003) *Le livre noir du colonialisme*. Paris: R. Laffont.

FONTAINE, A. (1983) *Histoire de la Guerre Froide*. Tomes I, II & III. Paris: Seuil Histoire.

GEORGE, S. (1990) *A Fate Worse Than Debt*. New York: Grove Weidenfeld.

HAREL, X., HOFNUNG, T. (2011) *Le scandale des biens mal acquis*. Paris: La Découverte.

HOLLAND, M. (2002). *The European Union and the Third World*. New York: Palgrave.

HOOK, G.D. and al. (2001) *Japan's International Relations: Politics, Economics and Security*, Routledge.

HUANG, Y.S. (2008) *Capitalism with Chinese characteristics: Entrepreneurship and the State*. Cambridge, Mass.: Cambridge University Press.

HUGON, P. (2009) *L'Economie de l'Afrique*. Paris: La Découverte.

JANSEN, M. (2000) *The Making of Modern Japan*. Harvard University Press.

JOVANOVIC, M. (2013) *The Economics of European integration*. 2nd edition, Edward Elgar.

KITANO, N., HARADA Y. (2014) *Estimating China's Foreign Aid 2001-2013*, Working Paper No. 78, June, JICA Research Institute, Japan International Cooperation Agency (JICA).

KOMIYA R., MOTOSHIGE I. (1988) Japan's International Trade and Trade Policy 1955-1984. In I. TAKASHI, D. OKIMOTO (eds), *The Political Economy of Japan. Volume 2: The Changing International Context*. Stanford: Stanford University Press.

LINCOLN, E.J. (1992) *Japan's rapidly emerging strategy toward Asia*. OECD/GD (92)59. Paris.

MARGOLIN, J.-L. (2007) *Violences et Crimes du Japon en Guerre*. Paris: Hachette-Armand Colin.

MATTHEWS, A. (2007) The EU and the Developing World. In EL AGRAA, A. (ed.) *The European Union: Economics & Policies*. 8th edition, Cambridge University Press.

MAYALL, J. (2005) The shadow of Empire. In HILL, C., SMITH, M. (eds), *International relations and the European Union*. Oxford University Press.

MC GREGOR, R. (2010) *The Party: The Secret World of China's Communist Rulers*. London: Penguin Books.

MOFA (Ministry of Foreign Affairs of Japan) (2015) Revision of Japan's Official Development Assistance Charter (Draft) <http://www.mofa.go.jp/policy/ODA/reform/revision0307.html>.

MOGHALU, K.C. (2014) *Emerging Africa.* London: Penguin Books.

MOYO, D. (2010) *Dead aid.* London: Penguin Books.

NIXSON, F. (2008) Aid, Trade & Economic Development. In NIXSON, F., ARTIS, M., *The Economics of the European Union.* Oxford University Press.

OECD (2015) Aid statistics, <http://www.oecd.org/dac/stats/>.

PETRI, P. (1993) The East Asian Trading Bloc: an analytical history. In FRANKEL, J., KAHLER, M., *Regionalism and Rivalry: Japan and the United States in Pacific Asia.* NBER: University of Chicago Press.

SENAT DE BELGIQUE (2003) Annales du Sénat de Belgique, version française, mardi 1er avril 2003, séance de l'après-midi, Sénat de Belgique, Brussels.

SCHMIDT, E. (2013) *Foreign Intervention in Africa.* Cambridge University Press.

SHAMBAUGH, D. (2013) *China Goes Global: The Partial Power.* Oxford: Oxford University Press.

SHIN, D., EISENMAN, J. (2014) *China in Africa: a century of engagement.* Philadelphia: University of Pensylvania Press.

VERSCHAVE, F.-X. (2000) *Noir Silence.* Paris: Les Arènes.

WANG, J.-Y. (2007) *What drives China's Growing Role in Africa?* IMF Working Paper, WP/07/211, Washington DC.

YAMAMURA, K., HATCH, W. (1997) *Asia in Japan's embrace: building a regional production alliance.* Cambridge University Press.

YOSHIHARA, K. (1988) *The rise of Ersatz capitalism in Southeast Asia.* Oxford: Oxford University Press.

Part 2.

Euro-Asian cooperation in ODA: achievements and challenges

China as a (re)emerging donor in Africa: Opportunities and challenges for cooperation with the European Union

Anna Katharina STAHL

Introduction

Since the turn of the century, the international development landscape has witnessed fundamental shifts. In particular, a multiplicity of actors has started to engage in new forms of development cooperation. In particular, middle-income countries from Asia are now playing the role of so-called "emerging donors". In this context, China's engagement in Africa has witnessed growing attention.

After a period of isolation, the Peoples Republic of China (China) has started to exert a growing international influence, in particular in the field of international development cooperation. China is not only expanding its cooperation with international organisations like the World Bank's International Development Association (IDA) and the OECD's Development Assistance Committee (DAC), but it has also become one of the world's biggest suppliers of finance to developing countries (Chin, 2012; Stahl, 2013). Alongside its growing commitment to international financial institutions, China has also started to put forward new development strategies and institutions. Most importantly, China has initiated the establishment of a new international financial institution, the Asian Infrastructure Investment Bank (AIIB). Under the label "One Belt, One Road" (OBOR), the Chinese leadership has also initiated a new development strategy, which is based on two main components: the land-based "Silk Road Economic Belt" and the "Maritime Silk Road". China's New Silk Road Initiative is accompanied by a specific fund, of which developing countries in Africa will be prime beneficiaries as the Maritime Silk Road is reaching across the Indian Ocean to the African continent (Stahl, 2015).

China's engagement in Africa has become a symbol for the changing international development landscape. The increase of Chinese development assistance to Africa bears important consequences for traditional donors like the European Union (EU). On one hand, EU-China relations have traditionally been based on development cooperation. On the other hand, the EU is the biggest aid donor to Africa. Hence, China's growing engagement in Africa did not only contribute to a rebalancing of the EU's relations with Africa, but also set the stage for the formulation of new trilateral EU-China-Africa partnership.

This chapter is divided into three sections. The first section sheds light on China's role as an emerging donor and its growing role in Africa. Against this background, section two examines the how China's rise in Africa has contributed to changing the nature of the EU's development cooperation with Africa. Finally, section 3 explores the growing collaboration between the EU and China to foster African development, as well as initial attempts of establishing a new type of EU-China-Africa trilateral dialogue.

1. China's Engagement in African Development

Due to the fact that China does not share the same historical legacy with Africa as traditional donors like the EU, China is commonly described as an "emerging" donor in Africa. Yet, China is not a completely "new" player in the region and current Sino-African relations are based on deep historical roots (Lum et al., 2009). In addition to its long-lasting diplomatic relations with Africa, China has also gained some experience as a donor of development assistance in other parts of the world. In fact, 2010 marked the 60th anniversary of China's foreign assistance, which shows that China has a longer history of being a donor than a recipient of aid.

China's foreign aid began in 1950, only one year after the founding of the People's Republic of China (PPC). During this period, China's foreign aid was influenced by the Cold War and mostly driven by ideological motivations. For this reason, China provided most of its economic and technical assistance to neighbouring socialist countries such as North Korea and Vietnam. Following the Asian-African Conference in Bandung in 1955 (known as the Bandung Conference), China expanded the range of its aid recipients to include non-socialist countries in Asia and Africa. In this context, Chairman, Mao Zedong, provided support to national independent movements in Africa through development and technical assistance (Mawdsley, 2007). An important symbol of China's presence in Africa during this period was the construction of the Tazara or TanZam railway, linking Zambia to the port of Dar es Salaam in Tanzania and thereby eliminating Zambia's economic dependence on the apartheid regimes of South Africa and Rhodesia (now Zimbabwe) (Snow, 1988). The example of the Tazara railway shows that Chinese development assistance primarily focuses on solving concrete development challenges and building large-scale infrastructures projects (Zhang et al., 2015:23).

Since the 1950s, Chinese assistance to Africa is characterised by the "Five Principles of Peaceful Coexistence" that were formulated by the Chinese Premier Zhou Enlai in the wake of the Bandung Conference. They present guiding principles for China's relations with other countries and are enshrined in the constitution of the People's Republic of China. Among the five principles[1], Chinese leaders have put particular emphasis on the principle of sovereignty and of non-interference. On the basis of the Five Principles of Peaceful Coexistence, the Chinese leadership adopted a set of more specific norms to guide Chinese aid and technical assistance to developing countries, known as the "Eight Principles for Economic Aid and Technical Assistance". These eight principles were put forward by then Premier Zhou Enlai during his visit to several Asian and African countries in 1964. According to these principles, China's relations with developing countries are based on equality and mutual benefit, as well as on the respect of the sovereignty of the recipient countries.

Although both sets of principles date from the 1950s and 1960s, they still guide current Chinese aid to Africa. Unlike traditional donors, Chinese aid to Africa reflects China's unique experience as both a developing country/recipient of development assistant and a growing economic power/aid donor. Chinese policy documents therefore do not refer to the notion of Official Development Assistance (ODA), but rather to the concepts of "foreign aid" and "South-South cooperation" (SSC). Moreover, Chinese leaders argue the practice of aid conditionality advocated by traditional donors stands in contrast to China's principle of non-interference. Sino-Africa relations therefore contrast with the classical donor-recipient relation between the EU and Africa.

As a consequence of China's "Going Out" strategy and the economic reforms of the 1980s, China's economic activities in Africa witnessed an exponential growth. Sino-African trade has passed from 10 billion USdollars (USD) in 2000 to 200 billion USD in 2012 (OECD, 2012). In order to respond to this new economic trend, the Chinese government has established a specific institutional architecture and elaborated policy guidelines to foster cooperation with Africa.

In terms of institutions, the Forum on China-Africa Cooperation (FOCAC) plays a leading role. It was established in 2000 in order to serve as a high-level platform of exchange between China and different Africa countries. Initially, the FOCAC was based on the mechanism of ministerial conferences, bringing together Chinese and African foreign affairs and finance ministers (Taylor, 2011).

---

[1] Mutual respect for each other's territorial integrity and sovereignty, Mutual non-aggression, Mutual non-interference in each other's internal affairs, Equality and cooperation for mutual benefit, Peaceful Co-existence.

These ministerial conferences were held every three years, alternating between Africa and China. Whereas the creation of the FOCAC remained rather unnoticed, it was the third ministerial conference held in Beijing in November 2006 that drew wide international attention. On this occasion, the FOCAC summit was initiated, bringing together for the first time different African heads of state and government.. The second FOCAC summit and 6th FOCAC ministerial conference took place in December 2015 in South Africa.

Together with the establishment of the FOCAC summit structure, the Chinese government also issued a specific White Paper on China's Africa Policy (Chinese State Council, 2006). The 2006 White Paper, was followed by other key policy documents on China's role as an emerging donor in Africa, including the 2011 and 2014 White Papers on China's Foreign Aid (Chinese State Council, 2011). The 2011 White Paper on China's Foreign Aid was mostly published as a response to the criticism of the international community regarding Chinese development assistance to Africa. It was meant to send a signal of increased transparency of China's role as a donor in Africa (Castillejo, 2013; Grimm et al., 2011). In light of the important increase of Chinese aid to Africa, the most recent White Paper from 2014 provides an update of data provided by the first Foreign Aid White Paper. According to the latest data, China's overall foreign aid in the period between 2010 and 2012 accounted for 14.41 billion USD (Chinese State Council, 2014). Chinese foreign assistance usually takes the form of grants, loans (Interest-free and concessional), debt relief a humanitarian assistance and disaster relief (Bräutigam, 2011).

2. The European Union's Development Cooperation with Africa

Despite the important increase of Chinese aid to Africa in recent years, China's role in the area of international development cooperation as compared to that of the European Union (EU) remains rather limited. Together with its Member States, the EU accounts for more than 50% of global aid (Carbone, 2007; Holland and Doidge, 2012:216). Moreover, the European Commission, alongside most of the 28 European Member States, is a member of the OECD's Development Assistance Committee. DAC members quantify their aid to developing countries according to the concept of Official Development Assistance (ODA)[2]. Most of the members of the DAC belong to the EU and have a

[2] According to the OECD DAC, ODA are "flows of official financing administered with the promotion of the economic development and welfare of developing countries as the main objective, and which are concessional in character with a grant element of at least 25 percent (using a fixed 10 percent rate of discount)."

legacy of colonial rule in Africa. Other DAC members include Western countries like the United States (US) and Canada. Japan and South Korea are the only Asian members of the DAC. The OECD DAC is therefore commonly considered as a club of so-called "traditional donors".

Figure 1 provides a comparison between China's net foreign aid and the net ODA provided by six major DAC donors (France, Germany, Japan, South Korea, UK, US) over a period of around 10 years. It shows that Chinese net foreign aid is still relatively low compared to that of most DAC members. It was only in 2005 that China began to catch up with the US, the UK, Germany, France and Japan (the top five DAC donors) (Kitano and Harada, 2014). Other data confirms that in particular in Africa Chinese development assistance remains rather low as compared to that of DAC donors (Strange et al., 2013). In fact, the EU (European Commission and single EU Member States) is the largest donor in Africa.

Figure 1: Comparison between net ODA from DAC members and China's net foreign aid

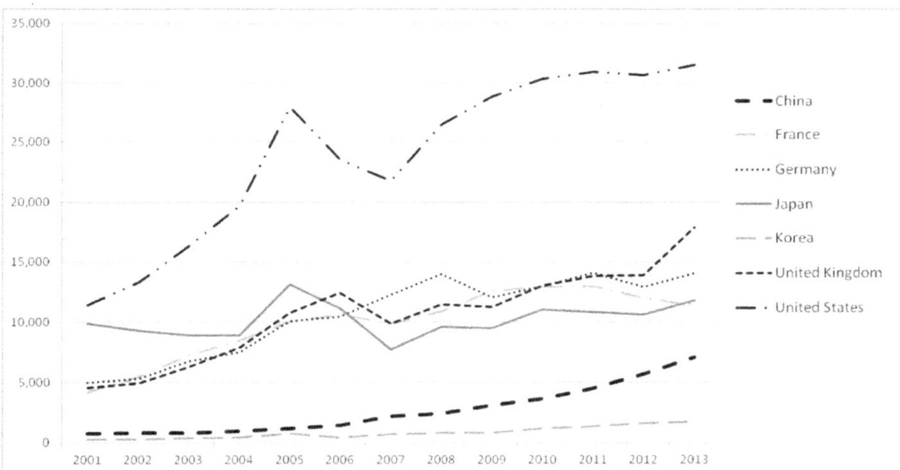

Source: Kitano and Harada, 2014

Since the creation of the EU in the 1950s, there has been an institutionalisation of the cooperation between the EU and Africa. Yet, the EU's development cooperation structures with Africa have been established in a fragmented way, dividing the African continent into three main regions: Sub-Saharan Africa, North Africa and South Africa.

A first structure of cooperation was created when many of the colonies of Sub-Saharan Africa became independent states in the 1960s. Through the signature of successive agreements the EU has created a special framework of cooperation with Sub-Saharan Africa along Caribbean and Pacific states, called the ACP regional group. The current legal framework for the cooperation between the EU and the 48 Sub-Saharan African countries, members of the ACP group, is the Cotonou Partnership Agreement (CPA) adopted in 2000. In order to facilitate the negotiation and implementation of the CPA, joint institutions were established, including an ACP Secretariat, an EU-ACP Council of Ministers, an EU-ACP Parliamentary Assembly and an EU-ACP Committee of Ambassadors. The main financial instrument of the EU for ACP countries is the European Development Fund (EDF). The current EU-ACP Partnership Agreement will expire in 2020 and the EU has therefore launched a consultation process in order to explore the future of EU-ACP relations

In addition to the ACP framework, the EU initiated a specific structure of bilateral cooperation with South Africa. Although South Africa is a member of the ACP group, it has also signed in 1999 a bilateral Trade, Development and Cooperation Agreement (TDCA) with the EU. In 2007, relations between EU and South Africa have been enhanced with the adoption of a Strategic Partnership, which involves, among others, regular bilateral summits between representatives of the EU and South Africa. Finally, the EU's collaboration with countries of North Africa (Algeria, Egypt, Morocco, Syria, Tunisia and Libya, which has an observer status) is part of a third structure, known as the European Neighbourhood Policy (ENP).

Traditionally, the EU's Africa policy has been characterised by a development-driven approach focused mostly on countries of sub-Saharan Africa within the ACP framework. Yet, since 2000, the EU has started thinking about ways how to develop a continental approach and treat Africa as "one", as well as to overcome the purely development-oriented agenda of the past (Bach, 2011; Grimm and Kielwein, 2005). The EU's desire of engaging with the whole African continent on topics beyond development cooperation was favoured by the adoption of the Constitutive Act of the African Union (AU) in 2000, as well as by the establishment of the New Partnership for Africa's Development (NEPAD) in 2001, as on overarching policy framework for strengthening economic cooperation and integration among Africa countries.

A first sign of the shift in the EU's policy towards Africa was the first EU-Africa summit, held in 2000, bringing together EU representatives and Africa heads of state and government. Subsequently, the European Commission issued a Communication in October 2005 providing the basis for an EU Strategy for Africa (European Commission, 2005). Yet, following criticism that the EU's Africa Strategy was based on a unilateral European endeavour, negotiations over a Joint Africa-EU Strategy were initiated. They led to endorsement of the Joint Africa-EU Strategy (JAES) and adoption of a bilateral EU-Africa Strategic

Partnership at the second EU-Africa summit held in Lisbon in December 2007. Although the current EU-Africa Strategic Partnership covers a variety of different policy fields, development cooperation remains a key area.

The EU's development policy is outlined in different policy documents. The most important documents are the "European Consensus on Development" and the "Agenda for Change". The European Consensus for Development was formulated in 2005 as a common European vision of development for both EU institutions and EU Member States (European Parliament et al., 2006). In 2011, the Commission presented a new policy proposal entitled "Increasing the Impact of EU Development Policy: an Agenda for Change" known as the "Agenda for Change" (European Commission, 2011). These two policy documents put forward a set of principles and values. Since 1990s, the EU has placed particular emphasis on the notions of good governance, human rights, rule of law and democracy (Crawford, 2007; Müller-Brandeck-Bocquet et al., 2007:48). In order to ensure that the recipient countries respect these principles, the EU relies on the instrument of aid conditionality (Holland and Doidge, 2012:190; Wissenbach, 2011). The EU therefore attaches political conditions such as human rights to the delivery of its aid to Africa.

China's growing influence in Africa, characterised by its policy on non-interference, is increasingly challenging the EU's approach of aid conditionality. The second EU-Africa summit in December 2007 can serve as a good example for this trend. At the Lisbon summit, African leaders have openly expressed criticism regarding the EU's approach of political conditionality. Due to the rise of alternative partners like China, the EU abided to African demands of inviting all African leaders, including those facing sanctions like the President of Zimbabwe, Robert Mugabe and the President of Sudan Omar al-Bashir. According to experts, "the Lisbon summit could only be held because of the decision of the EU to take stock of new limitation to its emphasis on norms and democratisation [...]" (Bach, 2008).

3. Attempts of EU-China collaboration to foster African development

Despite major differences between European and Chinese development approaches, some complementarities exist that have provided the basis for Sino-European cooperation in Africa (Grimm, 2014). In 2003, the EU and China agreed to build a Strategic Partnership as a specific institutional framework for their bilateral diplomatic relations. The bilateral EU-China Strategic Partnership finds its origins in the 1985 EU-China trade and cooperation agreement. Since then, the bilateral cooperation between the EU and China has expanded significantly, moving from an economy-oriented relationship to a wider political partnership. The institutional architecture of the EU-China Strategic Partnership is structures around 3 pillars: the Political Dialogue, the Economic and Sectoral Dialogue and the People-to-People Dialogue. The annual EU-China Summit, bringing together European and Chinese leaders, provides an overarching diplomatic platform for all three pillars.

First steps to integrate Africa in the bilateral EU-China Strategic Partnership have emerged in the mid-2000s. In 2005, the EU for the first time officially acknowledged China's presence in Africa in its "Strategy for Africa". The 2005 policy document underlines that "recent years have seen a number of new external players emerge in Africa, attracted by the continent's economic potential and political and strategic importance." Moreover, it underlines that "China merits special attention given its economic weight and political influence" (European Commission, 2005). Subsequently, the EU started to engage with China on Africa through informal exchanges between European officials and Chinese counterparts working on Africa (Berger and Wissenbach 2007:4). It was, however, only in 2006 that Africa was formally put on the agenda of the EU-China Political Dialogue (Carbone, 2011; Huliaras and Magliveras, 2008). This acceleration can be explained by the fact that the first FOCAC summit held in Beijing in 2006 was a wake-up call for the EU. It showed to European policymakers that China succeeded in organising a high-level event with Africa, whereas the EU had failed to hold the third EU-Africa summit scheduled for 2003 due to political controversy between both sides.. The EU's intention to include Africa as a new issue in the diplomatic exchanges with China was officially announced in the Commission's Communication "EU-China: Closer partners, growing responsibilities" from October 2006. In this document, the EU explicitly highlights its objective of establishing a "structured dialogue on Africa's sustainable development" with China (European Commission, 2006).

Initially, China responded to the EU's offer of joint collaboration in Africa in a cautious manner (Alden and Sidiropoulos, 2009). Yet, at the ninth EU-China Summit in September 2006, both sides agreed to mention Africa for the first time in a joint EU-China policy document. Moreover, European and Chinese leaders agreed to establish a structured dialogue on Africa (Council of the EU, 2006). One year later, at the tenth EU-China Summit in Beijing, the EU and China reiterate their commitment to "continue their dialogue on Africa issues, and actively explore ways and channels of cooperation among China, the EU and Africa in appropriate areas" (Council of the EU, 2007). In contrast to the joint statement adopted at the ninth EU-China Summit, European and Chinese leaders abstained from making any reference to their diverging values and development principles in 2007 (Wu, 2011). This highlights the commitment of both partners to look at the synergies, rather than the differences, of their policies in Africa.

Following the institutionalisation of the bilateral EU-China dialogue on Africa, the EU proposed in 2008 to establish another framework of collaboration, both with China and Africa, referred to as the EU, Africa, China trilateral dialogue. For this purpose, the Commission issued a specific Communication under the title "The EU, Africa and China: Towards trilateral dialogue and cooperation". The policy document suggests four sectors of trilateral cooperation with China and Africa, namely peace and security, infrastructure, environment and natural resources, as well as agriculture and food security (European Commission, 2008). In addition, it states that the EU, China, Africa trilateral dialogue should follow the three guiding principles of a pragmatic approach, a shared approach and effective aid.

Despite the two promising policy initiatives put forward by the EU and some efforts by single EU member states to reach out to China as a donor in Africa, Sino-European development cooperation in Africa remains rather limited. A major reason for the difficulties in EU-China collaboration on African development is related to the different understanding of development cooperation. Whereas the EU continues to approach development cooperation primarily in terms of Official Development Assistance that is accompanied by certain standards, China's relations with Africa are defined in terms of South-South Cooperation with mutual economic interests (Grauls and Stahl, 2010). The adoption of a specific resolution on China's Africa policy by the European Parliament has revealed the difficulties in finding a common ground between the European and the Chinese development approach. In this process, European policymakers were not able to find a compromise between the EU's principle of aid conditionality and China's commitment to state sovereignty and of non-interference. Hence, the resolution on "China's policy and its effects on Africa" adopted by the European Parliament in April 2008, mostly stressed the dangers of China's Africa policy regarding human rights, democracy and good governance (European Parliament, 2008). The policy document therefore led to strong reactions on the Chinese side and the Chinese Ministry of Foreign Affairs urged "the European parliament to stop the confrontational and provocative act and do more in the interest of China-EU relations" (Chinese Foreign Ministry, 2008).

Conclusion

This chapter has shown that China's engagement as a (re)emerging donor in Africa significantly alters the international development landscape. As Africa's traditional development partner, the EU is particularly affected by China's growing presence in Africa. Overall, China's development cooperation with Africa poses challenges, as well as offers opportunities for the EU. One on hand, China's South-South Cooperation with Africa undermines the EU's development approach, based on ODA and aid conditionality. On the other hand, it offers an opportunity of transforming the EU's traditional donor-recipient relation with Africa into a new type of development partnership, driven by common economic and geopolitical motivations.

Bibliography

ALDEN, C., SIDIROPOULOS, E. (2009) *Africa-China-EU Cooperation in Africa, Prospects and Pitfalls*. Nordic Africa Institute Policy Notes, Uppsala. <http://www.nai.uu.se/ publications/series/notes/PN-EU-0911.pdf>.

BACH, D. (2008) The EU and China in Africa. In K. AMPIAH and N. SANUSHA (eds), *Crounching tiger, hidden dragon? Africa and China*. Durban: University of KwaZulu-Natal Press, pp. 278-293.

BACH, D. (2011) The European Union and Africa: Trade Liberalization, Constructive Disengagement, and the Securitisation of Europe's External Frontiers. *Africa Review*, 3(1): 33-46.

BERGER, B., U. WISSENBACH (2007) EU-China-Africa trilateral development cooperation, DIE Discussion Paper 21/2007, German Development Institute (die), Bonn. <http://www.die-gdi.de/discussion-paper/article/eu-china-africa-trilateral-development-cooperation-common-challenges-and-new-directions/>.

BRÄUTIGAM, D. (2011) *The Dragon's Gift: The Real Story of China in Africa*. Oxford University Press.

CARBONE, M. (2007) *The European Union and International Development - The politics of foreign aid*. London and New York: Routledge.

CARBONE, M. (2011) The European Union and China's rise in Africa: Competing visions, external coherence and trilateral cooperation. *Journal of Contemporary African Studies*. 29(2): 203-221.

CASTILLEJO, C. (2013) Engaging China on development, FRIDE Policy Brief n°151, FRIDE, Madrid. <http://www.fride.org/.../PB_151_Engaging_China_on_development.pdf>.

CHIN, G. T. (2012) China as 'net donor': tracking dollars and sense. *Cambridge Review of International Affairs*. 25(4): 579-603.

CHINESE FOREIGN MINISTRY (2008) Press Conference by the Foreign Ministry Spokesperson Jian Yu, Beijing, 24 April.

CHINESE STATE COUNCIL (2006) White Paper on China's African Policy. Information Office, Beijing.

CHINESE STATE COUNCIL (2011) White Paper on China's Foreign Aid. Information Office, April, Beijing.

CHINESE STATE COUNCIL (2014) White Paper on China's Foreign Aid. Information Office, July 2014, Beijing.

COUNCIL OF THE EU (2006) Joint Statement of the Ninth EU-China Summit, Helsinki, 9 September 2006, 12642/06, PRESSE 249, Brussels, 11 September 2006.

COUNCIL OF THE EU (2007) Joint Statement of the 10th EU-China Summit, Beijing, 28November 2007, 16070/07, PRESSE 279, Brussels, 28 November 2007.

CRAWFORD, G. (2007) The EU and Democracy Promotion in Africa: High on Rethoric, Low on Delivery? In A. Mold (eds), *EU Development Policy in a Changing World: Challenges for the 21st Century*. Amsterdam: Amsterdam University Press, pp. 169-197.

DAC (2012) European Union Peer Review 2012, Paris, OECD Development Assistance Committee (DAC).

EUROPEAN COMMISSION (2005) EU Strategy for Africa: Towards a Euro-African pact to accelerate Africa's development, COM(2005) 489 final, Brussels, 12 October 2005.

EUROPEAN COMMISSION (2006) EU-China: Closer partners, growing responsibilities, COM(2006) 631 final, Brussels, 24.10.2006.

EUROPEAN COMMISSION (2008) The EU, Africa and China: Towards trilateral dialogue and cooperation, COM(2008) 654 final, 17.10.2008, Brussels: European Commission.

EUROPEAN COMMISSION (2011) Increasing the impact of EU Development Policy: an Agenda for Change, COM(2011)637 final, Brussels, 13.10.2011.

EUROPEAN PARLIAMENT, COUNCIL AND COMMISSION (2006) The European Consensus on Development, Joint statement by the Council and the representatives of the governments of the Member States meeting within the Council, the European Parliament and the Commission on European Union Development Policy: 'The European Consenus', 2006/C46/01, Offiicial Journal of the EU, 24.2.2005.

EUROPEAN PARLIAMENT (2008) Resolution on China's policy and its effects on Africa, T6-0173/2008, T6-0173/2008, 23 April 2008, Strasbourg: European Parliament.

GRAULS, S., STAHL A. (2010) European development policy towards Sub-Saharan Africa: challenges of the growing Chinese presence. *Émulations*. 7: 71-83.

GRIMM, S., KIELWEIN, N. (2005) The European Union's Startegy for Africa-Coherence in the Face of a Complex, Changing Continent?, DIE Briefing Paper 9/2005, German Development Institute (die), Bonn. <http://www.die-gdi.de/CMS-Homepage/ openwebcms3.nsf/(ynDK_contentByKey)/ENTR-7BRE69/$FILE/9 2005 EN.pdf>.

GRIMM, S. (2014) The EU-China strategic partnership on development: unfulfilled potnetial, Policy Brief 12, European Strategic Partnerships Observatory. <http://www.egmontinstitute.be/wp-content/uploads/2014/09/ESPO-PB12.pdf>.

GRIMM, S., RANK, R., MCDONALD, M., SCHICKERLING, E. (2011) Transparency of Chinese Aid. *Journal, Centre for Chinese Studies* (CCS) & Publish What YouFund, City, available.

HOLLAND, M., DOIDGE, M. (2012) *Development Policy of the European Union.* Macmillan Basingstoke and New York: Palgrave.

HULIARAS, A., MAGLIVERAS, K. (2008) In Search of a Policy: EU and US Reactions to the Growing Chinese Presence in Africa. *European Foreign Affairs Review.* 13(3): 399-420.

KITANO, N., HARADA, Y. (2014) Estimating China's Foreign Aid 2011-2013, Japan International Cooperation Agency (JICA) Research Institute, Tokyo.

LUM, T., FISCHER, H., GOMEZ-GRANGER, J., LELAND, A. (2009) China's Foreign Aid Activities in Africa, Latin America, and Southeast Asia, Congressional Research Service Report, Congressional Research Service Washington D.C., 25 Feburary 2009. <http://www.fas.org/sgp/crs/row/R40361.pdf>.

MAWDSLEY, E. (2007) China and Africa: emerging Challenges to the Geographies of Power. *Geography Compass.* 1(3): 405-421.

MÜLLER-BRANDECK-BOCQUET, G., SCHMIDT, S., SCHUHKRAFT, C., KEßLER, U., GIEG, P. (2007) *Die Afrikapolitik der Europäischen Union: Neue Ansätz und Perspektiven.* Opladen & Farmington Hills: Barbara Budrich.

OECD (2012) African Economic Outlook 2012, Special Theme: Promoting Youth Employment. <http://www.africaneconomicoutlook.org/en/outlook/external-financial-flows/>.

SNOW, P. (1988) *The Star Raft: China's Encounter With Africa.* London: Weidenfeld and Nicolson.

STAHL, A. K. (2013) Fostering African Development, Governance and Security through Multilateral Cooperation between China and Western Donors: The Case of the China-DAC Study Group. In G. MULUGETA GEBREHIWOT and H. LIU, *China-Africa Relations: Governance, Peace and Security.* Institute for Peace and Security Studies (IPSS) of Addis Ababa University and the Institute of African Studies (IAS) of the Zhejiang Normal University (ZNU), Ethiopia, pp. 74-96.

STAHL, A.K. (2015) China's New Silk Road Diplomacy: Implications for China's relations with Europe and Africa. *EU-China Observer.* 1(15): 16-19.

STRANGE, A., BRADLEY, P., TIERNEY, M.-J., FUCHS, A., DREHER, RAMACHANDRAN, V. (2013) *China's Development Finance to Africa: A Media-Based Approach to Data Collection,* CGD Working Paper, Centre for Global Development, Washington D.C.

<http://international.cgdev.org/sites/default/files/chinese-development-finance-africa_0.pdf>.

TAYLOR, I. (2011) *The Forum on China-Africa Cooperation (FOCAC)*. New York: Routledge.

WISSENBACH, U. (2011) China-Africa relations and the European Union: Ideology, conditionality, realpolitik and what is new in South-South cooperation. In C. M. DENT (eds), *China and Africa Development Relations*. Oxon and New York: Routledge, pp. 21-41.

WU, C.-H. (2011) Beyond European Conditionality and Chinese Non-Interference: An inclusive approach in regulating EU-China-Africa trilateral relations. In J. WOUTERS, T. de WILDE, P. DEFRAIGNE, J.-C. DEFRAIGNE (eds), *China, EU and the Restructing of Global Governance*. Edward Elgar Publishing.

ZHANG, Y., GU, J., CHEN, Y (2015) *China's Engagement in International Development Cooperation: The State of the Debate*, IDS Evidence Report No. 116, University of Sussex, Institute of Development Studies (IDS).

EU-India development partnership in Africa: Cross-cutting issues of contention and cooperation

Pooja JAIN-GRÉGOIRE

Introduction

Authors such as Lancaster or Alesina and Dollar have suggested how intricately aid is related to foreign policy of a country (Lancaster, 2007; Alesina and Dollar, 2000). The motivations behind aid depend largely on the country from which it emanates. Lately, the pillars of India's foreign policy on various fronts and in a multitude of bilateral and multilateral fora have been a sustained rate of growth which outshines most parts of the developed world, deep functioning democratic institutions and a demography which makes up one sixth of the humanity. These pillars subsume one another and are more or less important depending on the country or region with which India interacts. When it comes to the policy front, it is the schizophrenia inherent in India's status as an emerging power and a developing country belonging to the global south which is both a source of contention and cooperation. As we know and understand, the collective appellation of the south is not just a geographic etiquette but has a historic connotation as well as a reference to the level or stage of development. This southern identity manifests itself in India's refusal to don more labels such as that of donor which it considers are constructed in institutions dominated by the north. We shall see whether common ground can occur between identities so divergent as they exist between the European Union and India (Mawdsley, 2014).

In order to understand whether there are incentives for the EU and India to cooperate, I choose to begin exploring the motivations to cooperate that exist between India and Senegal, both belonging to the global south.

1. India-Senegal

A counterintuitive pairing at first glance, India and Senegal have mutual interests to cooperate. These motivations have been drawn from my fieldwork in the two countries in 2010, 2011 and 2012.

1.1. Dignity, distributive justice, equity, respect and recognition

The demand of the South to participate on an equal footing in the world is not a recent phenomenon; claims to a new world order have been resonant since the 1970s. For years, the south has tried to speak in unison for its rights and to add collective voice to a collective claim. In spite of unequal relations and lack of consensus within the South, commitment to the endeavor of distributive justice prevails. The interviews conducted in India and Senegal suggested a mutual understanding of each other's rights. Senegal expressed support for India's nomination to the Security Council (Embassy of India, 2013) and it was pointed out that the emerging countries were in favor of a permanent representation of Africa at the Security Council.

1.2. Organised interests[1]

Kohli has suggested that in India there lies a link between the state's goals and capacities and the institutionalizing of the state's relationship with the private sector (Kohli, 2004:13). Chanana has suggested that "India's private sector is subsumed as an extension of the donor mechanism or, conversely, that the donor programme becomes an extension of the private sector's promotion strategy" (Chanana, 2010). Green states, "to preserve a chance of selling to the "left out" countries, the MNCs favor concessional aid" (Green, 1974:107). A senior officer from the public debt section of the Ministry of Finance in Senegal suggests that "emerging countries are in Africa for finding markets for their enterprises. It was for Africa to exploit that opportunity" (Interview conducted on January 20, 2012). The lines of credit from the Export Import Bank of India (EXIM) were considered as means to provide and access low cost capital. The lines of credit come with the condition that 75% of material or service is sourced from India from the public or the private sector (Indian Ministry of Finance, 2010). Joint ventures with the Indian companies are encouraged by the Senegalese government. The lines of credit are allocated to Senegal at a rate of 1.75% over a period of 20 years (GOI Exim Bank, 2011). Senegal has eight lines allocated to it in sectors ranging from urban transport to agriculture and rural electrification. It also shares a line of credit with Mali for the acquisition of locomotives and passenger coaches suggesting the regional focus of TEAM 9 credit lines.

---

[1] Lancaster (2007: 5-6) defines interests being typically, "private organizations and informal networks as well as government agencies supportive of the diplomatic uses of aid, those pushing for the commercial uses of aid, and those engaged in the development uses of aid. While one of these interests is weak or lacks access to the political process, as is the case with development interests in Japan and France, the purpose of aid associated with those interest s will be weak".

1.3. The pursuit of 'emerging'

Nye says that "a robust and growing economy provides the basis for all instruments of power" (Nye, 2011: 80). Interviews[2] in India suggested that being an emerging country has provided it with the capacity and reinforced its will to contribute. India always wanted to cooperate and thanks to its economic growth, it now has the means to do it. The West African Bank for Development's (BOAD) annual Report for the year 2012 mentions that the growth of emerging countries, principal trade partners of most African countries have helped in reducing the effect of the crisis on the world economy (BOAD, 2012)[3]. It says that the emerging countries have resisted the crisis better and could be prospective sources of financial assistance and investment (World Bank, 2012; Chanana, 2010). The 2013 report of the Bank (BOAD) says that developing countries have benefitted from positive spin-offs of growth in China and India. This was encouraged by south-south trade, investment and technology transfer (BOAD, 2013). Similar sentiments were aired by a financial analyst at the Bank (BOAD)[4]: "The African countries were becoming more and more opportunist. The traditional donors imposed a lot of conditions, for example environmental conditions, which increased the project cost. However, additional finance to meet the conditions was not provided for. The emerging countries were more realistic and practical. Traditional donors were no longer indispensable and there are more financing opportunities available today than a few years ago".

1.4. Common development challenges

Poverty has been suggested as one of the important motivating factors for donors to provide aid (Chakravarti, 2005:5). Interviews conducted during fieldwork in both India and Senegal (2011 and 2012) as well as official statements evoke that India faces common development challenges with Senegal and Africa on the whole. Common development challenges legitimize partnerships based on mutual benefit. An overrunning sentiment observed during interviews in Senegal suggested that Senegal finds empathy in the Indian democracy's problems and considers that the possibility of mutual dialogue for mutual solutions in its partnership with India. The interviews suggested that Senegal considered India's emergence as inspiring but the common development challenges make India a less condescending a partner to deal with, reducing the chances of domination. Morais de Sá e Silva suggests that: "The special feature of south-

---

[2] Interview conducted by the author in January and February 2011, India.

[3] However, the BOAD Annual Report 2010: 11-12 also suggested the downturn in the economy of South Africa, the trade and finance of which is more intricately linked to the developed countries.

[4] Interview conducted by the author on January 17, 2012, Dakar.

south modality is that perceptions tend to be positive and there are fewer impediments to achieving mutual trust" (Morais de Sá e Silva, 2009:56). On the other hand, there is perceived mistrust especially on the causes of development in the north.

1.5. History and civilization as a precursor

Large has suggested that India's image in Africa benefits from a shared colonial history (Large, 2013). At the occasion of the 50th anniversary of the African Union in Addis Ababa, the Vice-President of India revoked India's role as one of the foremost nations to have placed apartheid on the agenda of the very first session of the UN General Assembly (Indian Ministry of External Affairs, 2013). Senghor highlighted the civilizational links between southern India and Africa in his poems. While on a trip to Chennai in South India, he was struck by the physical resemblance between Africans and South Indians who he called 'black Indians' (Koumarane, 2013; Vander Steene, 2008:124). However, positive perceptions based on historical empathy linked to colonial resistance are not exclusive to India alone. Arguments regarding colonial history have been put forward in favour of countries like the United States where the journalist of Jeune Afrique asserted that Obama enjoys greater credibility in Senegal unlike Nicolas Sarkozy because the former was not a colonial power and is free of such tainted history (Soudan, 2009).

2. India-European Union

The motivations behind Indo-Senegalese cooperation bring out the cross-cutting and comprehensive nature of south-south cooperation. Taking cue from these motivations, the next section will explore the impediments and possibilities for the EU and India to cooperate with countries in Africa. Given the cross-cutting nature of SSC, often the disincentives and incentives for a trilateral cooperation are not isolated but are interdependent and are affected by spill overs from other issues.

2.1. Disincentives

The very notion of South-South Cooperation leaves little room for cooperation with an actor like the European Union. There has been an insistence that SSC has a paradigm of its own which grows out of the traditional concept of aid (Japan International Cooperation Agency, 2012:40). Indeed, in its strategy paper for relations with the EU (2004), India stresses on a relationship based on sovereign equality based on comparative advantage and mutuality of interests and free from either side's relationship with a third party (Jain, 2007). On a discursive level, there has been a convergence where all parties seek to put aside the labels of donors and recipients. 'Partnerships' which embody equality and trust are what Africa, European Union and India employ for their relationships based on development cooperation. The Cotonou Partnership Agreement 2000 suggests the EU building on comprehensive partnerships with the ACP group of countries. However, notwithstanding the words we choose to describe a relation, inequalities persist due to difference in the resource base and international power structures of the countries. And as mentioned earlier, contrary to North-South relations, SCC benefits from inherent mutual historic trust.

The principle of sovereignty and non-interference in the domestic affairs of a country for promotion of human rights or democracy is another issue on which the European Union and India beg to differ. This is reflected in the voting patterns of the EU and India in the United Nations General Assembly. The common denominator has been of 25% in cases where the EU members vote in cohesion (Keukeleire and Hooijmaaijers, 2013). The voting patterns of India and Senegal do not converge on all issues either. For instance, while India contributed USD 2.5 million in the form of humanitarian assistance to Syria, it chose to abstain from a UN Resolution on the deterioration of human rights and escalating violence in Syria; unlike Senegal which voted in favor.

There are differences in opinion and positioning on matters related to climate change and the World Trade Organization. However, in the case of climate change there has been an increased trend of convergence in the positioning of the European Union and the ACP countries. Although, India has been largely backed by Africa on common and differentiated responsibilities regarding climate change talks, the small island states and the least developed countries (of which Senegal is one) have come to identify themselves with the European position on climate change. The demand for the developed countries to respect their commitments persists (Sethi, 2012). It needs to be seen whether the relationships within the global south could have an isolating effect on India's position on climate change negotiations. A global south which aligns with the European position on climate change could be a game changer. Besides, in spite of a suggested leaning to pro-climate change positioning in international negotiations, the interviews conducted in Senegal (January and February 2012) reflected dissatisfaction with environmental conditionalities attached to aid. The said conditionalities were not met with additional financing needed to fulfil them.

However, WTO narrates another story of its own. Recently, India stalled the latest round of negotiations at the WTO with the new government not standing by the stance of the previous one. This was an instance of India's exceptionalism based on safeguarding its domestic population. The historic value based morality of India is now replaced by a pragmatic morality based on demographics which tends to complicate the value based cooperation that could exist between the EU and India. Be it climate change or trade, India has had a penchant to 'exceptionalism'. This extends to its development cooperation policy and implementation as well which seeks and sees its cooperation as 'distinct'. This does not align well for a European Union seeking an universal norm based development aid policy.

Fractured policy making in the EU where the common policy overlaps with those of member states especially ones with a deep history in Africa also tend to blur the lines for future cooperation with a third party like India. For instance, the EU along with France and Belgium are shareholders of the West African Bank for Development (BOAD). Speaking of Senegal, though independent, it relied heavily on France. Initially reluctant, France started providing economic assistance to its former colonies maintaining its sphere of influence (Lancaster, 2007: 29). 80% of Senegal's trade was with France and the latter provided two-thirds of Senegal's public development investment and 90% of private capital. The trade deficits of Senegal were covered by the French treasury. At the same time other European Economic Community members were getting closer to Senegal and the European Development Fund became a new source of multilateral aid. However, the peanut economy of Senegal was intricately linked to the French demand. In 1967 the French stopped buying peanuts at subsidized prices from Senegal resulting in a 20% fall in the exports of the commodity (Gellar, 1982:51). This goes on to suggest that traditional aid is not isolated either and can be mitigated by spill overs from other issues.

The development cooperation institutions in India and EU are structured very differently. The newly created development partnership administration in India is not necessarily a policy making institution. At the same time, the current donor mechanism is ill-suited to India's development cooperation and progress needs to be made in this direction (Castillejo and Hackenesch, 2014). Conditionality and tied aid are matters of deep contention. There is reluctance on the part of India to share information and statistics about its development cooperation. What the EU or the OECD sees as tied aid, India sees as export promotion strategy aimed at benefitting both India and the partner country through enhanced trade, adaptable, low cost products and services and provision of financing at lower interest rates.

While statistics are elusive for India, the OECD statistics for the EU show that bilateral ODA from the EU was focused on Eastern Europe and Sub-Saharan Africa (SSA). 31% aid was allocated to Eastern Europe and 28% to SSA. 49% of aid was allocated to the top ten recipients. The recipients in that list from SSA were Congo Democratic Republic and South Africa. There has been a rising trend in aid allocation from the EU except in 2013 where aid fell by 13.1% in real terms from 2012 (OECD, 2015).

On the other hand, the Annual Report of the Ministry of External Affairs of India for 2013-14 gives up a break up of budgetary grant expenditure by the Indian Government to Foreign countries (Indian Ministry of External Affairs, 2014: 206-207). 45%, the maximum share is granted to the ITEC (Indian Technical and Economic Cooperation Programme started in 1964). Of the total aid budget, 4.62% were allocated to the African countries with Bhutan (48.79% of the total aid budget) being the highest beneficiary followed by other neighbouring countries in the region. Total grants allocated in 2013 were of 48 447 000 USD. In 2013-14, lines-of-credit for USD 1176.40 million were sanctioned for African countries (Indian Ministry of External Affairs, 2014). Indeed, these figures suggest that budgetary aid in the form of grants from the MEA privileges the neighbouring countries where India has higher strategic interests. Aid in form of grants could be a material pays off for the policy of non-interference as well as other interests such as hydroelectricity. The Indian Budget 2014-2015 indicates a steady rise in grants to African countries but a decline in SCAAP (Special Commonwealth Assistance for Africa Programme).

On the Indian side, it is understood that even though India has had relations with the European Union back in the 1960s, India does not understand EU as a political bloc and prefers bilateral relations (Wülbers, 2011). Additionally, when it comes to international cooperation, Indian Foreign Service is deficient in personnel given the size of the country. There is a prevalent perception in the public that the EU is on a downturn which does not provide enough motivation to deepen cooperation. The EU does not figure in the international visits of the newly elected Prime Minister of India. His international visits suggest the importance of regionalism and the United States in India's foreign policy. At the same time, EU as a trade bloc is the most important trading partner of India. This needs more media attention.

On the African side, the multitude of partners has helped it gain negotiating space and circumvent conditionalities as was manifest in the interviews in Senegal. Additionally, Indian joint ventures with Senegalese companies like Senbus and TSE were not exclusive. These Senegalese companies had joint ventures and partnerships with Asian and European companies as well. Would these Senegalese companies seek a cross-partnership with their Asian and European partners? Lancaster (1999: 33) identifies three main strategies African governments adopted in managing their relations with aid donors during the first two decades of independence: "switching (that is playing of one side against the other), balanced benefaction and reliance/penetration".

On similar lines Carlos Oya suggests that countries in Africa have the potential to take advantage of development cooperation with emerging countries as a lever to gain more 'policy space' (Oya, 2008:2) and negotiating capacity facing both traditional and emerging donors (Helmut and Stijns, 2011). A partnership with a joint EU-India axis carries the risk of making the relationship lopsided bringing with it unfavorable power and negotiating terms for African countries. Would countries in Africa be willing to take the risk and make changes to their negotiating space? These risks could be allayed by stringent rules, shared responsibilities, performance and result-based partnership. Another way would be to include informal or non-governmental networks. Transparency of the partnerships and local media checks and coverage which affects the international standing and positioning of the partners would be a practical buffer against such risks. However, until recently TDC (Trilateral Development Cooperation) has been very shy largely due to lack of engagement from Africa (Fejerskov, 2013:16).

2.2. Incentives or possibilities for cooperation

In spite of the impediments mentioned above, there exist avenues for future cooperation. The differences in paper could hide the potential for cooperation on the ground.

To illustrate the above mentioned point: "For a newly-independent nation, there was a strong conviction that some of the economic and other prescriptions that came with the aid received were simply not applicable to the prevailing socioeconomic conditions. At the same time, the assistance received in capacity building was invaluable and had a tremendous impact on India's development. This was the inspiration for the ITEC – the idea genuinely was to share the lessons in development that we were imbibing" (Indian Ministry of External Affairs, 2015:1-2). The statement begins by pointing out the unsuitability of certain conditions which are at odds with the socio-economic situation of the beneficiary. This statement suggests that Indian aid policy and implementation is shaped by its own experience as a receiver. It is not a statement that refuses aid but makes a case for the positive effect aid from traditional donors has had on India's development. Mutual recognition of comparative advantages of different partners is not non-existent. For instance, the Pan Africa e-network programme launched by India was awarded the Hermes Prize for innovation and sustainable development by the European Institute of Creative Strategies and Innovation, a think tank (Indian Ministry of External Affairs, 2014).

Trade, technology and training are the pillars of India's cooperation with Africa according to the latest statement published by the MEA website (Indian Ministry of External Affairs 2015b). Terrorism and security are other areas of cooperation. These also form the basis for EU-India cooperation along with sustainable development. These common interests can form a basis for trilateral cooperation. Possible areas of convergence would be more on innovation and technology based development cooperation (EU-Africa Summit, 2014) and pooling of resources rather than rule or common policy formulation. Regarding rules and policy, there is skepticism in the diplomatic circles and in some parts of academia that norms are mostly western, malleable and too soft to be complied with. Instead of relative compliance, India will have to find its own rationale for following norms.

India would look for partnerships which help it expand and preserve its development space. It does not seek alienation, but partnerships that help India propel its growth and move up the global trade and value chain. India will not walk into alliances which have a locking effect but will cautiously stay in the middle camp. India will emphasize on a bargaining tactic which works through entitlements (Mehta, 2015). Such bargaining would require a more embedded relationship between the EU, India and Africa with the latter two pushing hard to move up the global value chain.

India's development assistance is driven by the private sector which is a possible area of cooperation through international and African channels. Large scale national agricultural projects in Senegal like the self-sufficiency in production of rice has a multitude of development partners from the Indian EXIM Bank funded supply of Kirloskar pumps to other partners such as the Arab Bank for Economic Development, IDRC, JICA and USAID. The local transport project in Dakar in part commenced with Tata winning the bid for a World Bank contract through competitive pricing and local value addition. Indeed, Tata's case highlights the importance of local value addition and cost reduction. As Wagner (2008) suggests, frugal innovation based on comparative advantages of the EU and India is an area the two need to work on in Africa. Information technology, infrastructure and capacity building would be areas the EU and India could work together in Africa. Cooperation through civil society could be a platform. For instance, Tata funded the initiative of local NGO-Dakar Women's Group[5] to cover the health expenses of destitute children[6].

Further convergence between the EU and India could come about with deepening economic and trade relations. The value of EU-India trade grew from €28.6 billion in 2003 to €72.7 billion in 2013[7]. With the newly coined 'Make in India' programme there will be more insistence on transfer of technology which opens channels for cooperation but contentions on intellectual property

---

[5] <http://dakarwomensgroup.org/>.

[6] <http://www.villagepilote.org/en/news/172-tata-accorde-une-subvention-au-refuge>.

[7] European Commission, <http://ec.europa.eu/trade/policy/countries-and-regions/countries/india/>.

rights especially regarding pharmaceuticals could hamper advances. The EU-India FTA (Free Trade Agreement) is still in the pipelines suggesting the need for mutual understanding and creation of linkages. Often the large Indian companies and conglomerates like Tata have operations in Africa as well as Europe. Such companies along with greater academic exchange could be stepping stones to creating epistemic communities which could play an important role in promoting cooperation between the three partners.

Indeed, India's partnership with Senegal suggests the role of historic value systems as espoused by Gandhi and Senghor and the private sector in building bridges between the two countries. The absence of a diaspora has not been a hindrance in India's relations with Senegal. The epistemic communities could play a pivotal role in India-EU cooperation in the absence of strong diaspora which has often been evoked when it comes to India's relations with the United States (Bawa, 2008). An important channel of image building and soft power for India in Senegal was its culture, especially its films. International brand names such as Tata confessed being unknown in Senegal. The company sponsored and organized Indian film festivals in Dakar to make it known. Joint Euro-Indian film and cultural festivals in Africa could be a step to ponder. Growing cooperation and embedded relations could lead to intertwining of interests. Future cooperation between EU, India and Africa would also move towards addressing common concerns of security, peacebuilding and peacemaking in conflict ridden zones.

The interests and priorities defined by NEPAD (New Economic Partnership for Africa Development) would steer the EU-India cooperation with Africa. With a demand-driven approach, areas of cooperation would be as requested by the NEPAD member countries. To illustrate the point, an interviewee from the CII (Chamber of India Industries) when asked about India's relation with Zimbabwe said that India respects the rules formulated by the AU (African Union) and not the International Monetary Fund (IMF) or the UN Security Council (UNSC).

Conclusion

"EU and India relation outcomes are poor, the joint communiqués are shallow, both entities may not disagree, but they just don't meet" (Vivet, de Lalande, 2014). Enhanced communication, interconnectedness and interdependence are what would pave the way for enhanced cooperation between the EU and India amongst each other and in Africa. Trust between the three partners is integral to all future cooperation. Indeed, triangular cooperation should be an incremental process where trust can grow with the development of projects. The partnerships will be nuanced with respect to the needs and interests of the African country. As for policy convergence, it is likely that the countries involved would seek material pay-off for the adherence to norms.

The key to the future lies in more and more interactions. Elsenhans notes that "repetition of cooperative behavior leads to norms and regimes, from which to digress implies costs" (Elsenhans, 2007:233). Moreover, personal leadership also can be an underlying force in moving things forward. Recently, the media has highlighted the personal chemistry between leaders in the India-US and India-China relationships. Literature on EU-India relations often credit Chris Patten for his efforts in cementing the relationship.

Bibliography

ALESINA, A. and DOLLAR, D. (2000) Who Gives Foreign Aid to Whom and Why? *Journal of Economic Growth*, March, pp. 33-63.

BAVA, U-S. (2008) The EU and India: challenges to a strategic partnership. In: Á. VASCONCELOS and G. GREVI, *Partnerships for effective multilateralism EU relations with Brazil, China, India and Russia. Cahiers de Chaillot* <P 8° 5772 > n°109, pp. 105-112.

BANQUE OUEST AFRICAINE DE DEVELOPMENT (BOAD) (2013) *Annual Report 2013.* <http://www.boad.org/sites/default/files/interactive_boads_annuel_report_2013. pdf

BANQUE OUEST AFRICAINE DE DEVELOPMENT (BOAD) (2012) *Annual Report 2012.* <http://www.boad.org/LinkClick.aspx?fileticket=wh8GwAejmys%3D&tabid=88&mid=444>.

CASTILLEJO, C. and HACKENESCH, C. (2014) EU and its partners on development: How strategic on ground? Analysis. *Eurasia Review.* October. <http://fride.org/ download/ 03.10.2014_EurasiaReview_US_CC.pdf>.

CHAKRAVARTI, A. (2005) *Aid, institutions and development: new approaches to growth, governance and poverty.* Northampton, Mass.; Cheltenham, UK: Edward Elgar.

CHANANA, D. (2010) *India's Transition to Global Donor: Limitations and Prospects.* ARI 123/2010. Real instituto elcano, July 23rd.

ELSENHANS, H. (2007) The global system, the European Union and India: the challenge of creating new identities. In: R.-K. JAIN (ed.), *India and the European Union building a strategic partnership.* New Delhi: Radiant Publishers.

EMBASSY OF INDIA (2013) Dakar, Senegal. India-Senegal Bilateral relations. <http://www.embassyofindiadakar.org/relationpages.php?id=81>.

EU-AFRICA SUMMIT (2014) *Roadmap 2014-2017*, Brussels, 2-3 April. <http://www.africa-eupartnership.org/sites/default/files/documents/2014_04_01_ 4th_eu-africa_summit_roadmap_en.pdf>.

GOI, EXIM Bank (2011) Lines of credit: an instrument to enhance India-Africa partnership, November 22. <www.indiainbusiness.nic.in/trade/presentation_loc/exim.pdf>.

GELLAR, S. (1982) *Senegal: an African nation between Islam and the West.* Boulder: Colo Westview press; London: Dartmouth.

GREEN, R.H. (1974) The Peripheral African Economy and the MNC. Joint Conference Multinational Corporations in Africa, 1974, Dakar.

INDIAN MINISTRY OF EXTERNAL AFFAIRS (2015) 50 years of ITEC. Indian Technical and Economic Cooperation Programme, New Dehli. <http://www.mea.gov.in/Uploads/PublicationDocs/24148_REVISED_50_yrs_of_ITEC_brochure.pdf>.

INDIAN MINISTRY OF EXTERNAL AFFAIRS (2015b) India and Africa: Sharing Interlinked Dreams. <http://www.mea.gov.in/in-focus-article.htm?24742/India+and+Africa+Sharing+ interlinked+dreams. 28 January>.

INDIAN MINISTRY OF EXTERNAL AFFAIRS (2014) Power of an Idea: Connecting India and Africa via e-network, 17 August. <http://www.mea.gov.in/in-focus-article.htm?23935/ Power+of+an+Idea+Connecting+India+and+Africa+via+ enetwork>.

INDIAN MINISTRY OF EXTERNAL AFFAIRS (2013) Address by Vice President at the 50th Anniversary Summit of OAU/AU in Addis Ababa, May 25. <http://www.mea.gov.in/in-focus-article.htm?21747/Address+by+Vice+President+at+the+50th+Anniversary+Summit + of+OAUAU+in+Addis+Ababa>.

INDIAN MINISTRY OF EXTERNAL AFFAIRS (2014) Annual Report of the Ministry of External Affairs of India for 2013-14. New Delhi, 8 August.

INDIAN MINISTRY OF FINANCE (2010) Terms and Conditions and Procedure to be adopted in respect of Government of India (GOI) Supported Exim Bank Lines of Credit (LoC's), 23 July. <http://www.eximbankindia.in/sites/default/files/C.pdf>.

JAIN, R.K. (2007) India and the European Union: The Parameters and Potential of Strategic Partnership. In: R.K. JAIN (ed.), *India and the European Union building a strategic partnership.* New Delhi: Radiant Publishers.

JAPAN INTERNATIONAL COOPERATION AGENCY (JICA) (2012) *An Overview of South-South Cooperation and Triangular Cooperation*, Tokyo, February.

KEUKELEIRE, S. and HOOIJAMAAIJERS, B. (2013) EU-India relations and multilateral governance: Where is the strategic partnership? In: *India-European Union Relations.* Foreign Policy Research Centre, New Delhi, pp. 117-122.

KOHLI, A. (2004) *State-directed development: political power and industrialization in the global periphery.* Cambridge, UK; New York: Cambridge University Press.

KOUMARANE, D. (2013) *Senghor et l'Inde*, Cercle Richelieu Senghor de Paris. <http://www.cercle-richelieu-senghor.org/index.php?option=com_content&view=article&id=61>.

FEJERSKOV, A.M. (2013) *European Union Development Cooperation in a Changing Global Context*, DIIS Report 2013:02. <http://subweb.diis.dk/graphics/Publications/Reports2013/RP2013-02-European-Union-Development-Cooperation-web.pdf>.

LANCASTER, C. (2007) *Foreign aid: diplomacy, development, domestic politics.* Chicago; London: University of Chicago Press.

LARGE, D. (2013) *Emerging Powers in Africa.* Special Report, SR016, LSE IDEAS, June, pp. 28-36. <http://www.lse.ac.uk/IDEAS/publications/reports/pdf/SR016/SR-016-Large.pdf >.

MAWDSLEY, E. (2014) *Development and the India-EU Strategic Partnership: Missing Incentives and Divergent Identities.* Policy Brief 14, October, European Strategic Partnership Observatory.

MEHTA, B.-P. (2015) *India in the World.* Presentation made during a conference at CERI-Sciences Po Paris, January 15.

MORAIS DE SA E SILVA, M. (2009) South-South Cooperation: Past and Present Conceptualization and Practice. In: L. CHISHOLM and G. STEINER-KHAMSI (eds), *South-South cooperation in education and development.* Cape Town: HSRC Press; New York; London: Teachers College Press, pp. 39-62.

NYE, J.-S. (2011) *The future of power.* New York: Public Affairs.

OECD (2015) Statistics from the Development Co-operation Report 2015, DAC Member profile. European Union. <http://www.oecd.org/dac/europeanunion.htm>.

OYA, C. (2008) *Greater Africa-China Economic Cooperation: Will This Widen 'Policy Space'?* Development Viewpoint, no. 4, Centre for Development Policy and Research, School of Oriental and African Studies, June.

SETHI, N. (2012) Emission cut targets may not be raised in Doha Summit. *Times of India*, December 3rd.

REISEN H. and STIJNS J.-P. (2011) Emerging partners create policy space for Africa. *Vox*, July 12.

SOUDAN, F. (2009) Le discours d'Accra. *Jeune Afrique*, July 20, 2009. <http://www.jeuneafrique.com/Article/ARTJAJA2532p022-028-bis.xml0/>.

VANDER STEENE, G. (2008) "Hindu" Dance Group and Indophilie in Senegal. In J.-C. HAWLEY (ed.), *India in Africa, Africa in India: Indian Ocean Cosmopolitanisms.* Bloomington and Indianapolis: Indiana University Press, pp. 117-148.

VIVET, E. and de LALANDE, V. (2014) EU *Strategic partnerships: Shallow political summits, active technical dialogues?* Paris, June. <http://www.ecfr.eu/page/-/EU_SP_word_article_June_2014_with_annexes_V4-1.pdf>.

WAGNER, C. (2008) The EU and India: a deepening partnership. In: Á. VASCONCELOS and G. GREVI, *Partnerships for effective multilateralism* EU *relations with Brazil, China, India and Russia.* Cahiers de Chaillot <P 8° 5772 > n°109, pp. 87-103.

WORLD BANK (2012) Global Mobility Unaffected by Financial Crisis, as Remittances Remained Resilient. Press Release No:2012/DEC/506, Washington, June 14. <http://web.worldbank.org/WBSITE/EXTERNAL/NEWS/0,,contentMDK:23219391~pagePK:34370~piPK:34424~theSitePK:4607,00.html>.

WÜLBERS, S-A. (2011) *The paradox of* EU*-India relations missed opportunities in politics, economics, development cooperation, and culture.* Lanham, Md: Lexington Books.

Korea's development cooperation policy:

Assessing opportunities for collaboration with the European Union

Axel MARX & Jadir SOARES

Introduction

The world of development cooperation is changing significantly. First, new players (donor countries) are manifesting themselves on the global scene. This does not only result in an increase of actors, but also in a diversification of models, each with their own objectives, for development cooperation (Walz and Ramachandran, 2010). Second, an increasing attention is emerging for partnerships and trilateral North-South-South cooperation (Busan Declaration, 2011). As a result, an increasing number of donors are developing partnerships.

The Republic of Korea has emerged as an especially interesting partner to further develop partnerships in the context of development co-operation. The Republic of Korea is not only an exceptional example of sustained economic development (Evans, 1995; Amsden, 2002) which in a few decades moved from being a recipient country in the context of development cooperation to a donor country. It has also taken a leading role in pursuing actively the advancement of the 'development agenda'. At its 2010 Seoul summit, the G-20, then led by the Republic of Korea, agreed to the so-called "Seoul Consensus" on development policy which aims to replace the Washington Consensus. The 'Seoul Development Consensus for Shared Growth is a set of principles and guidelines aimed to improve economic development and the achievement of the UN's Millennium Development Goals in the less developed countries. The core principles focus *inter alia* on economic growth, global development partnerships, private sector development and participation, complementarity of policies and tangible outcomes to address significant development problems. In 2011 the Republic of Korea hosted the 4th High Level Forum on Aid Effectiveness in Busan which resulted in the Busan Partnership for Effective Development Co-operation.

In this context, the ambitions of the European Union and the Republic of Korea seem to align in the context of development cooperation. In this chapter the Korean development cooperation policy is analyzed from the perspective of gaining a better understanding on how it relates to and potentially differs from EU development cooperation[1]. In the following sections, the chapter starts by contextualizing the rapid development experienced by Korea over the last half century, moving from a poor recipient to an emerging DAC donor (section 2). Next, section 3 presents the Korean objectives on development cooperation and discusses the Korean approaches to perform its assistance through different channels and types, comparing it with the European Union. Further, the chapter analyses the recipients of South Korean aid, both in terms of partners and sectors and discusses possibilities for further cooperation. Section 4 makes an assessment of the potential for collaboration between South Korea and the European Union. Section 5 presents some tentative conclusions.

1. The rise of Korea in development cooperation: from recipient to donor

Korean development in recent decades has been impressive (Evans, 1995; Amsden, 2002). The country was devastated after the Korean War (1950-1953) but, after a successful economic transformation, in half century the country became an OECD member, figuring among the most developed nations around the world.

The recent Korean economic development, in part is due to a well-managed development aid that the country received. According to the Korean government estimates, the country received USD 12.7 billion between 1945 and late 1990s, "which helped spur economic development and decrease poverty" (OECD, 2008:9). According to the Korean Deputy Minister of Foreign Affairs, Mr. Oh Joon, on his speech when Korea became member of the OECD's Development Assistance Committee (DAC) on November 2009[2]: "Half a century ago Korea was one of the poorest nations in the world, endeavoring to emerge from the ashes of the Korean War to rebuild itself"... "we worked hard to overcome poverty and achieve development". This aid was mainly supported by the United States, Japan, and European Union DAC Members as illustrated in graph 1.

---

[1] Development cooperation is a shared competence of the Union and its Member States (albeit with the particular feature that the exercise of EU competence does not prevent the Member States from exercising theirs (Art. 4(4) TFEU), and strategies have been developed to ensure that the policies of the EU and the Member States are consistent and effective.

[2] OECD Development Assistance Committee (DAC) welcomes Korean Membership, available at: <http://www.oecd.org/document/50/0,3343,en_2649_33721_44141618_1_1_1_1,00.html>, accessed on: 10/May/2012.

Graph 1: Net ODA flows to South Korea by donor

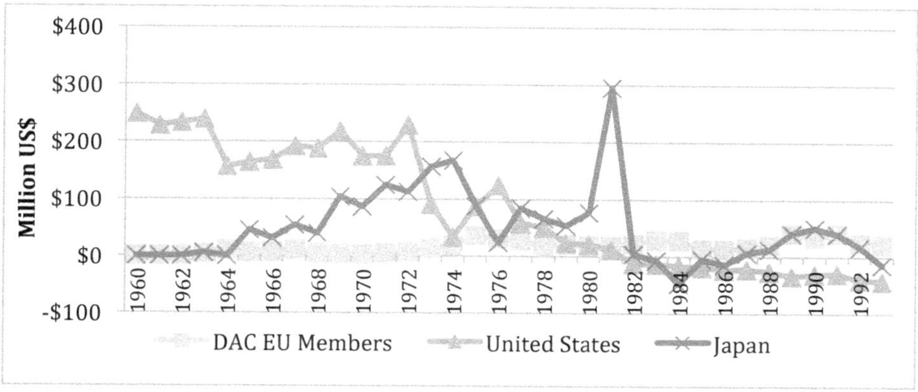

Source: OECD, 2012

During the period that Korea was a recipient country of aid, the Korean government had a strong commitment to use foreign aid effectively, and successfully managed to use this financial assistance to overcome various national challenges through state-led projects aimed to spur economic development. (Jiyoung Kim, 2011; Evans, 1995).

Following decades of sustained economic growth the Republic of Korea became a member of OECD in 1996 and, one decade later, the country began its application to become a member of OECD DAC, which succeeded at the end of 2009. However, Korea's Assistance started earlier, with the provision of technical cooperation in the late 1970s, during which Korea transferred its own development experience to developing countries (Chun et al., 2010:790). It was in the late 1990s that Korea made a more concrete effort to broaden and increase its assistance programs, which resulted in the creation of the Korea Eximbank's Economic Development and Co-operation Fund (EDCF) in 1987, and the Korea International Co-operation Agency (KOICA) in 1991 (OECD, 2008).

This rapid movement from being a recipient to a DAC donor country is illustrated in graphs 2 and 3. Graph 2 plots Korean net official development assistance (ODA) flows, i.e., the difference of donors' gross disbursements of grants and loans minus Korean repayments of principal on earlier loans, from 1960 to 2004. From the beginning of the 1990s the net ODA flows to Korea became negative, indicating that the Korean repayments to previous loans surpluses the assistance influx. Graph 3 shows the net disbursements from Korea (as a donor) to developing countries from 1987 to 2011. Note that it started modest but it is growing fast, mainly from the second half of the 2000s. In 2011, Korea net flows reached USD 1,321.32 million (0.12% of Korean GNI).

Graph 2: Total Net ODA flows to South Korea

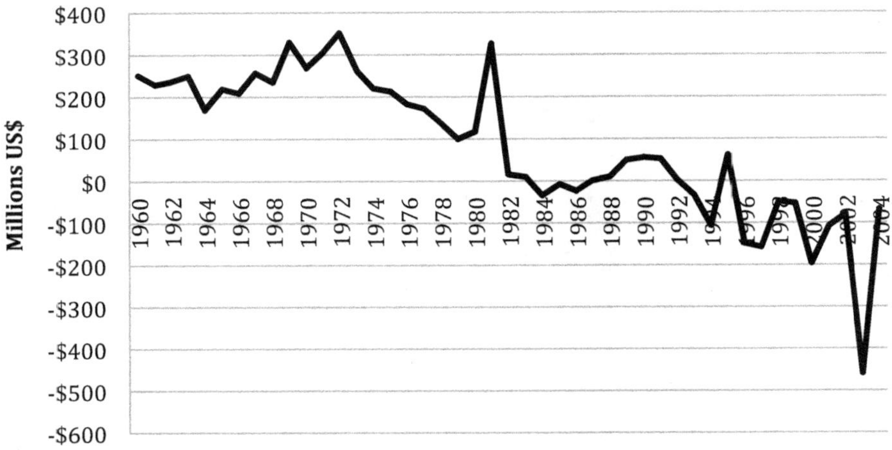

Source: OECD, 2012

Graph 3: Korean ODA (Net Disbursements)

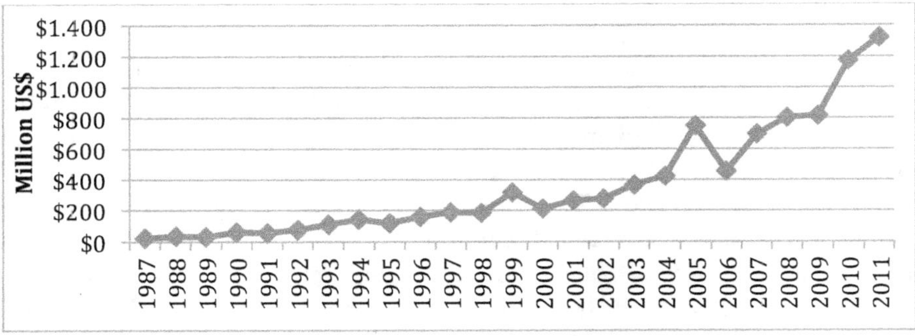

Korean ODA (% GNI)

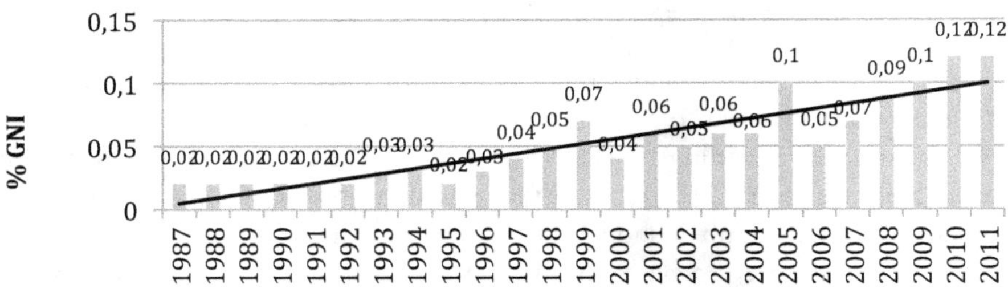

Sources : OECD, 2012

Even knowing that South Korean aid (% of GNI) is still modest when compared with leading donors such as Sweden and Norway, and also when compared with the average of European Union DAC members (see graph 4), the Korean rate of 0.12% of GNI should not be underestimated. When, in 2006, the government announced an ODA/GNI target of 0.118% by 2010 in its "Vision 2030" (The Reality of Aid, 2008), it was considered a huge challenge by its DAC peers (OECD, 2008). Although Korean rates are low when compared with top donors (that reached more than 1% of its GNI), Korean ODA is increasing fast (see graph 4) and it is almost reaching other DAC traditional members such as Japan (0.18% in 2011) and US (0.20% in 2011).

Graph 4: ODA as % of GNI - by Donor

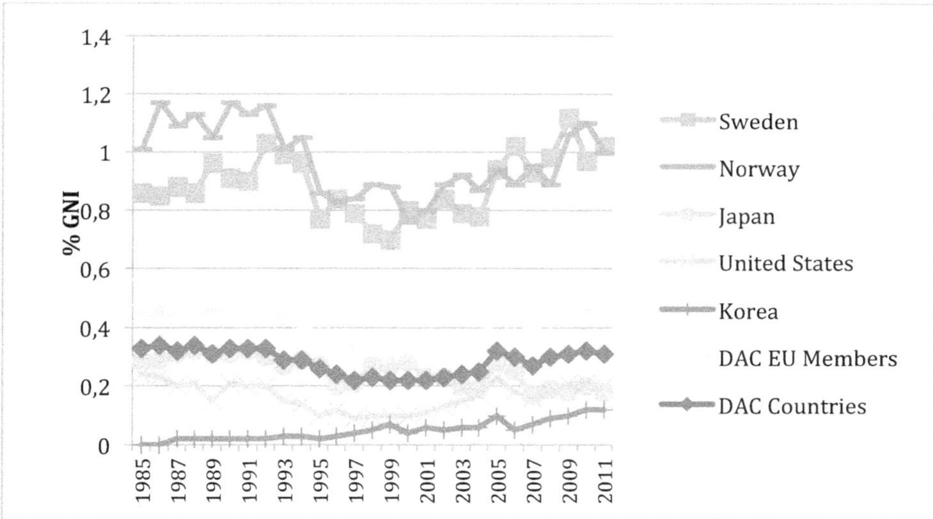

Source: OECD, 2012

Another interesting issue to be considered is the South Korea assistance to the northern part of the peninsula, estimated to be USD 558 million in 2007 (OECD, 2008). This assistance cannot be reported as ODA to the DAC, since South Korea constitution still recognizes the whole Korean peninsula as part of its territory (Chun et al., 2010:797). Consequently, it cannot be considered "foreign" aid. If we compute the assistance to North Korea, the South Korea ODA/GNI ratio in 2007 would increase from 0.07 to 0.13%.

2. Development strategies and practices in a comparative perspective[3]

2.1. Objectives of development assistance

The aim of the Korean Government on development assistance is to reduce poverty and promote sustainable development. In the words of President Lee, the country is "wholehearted committed to pay back its 'debts' to the world as an international donor" (Soyeun Kim, 2011:812).

The Korean' assistance structure is composed of mainly two actors. The Ministry of Foreign Affairs and Trade (MOFAT), responsible for grant aid policy, which is implemented by the Korea International Co-operation Agency (KOICA). Complementing, concessional loan policy is under responsibility of The Ministry of Strategy and Finance, and implemented by the Korea Eximbank's Economic Development and Co-operation Fund (EDCF). Additionally, a further 30 other ministries, agencies and municipalities are involved in providing small amounts of grant aid, mainly in the form of technical co-operation (OECD, 2008).

The intentions of the Korean development assistance program on helping developing countries to pursue their development can also be illustrated by statements from the Ministry of Foreign Affairs and Trade (MOFAT): "Korea is fully committed to supporting the global efforts to alleviate poverty, promote sustainable growth, address global challenges, and achieve the internationally agreed development goals, including the Millennium Development Goals (MDG)[4]".

The European Union objectives on development assistance align to a large degree to these of the Republic of Korea but also include other objectives. The promotion of inclusive and sustainable growth for human development and poverty eradication are the primary objective of the EU development policy (European Commission, 2011). As stated in the EU Agenda for Change (European Commission, 2011), the EU also includes the support of human rights, democracy and other elements of good governance in its development cooperation. These elements of good governance are considered as preconditions for sustainable and equitable development, for providing effective development assistance, as well as an objective in its own right (Hackenesch, 2011:8). We will return to this in section 4.

---

[3] This part is based on an earlier publication Marx & Soares (2013).

[4] <http://www.mofat.go.kr/ENG/policy/oda>.

The following sections compare South Korean and European Union development cooperation. Apart from each Member State, the EU alone was the third largest DAC member in 2010 (OECD, 2012b) and is one of the most important international actors on development cooperation and sustainable development in the current international debate. Although Korea and EU have a different background on development assistance, their policies on development cooperation share several principles, with the primary focus on poverty eradication and the achievement of the Millennium Development Goals. The main difference is the EU focus on promoting European values such as respect to human rights, freedom, peace, democracy, gender equality, among others (European Commission, 2006).

Besides comparing South Korean and EU development cooperation the following sections will also highlight some criticisms which have been raised in the literature concerning South Korean Assistance program. Many of these criticisms, aligning development cooperation objectives with strategic political and economic objectives, mirror criticisms which have been voiced towards other countries including many OECD-DAC. First of all, some authors have criticized Korea's performance on development assistance, much in line with a general criticism on the development cooperation policies of emerging donors, for being selective. Chun et al. (2010) note that the Korean commitment to poverty alleviation and the MDG's are probably not the only objectives of development cooperation policy, since a high amount of Korea's ODA goes to relatively wealthier Asian countries with which Korea has strategic economic interests (Sri Lanka and Indonesia, for example), instead of least developed countries. Another critical issue found in the literature is over the high volume of ODA flow to Iraq and Afghanistan (Chun et al., 2010; Soyeun Kim, 2011). Some authors link this with the objective of supporting the Korean strategic alliance with the US, instead of solely being focused on development and poverty eradication. Finally, lack of transparency is also an issue that is raised in the context of South Korean policy assistance. The country was ranked at 30 among 31 countries and multilateral agencies by Ghosh and Kharas 2011 Transparency Index in Foreign Aid[5]. Some of the critics will be discussed along this chapter when presenting data on Korea ODA.

[5] The Transparency Index is an attempt to measure the availability and accessibility of aid flow information in a timely, systematic and comparable manner. It rates 31 bilateral and multilateral donor agencies on six measures of transparency: membership in the International Aid Transparency Initiative (IATI); recording of project title and descriptions; detail of project descriptions; reporting of aid delivery channels; completeness of project-level commitment data;

3. Approach to development cooperation

This section discusses the different approaches towards performing development cooperation and compares them with the EU and DAC countries. The following three questions are addressed: is development cooperation pursued via multilateral or bilateral channels? is the assistance made via grants or loans? is aid tied or untied?

First, concerning the use of multilateral channels to implement development cooperation, some authors (Soyeun Kim, 2011; Kharas and Rogerson, 2012; Keohane, et al., 2009) argue that this channel has some specific benefits. Multilateral channels contribute to a better coordination of resources, and can improve efficiency on spreading the aid burden and leverages experience, expertise, geographic reach, and other assets that can be better deployed through joint efforts (OECD, 2011). This channel can also be considered more neutral (Soyeun Kim, 2011:804), since it limits the influence of domestic interests on using assistance for political or commercial ends (Keohane et al., 2009). The multilateral aid share of Korea and European Union Institutions are presented on graph 5, together with DAC members' averages.

Graph 5: Multilateral Aid Share

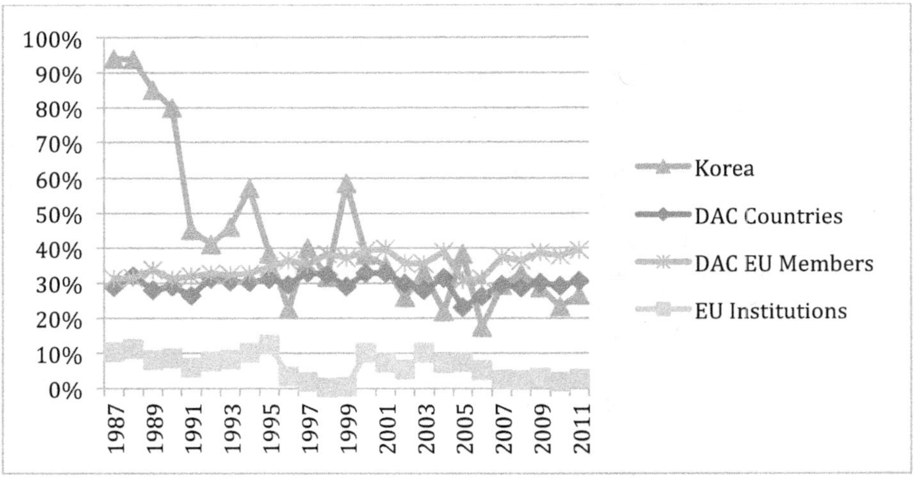

Source: OECD, 2012.

---

and the share of net ODA that donors give to recipients with good monitoring and evaluation framework.

Graph 5 shows that Korea channeled its development cooperation mainly through the use of multilateral organizations until the mid-1990s. In this period, South Korea assistance was mainly through World Bank and Regional Development Banks. For example, in 1990, 61% of the Korean multilateral assistance was addressed to World Bank and 29% was addressed to Regional Development Banks. However, from the mid-1990s Korea changed its profile, and has increased its aid mainly through bilateral agreements. In the last decade, Korean multilateral share has been below the average of DAC members (around 30%), but the IDA and other World Bank Institutions (with 35%) are still the top destination of Korean multilateral aid, followed by the Regional Development Banks, with 30% (see graph 6).

One possible explanation for the decline in aid channeled through multilateral organizations by Korea is that multilateral approaches can be difficult to implement due to problems in acquiring political or public support at home (Chun et al., 2010:798), since, as stated by Milner and Tingley (2010), the donor country (principal) loses control over the funds in favor of a multilateral actor (agent)[6]. However, the Korean government is aware of the necessity to increase their multilateral share. For example, among the development goals of EDCF, there is one specific goal to "Promote global partnership with development institutions such as Multilateral Development Banks (MDBs)" (EDCF, 2010). Also note that a decrease in the percentage of aid channeled through multilateral organizations can also be partially be explained by the increase of the aid assistance volume in total if the additional volume of aid is exclusively allocated for bilateral use.

With regards to the European Union, the multilateral share of its assistance is low, which is not surprising since the EU itself is a supra-national organization which receives significant funds from its member states. However, if we look at graph 5 we can see that the DAC EU members perform a high percentage of their aid via multilateral channels, representing around 30 to 40% of their total development assistance. If we look at graph 6, it is evident that the top destination of the DAC EU members' multilateral assistance is the EU (48%). With regards to the destination of the EU multilateral aid, the top destination in 2011 was The United Nations Agencies, with 42% of the total multilateral share, followed by Regional Development Banks, with 11%. Other 46% of the EU multilateral aid goes to other smaller agencies or are not specified in the DAC dataset. Given the high percentage of aid of the DAC EU members going to the EU one should be careful with comparing the percentages to Korea and the EU.

---

[6] See Milner and Tingley (2010) for more details on a principal-agent model.

Graph 6: 2011 Percentage of Multilateral Flows by Destination

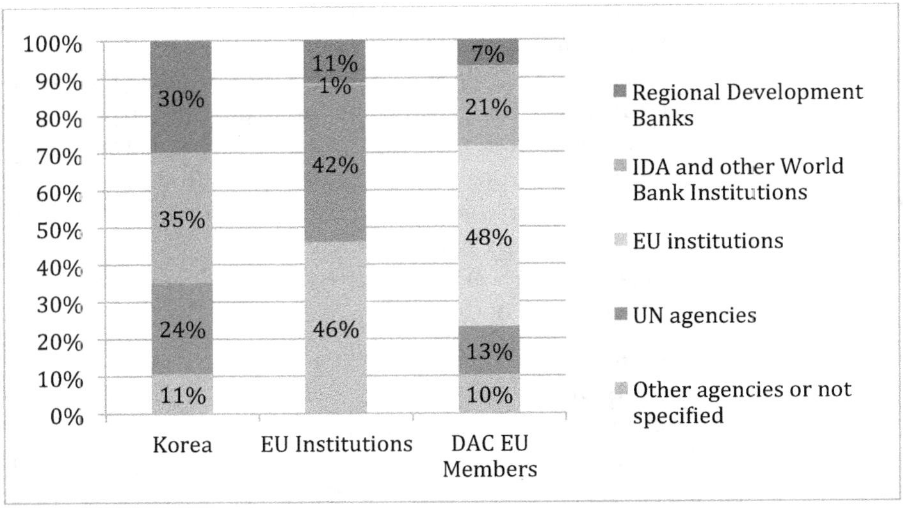

Source: OECD, 2012

Secondly, we compare the use of loans versus grants. Grants are transfers in goods, services or cash for which no repayment is required. These are increasingly preferred in a context of highly indebted developing countries. Korean aid is still characterized by a large use of concessional loans. As one can see in graph 7, loans represented 65% of the total Korean aid in 2000, against 22% on average for all DAC members and 11% on average for the European Union donors. Although loans are a valid aid mechanism and Korea had a successful experience receiving this kind of aid in the past (Kim, 2011:809), it has been kept under concerns due to international efforts to ensure debt sustainability, mainly in the case of least developed countries (LDC). Korea is aware of this issue and has changed this profile. Ten years later, the loan share has decreased, but still represents 39% of the Korean aid, a high proportion when compared with DAC EU members (15%), or if compared with the EU, that in 2010 performed 100% of its aid through grants.

Finally, the issue of tied versus untied aid is discussed and compared. Tied aid, i.e., aid that must be spent in the providing country, should be reduced, since it raises the cost of goods and services by 15-30% on average (OECD, 2008: 23). In other words, tied aid is aid that must be spent in the country providing the aid (the donor country) or in a group of designated countries. A donor country will only provide a loan or a grant to a recipient country if this recipient country spends the money on goods and services produced in the donor country or a group of countries that is identified by the donor country. In contrast, untied aid has no geographical limitations or conditionalities.

Graph 7: Grants x Loans

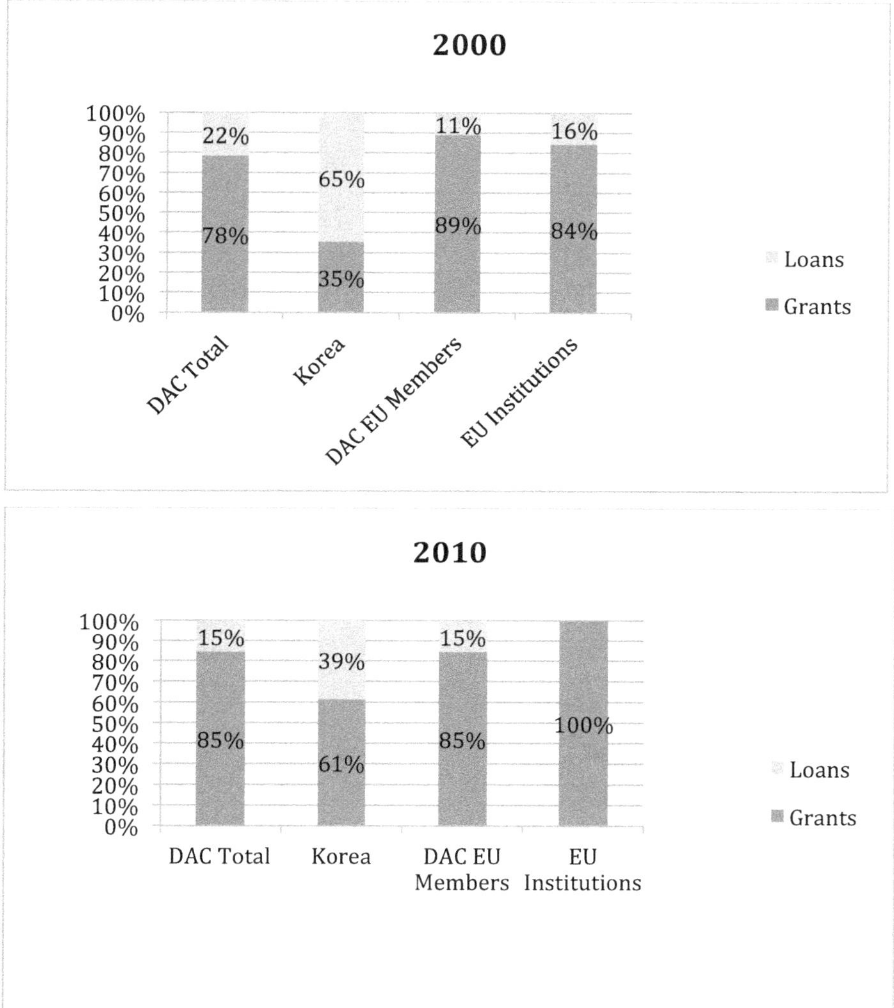

Source: OECD, 2012

Some European countries, such as Luxembourg, Norway and Sweden, have already fully untied their bilateral aid programs, but the average of DAC members is still 16% in 2010 (see graph 8). Until 2006, almost all Korean bilateral aid was tied (98% in 2006). This high proportion of tied aid in the Korean program has been criticized because it reduces the aid value and effectiveness but also due to the likelihood of neglecting the ownership of recipient countries and inadvertently promoting donor' export interests (Chun et al., 2010).

However, recently efforts have been made to reduce tied aid to the least developed countries, following DAC recommendations (OECD, 2008:24). The Korean government created a roadmap to untie 75% of its overall ODA by 2015. In 2010, only 36% of Korean aid was untied. This figure is still low when compared with the 2015 goal, but the progress is clear if we consider the performance until 2006.

With regards to the European Union Institutions, 54% of the bilateral aid was untied in 2010. However, as data from previous years are not available, we cannot analyze its trend. Anyway, 46% of EU aid is still tied or partially tied, what indicates that EU also has improvements to enforce with regards to aid channels. The nature of this tied aid needs to be further investigated.

Graph 8: Tying Status of Bilateral Aid

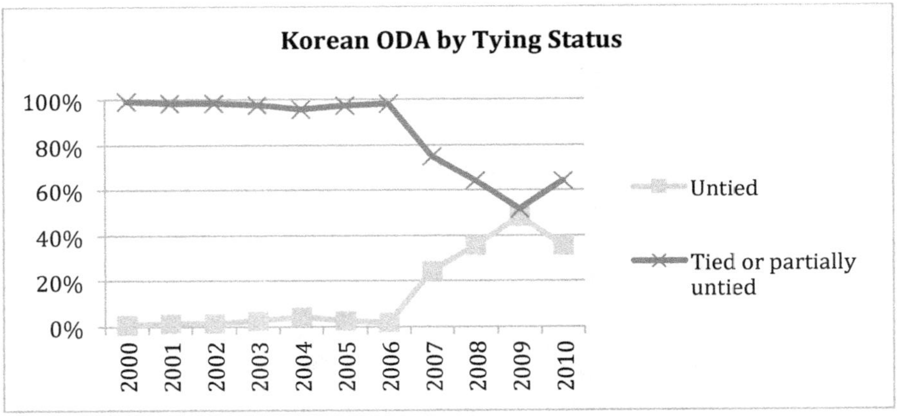

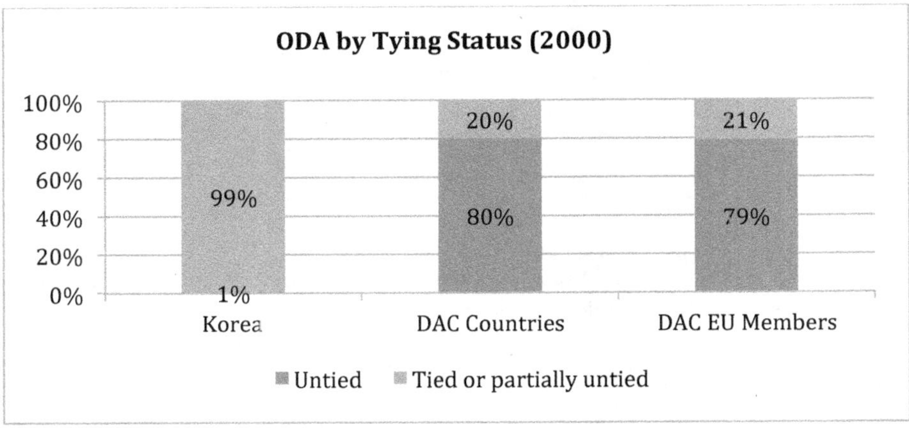

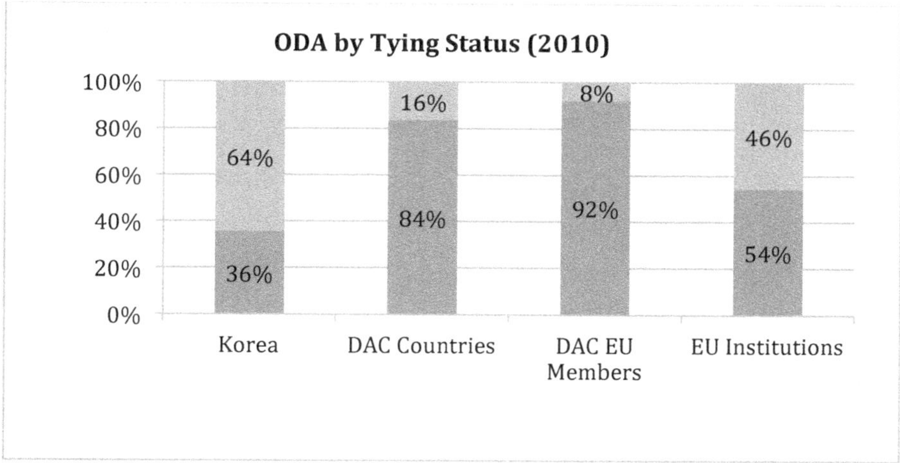

Source: OECD, 2012

3.1. Recipient countries of aid

As illustrated in graph 9, Korea has a clear focus on aid to Asia, especially on Iraq, Vietnam, Indonesia and Sri Lanka. For example, in 2005, 81% of the whole Korean aid was addressed to Asia. Although this focus is understandable from its own geographical location, some authors have criticized this focus, mainly because it does not seem to be aligned with poverty alleviation purposes and seem to focus more on commercial interests. Vietnam, Indonesia and Sri Lanka are economically fast growing countries and are not among the most needed ones (Chun et al., 2010). The high amount of aid to Iraq and Afghanistan has been criticized due to its security purpose, i.e., its main purpose seems to be the maintenance of the Korean strategic partnership on security with the United States (Chun et al., 2010; Soyeun Kim, 2011).

However, in recent years The Republic of Korea has started to balance its aid destination to other parts of the world, mainly to Africa. In 2010, the Asian share was reduced to 65%, while aid to Africa increased to 16%, followed by the Americas with 7%. The Korean presence in Africa seems to continue the upper trend, since recent news pointed to the increased presence of Korea in Uganda, and in Africa as a whole (Devex, 2012).

Graph 9: Korean ODA by region and countries

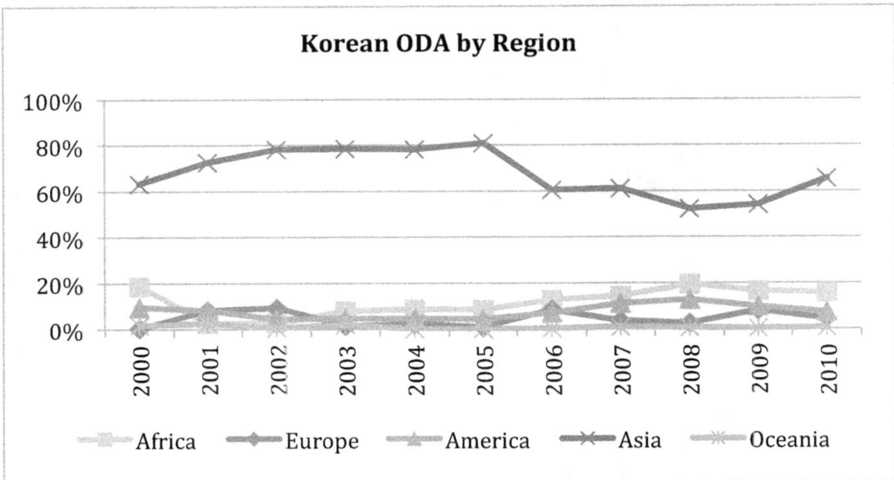

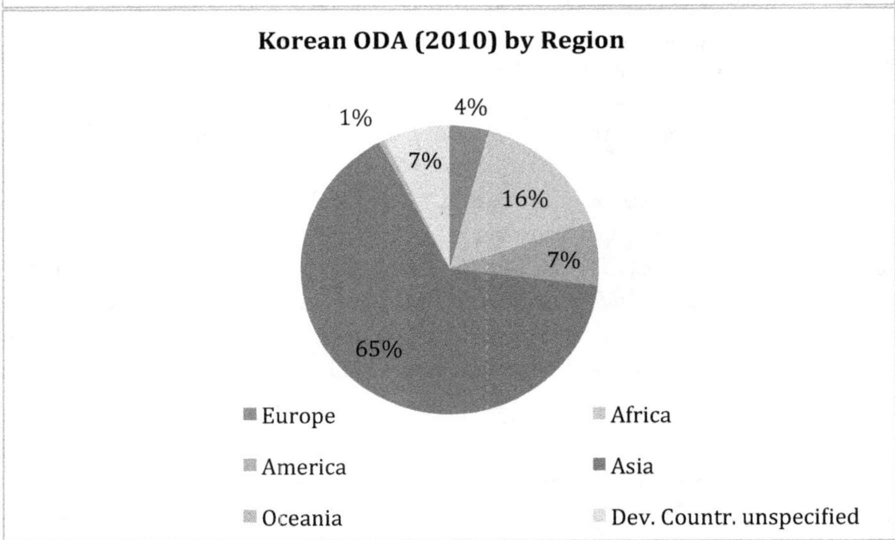

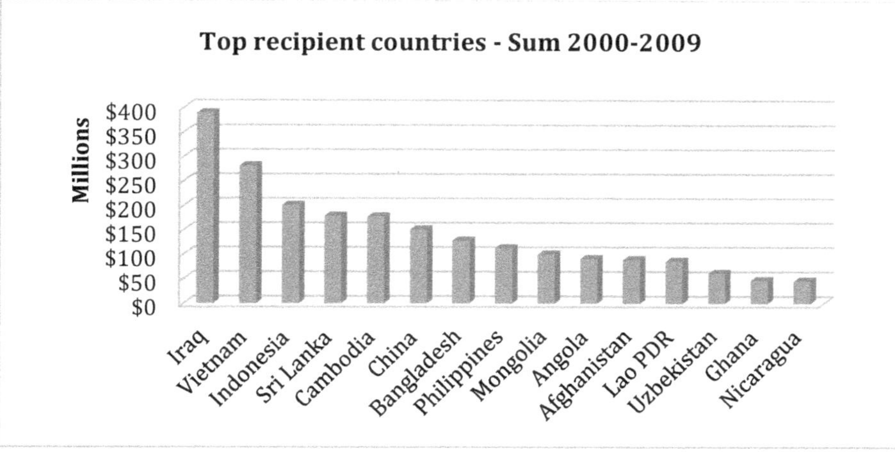

Source: OECD and World Bank Development Indicators

The recipients of European aid are more balanced across countries and regions. Graph 10 presents EU ODA by destination from 2000 to 2010. In this case one can observe a clear focus on Africa, followed by Asia and Europe. The distribution of EU aid among regions has been kept consistent during the last decade, without large variations over time and regions. In 2010, 44% of the EU aid was sent to Africa, 20% to Asia, 16% was sent to other European recipient countries such as Kosovo, Serbia and Moldova, and 10% to the Americas. The pie chart shows that, EU aid is more distributed than the Korean one, which is mainly focused on Asia. Also, if we look at the top recipient countries over the last decade, the European distribution is spread more evenly across the world.

Graph 10: European Union Institutions - ODA by region and countries

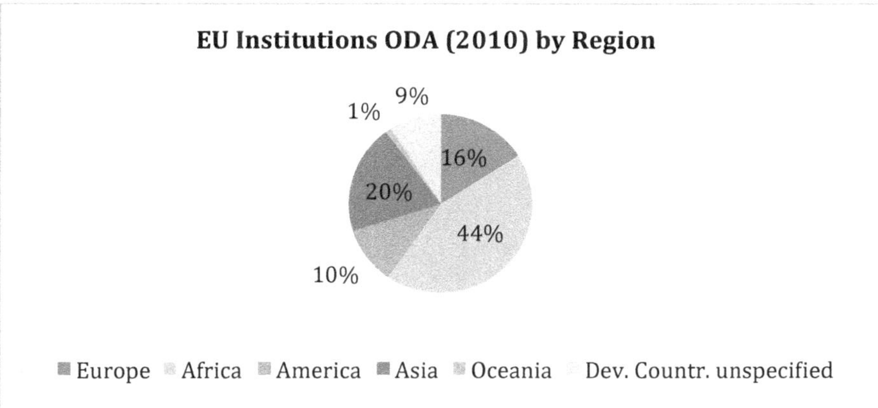

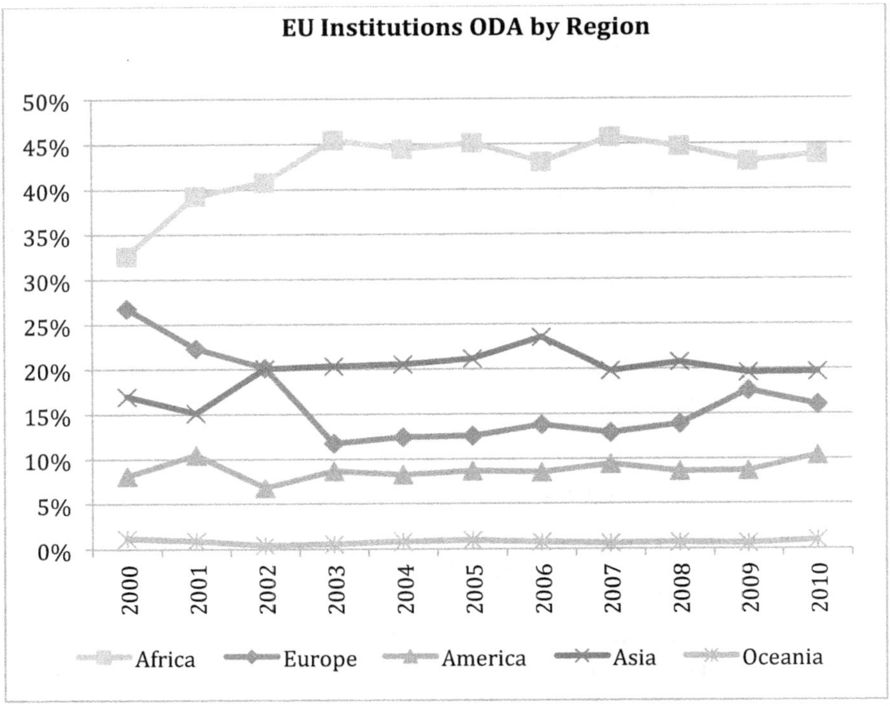

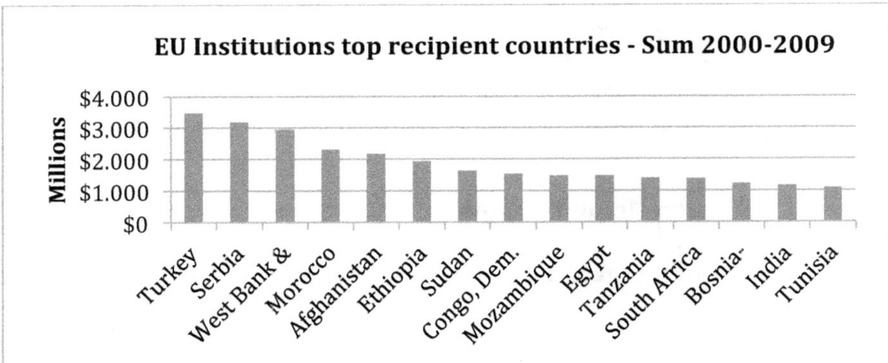

Source: OECD and World Bank Development Indicators

Returning to the Republic of Korea, the increase of aid to Africa was expected, since Korea agreed to it in its Initiative for Africa Development, announced in 2006 (DAC Special Review of Korea, 2008:16). But apart from Asia and Africa, Korea has also increased its aid to the least developed countries (LDC) and low income countries (LIC), which is in line with poverty reduction and Millennium Development Goals (MDG). The figures for LDCs and LICs countries[7] are highlighted in graph 11, and compared with aid to Africa. We can see that since 2000 Korea has increased aid to LDCs and LIC countries at a similar pace to Africa. In 2000, 44% of Korea aid was addressed to LDCs and LIC countries. This proportion oscillated in the mid 2000s but started to grow fast since then, reaching 56% in 2010. Considering this improvement, Korean share of aid to LDCs and LICs countries surpluses both the average share of all DAC members (41%) and the European Union Institutions (42%) in 2010. These figures put previous mentioned criticism on the possible commercial focus of Korean aid in another light.

However, it should be noted that Korea needs to be careful with regards to concessional loans to the least developing countries. As one can observe on graph 12, the loan share for LDCs and LICs countries are still high. Both shares have oscillated during the last decade, but the trends shows that the figures for LIC countries have decreased faster than the LDC share, although it seem to have a setback in the LICs loan share since 2008.

Graph 11: Aid to Africa and LDCs countries

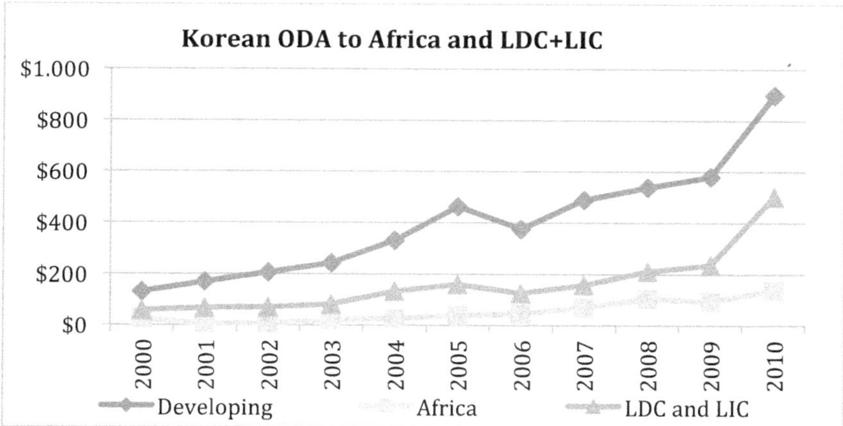

---

[7] Least Developed Countries are countries listed by the United Nations which are poor (GNI per capita less USD 750), weak on human resources and are economic vulnerable. The list includes 33 African countries, 14 Asian and 1 Latin American country (Haiti). Low Income Countries are listed by the World Bank, and includes countries with GNI per capita of USD 1025 or less. The list also includes African, Asian and Latin American countries. Some countries (for exemple, Benin and Congo Dem. Rep.) are listed both as LDCs and LICs, but the data presented on graph 11 do not overlap the ODA received by these countries. However, the ODA to African countries that are in the list of LDCs and LICs in graph 11 are included in both lines.

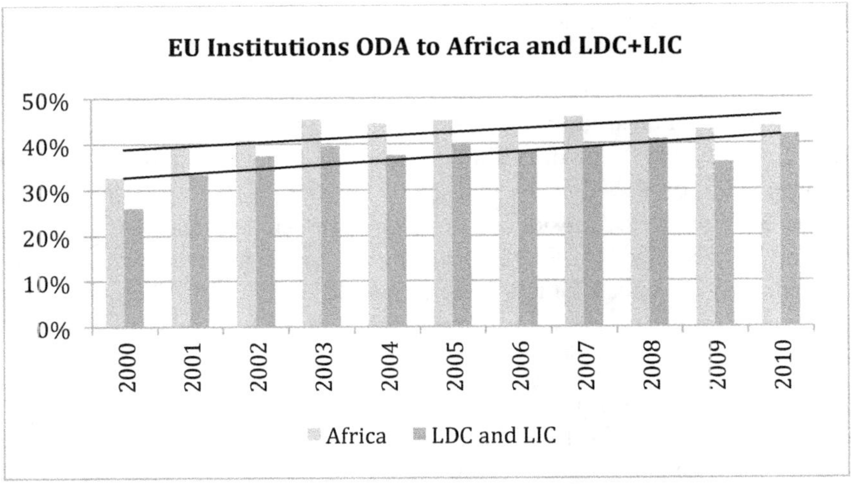

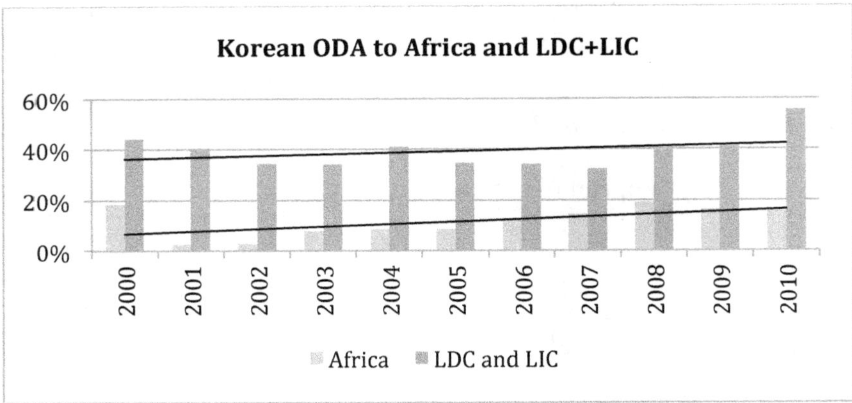

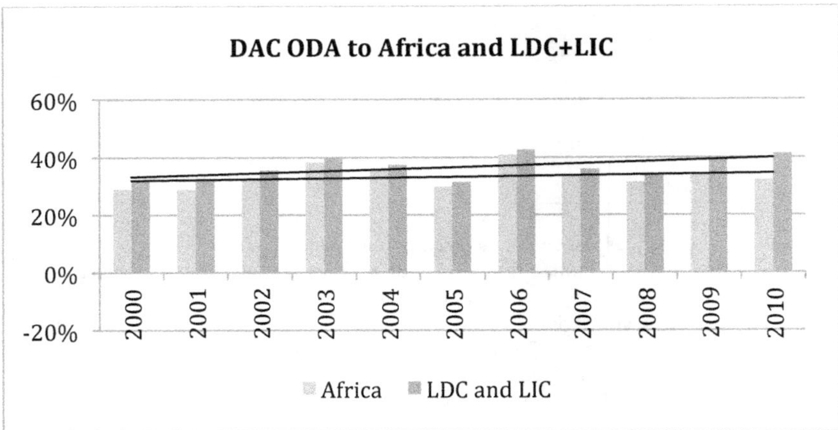

Source: OECD, 2012

Graph 12: Korean Loan Share to LDC and LIC countries

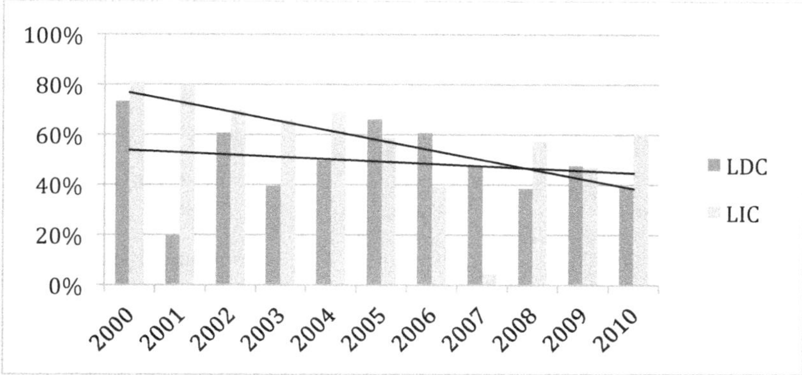

Source: OECD, 2012

3.2. Aid to which sectors

This section focuses on the sectors to which Korean aid is provided. DAC members are making efforts in a way that each donor country concentrates its assistance on a few sectors, increasing the "division of labor" in an attempt to increase aid effectiveness. Korea committed to focus on seven sectors: education, health, governance, rural development, information and communication technology, industry and energy, and environment and gender (OECD, 2008:17).

Korean ODA for each of these seven focus sectors from 2006 to 2010 are presented on graph 13. This graph also includes one extra sector, transport and storage, due to the high amount of investments. The graphs show a clear focus on Education, Health and Transport & Storage. Graph 14 highlights education and health and shows that Korean performance in these sectors is higher than the EU and the average of the DAC members.

It is interesting to note that the third sector on which Korea has more intensively performed its assistance since 2006 is not included in the list of its focus sectors. The high amount of investments on economic infrastructure, such as transport & storage, is understandable due to the Korean own development experience, and the belief that economic infrastructure and development come together (Soyeun Kim, 2011). However, Korea is investing on economic infrastructure in detriment of other sectors on which the country have committed to focus, such as gender equality, rural development and environmental protection. This can create potentially a skewed investment in some sectors to the detriment of other sectors which in the context of the agreed division of work with other donors may become problematic for some sectors in the area of development cooperation.

Graph 13: Korean aid by sector

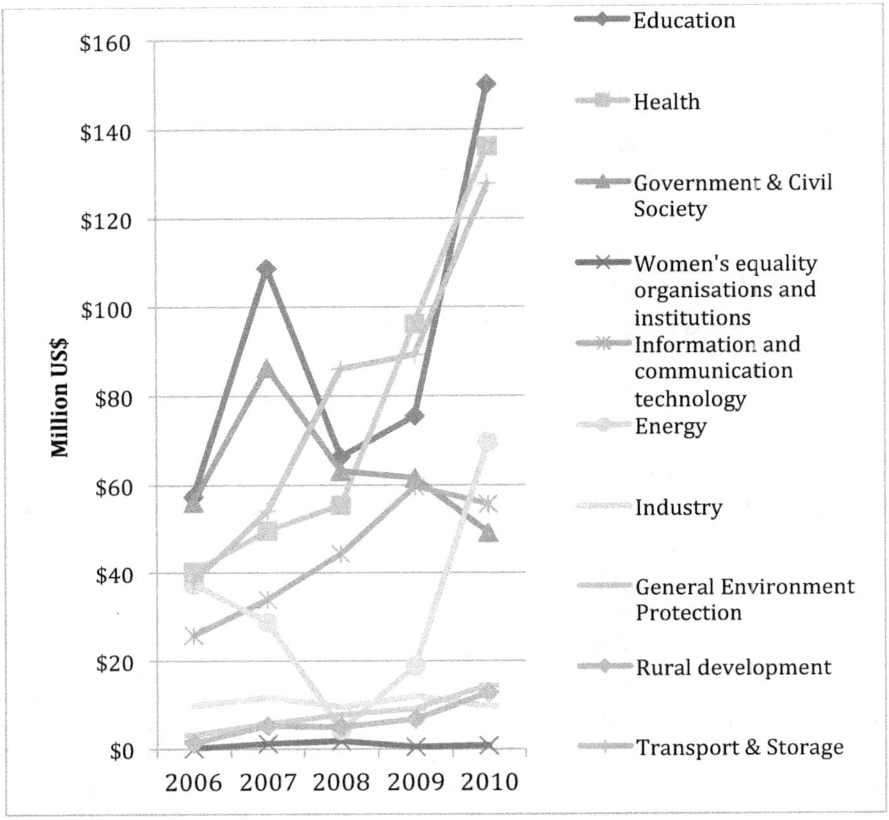

Source: DAC/OECD - Creditor Reporting System

Graph 14: Korean ODA in Education and Health

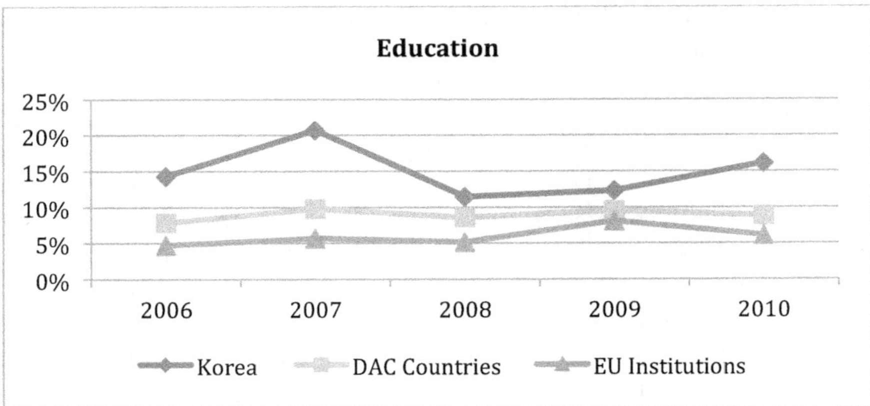

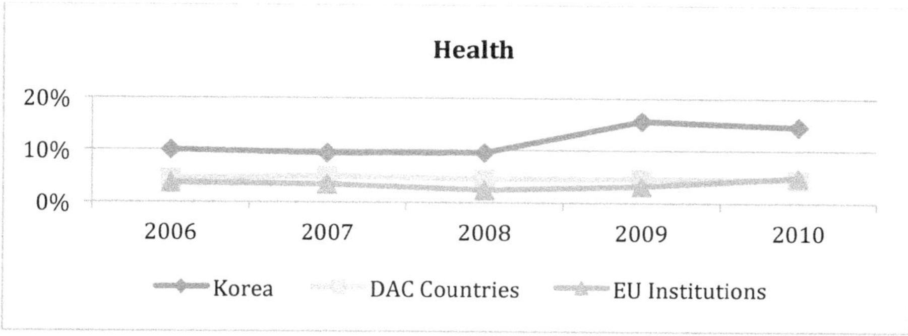

Concerning environmental protection, the developed countries that signed the Rio Conventions in 1992 committed themselves to assist developing countries in implementing the Conventions (Development Co-operation Report 2011:143). Korean assistance to environmental issues has been a small part of the Korean aid program as shown in graph 15. In graph 15 we compare Korean environmental performance with other DAC members. We can see that the share of Korean assistance to environmental issues, ranging from 1 to 1.5% of Korean ODA, has been below the average of DAC members (2-5%) and European Union Institutions (2-4%), and significantly lower than top environmental donor countries such as UK, France and Japan.

Graph 15: Environmental share of Assistance

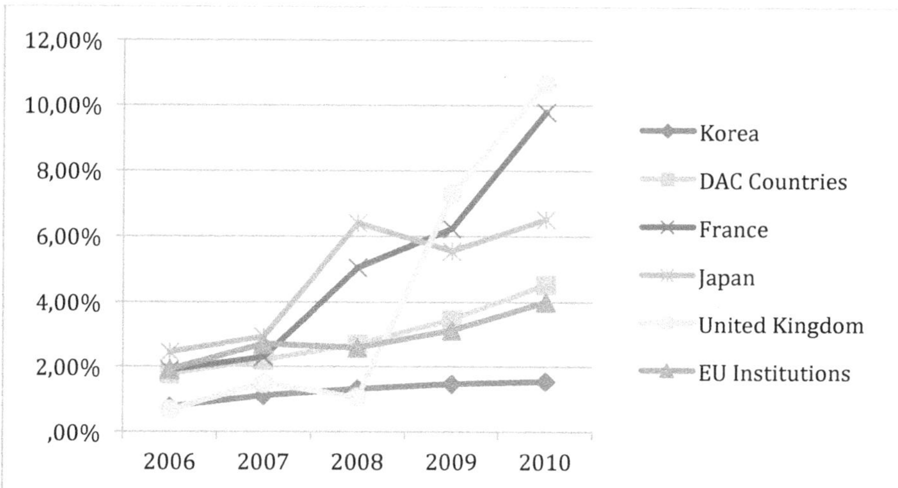

Source: DAC/OECD - Creditor Reporting System

Other focus sectors that haves received a small amount of Korean assistance are the promotion of gender equality and rural development. Graph 16 shows the figures for Korea, EU and the average of DAC members from 2006 to 2010.

For women empowerment the figures for Korea are small and there is no clear trend. Concerning rural development, there was a marked increase in the last years.

Graph 16: ODA to Women equality and Rural development

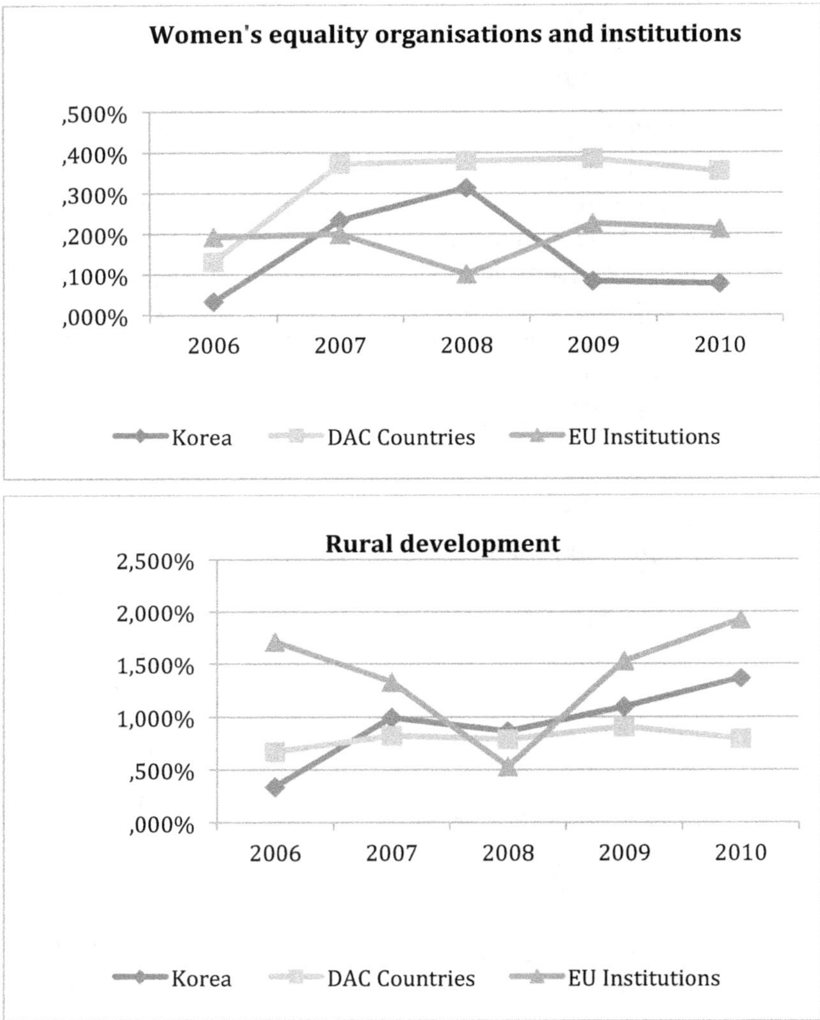

Source: DAC/OECD - Creditor Reporting System

Looking at the EU performance on their focus sectors (trade and finance, climate change, food security, migration and security) we also can observe incoherence between the priorities and actual disbursements. Graph 17 shows on the left side the five sectors that most received European investments from

2006 to 2010: government and civil society, transport and storage, education, multi-sectors without environment, and agriculture, forestry and fishing. The right side plots the European disbursements in their priority issues, as defined in the Policy Coherence for Development (European Council, 2009): trade and finance, climate change, food security, migration and security. As can be seen, only food security is among the sectors that most received European assistance. We should take into account that the Policy Coherence for Development was released in the end of 2009, and data is available by 2010, which could indicate that EU officials did not have enough time to adjust their disbursements according to the priorities defined in this document.

Graph 17: European Union aid by sector

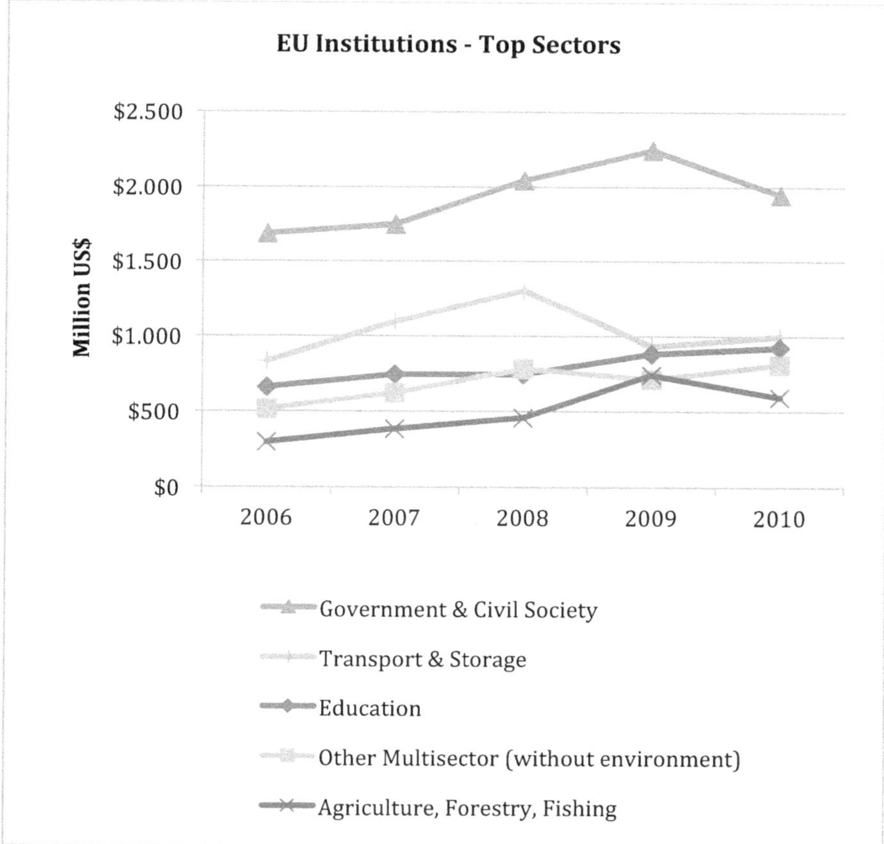

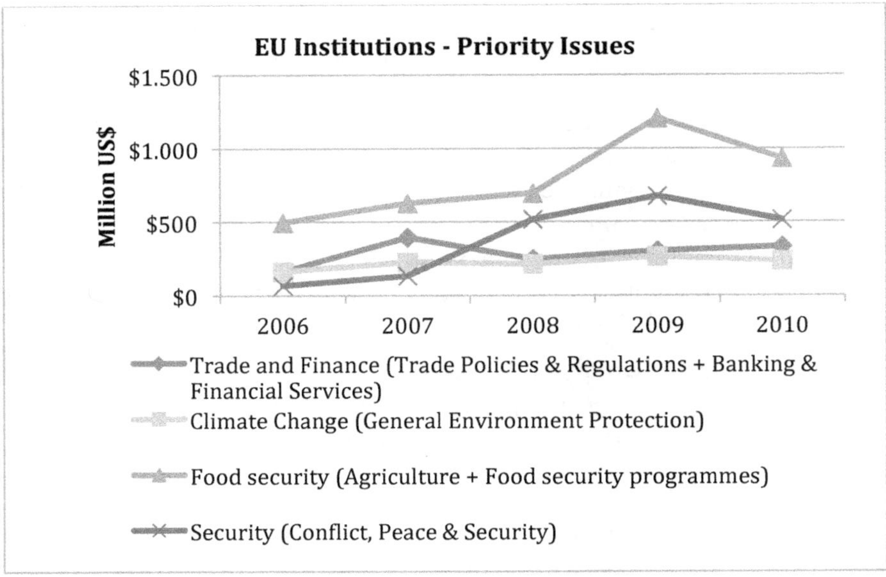

Source: DAC/OECD - Creditor Reporting System

More in general, the idea of the division of work between donor countries is an issue that needs to be further analyzed and addressed both by EU and Korea, and possibly other donors, in order to improve their cooperation. The OECD-DAC has recommended that each donor country concentrates its efforts on fewer sectors to make aid more effective (OECD, 2008). Similarly, in the "EU Code of Conduct on Division of Labour in Development Policy" the European Commission establishes eleven guidelines principles that, among other issues, ask the Member States to concentrate their activities on a limited number of recipient nations sectors, according to the comparative advantage of donor countries, as recognized by both the recipient countries and other donor countries (European Commission, 2007). However, the available evidence indicates that the division of labour is not materializing yet. Graph 18 plots the number of recipient countries and sectors that EU and Korea have assisted from 2006 to 2010. The figures in graph 18 are the sum of the number of sectors assisted by a donor in each recipient country. The figures for Korea show that they reduced the number of countries/sectors in the period 2007-2009, but then there was a setback in 2010, reaching a sum of 1977 sectors assisted by Korea in all recipient countries. In the European case, the figures show a steep increase from 2006 to 2010.

Graph 18: Total number of recipient countries and sectors assisted by EU and Korea

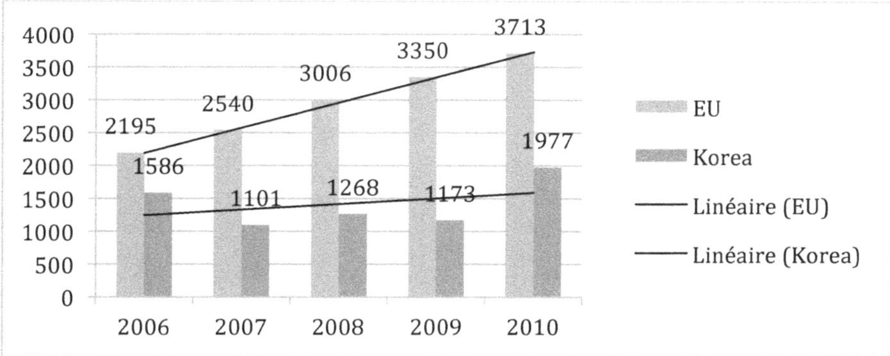

Source: DAC/OECD - Creditor Reporting System

Lastly, another important allocation of donor's assistance is humanitarian aid. As shown in graph 19, there was a steep increase in the Korean humanitarian aid from 2000 to 2008. In 2008 there was a peak of USD 56 million addressed for this purpose. In percentage terms, Korea reached the peak in 2005, with 5.6% of the total ODA allocated to humanitarian aid, what is modest figure if compared with the EU (11%). Further, there was a setback on the Korean humanitarian aid since 2009, with allocation of only 1% of the total ODA to this important issue.

Graph 19: Korean Humanitarian Aid

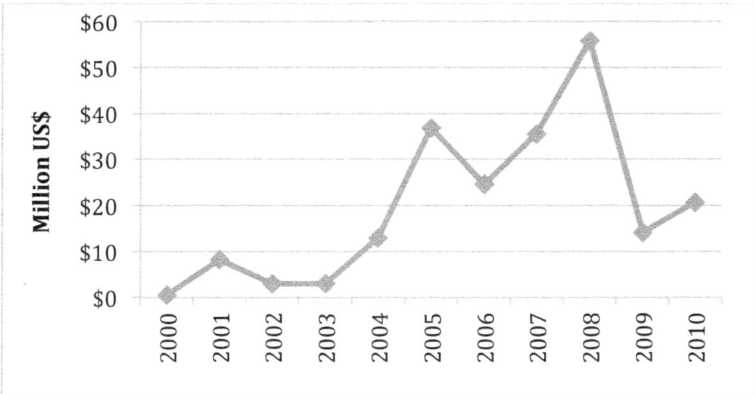

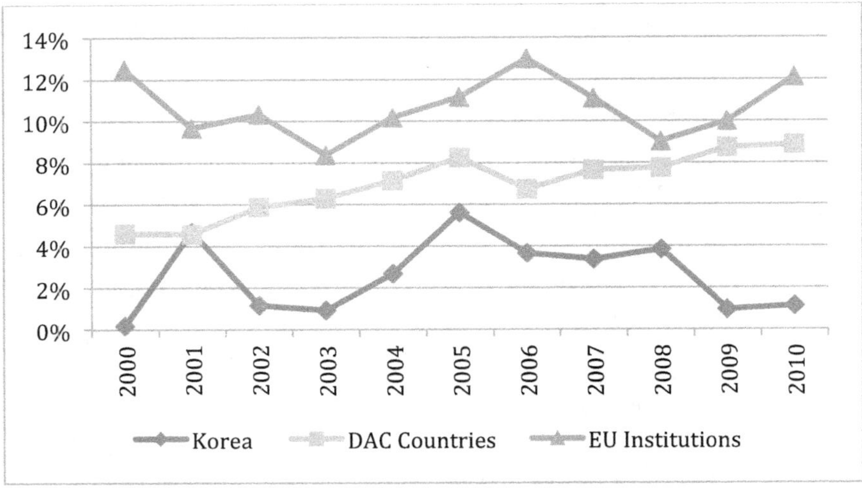

Source: DAC/OECD - Creditor Reporting System

4. Assessment of potential Korea-EU collaboration

4.1. EU-Korea collaboration in the context of triangular cooperation

The previous analysis shows that Korean has risen to become significant player in development cooperation and a potentially interesting partner for the EU to further coordinate development cooperation efforts. Both are examples of the so-called DAC-model (Walz and Ramachandran, 2010) and spend significantly on development cooperation geared towards different countries and sectors. In a new era with a strong focus on the emergence of new donors and the development of partnerships in the context of triangular cooperation following the emphasis on South-South cooperation several opportunities might emerge for closer cooperation between the EU and the Republic of Korea.

South-South cooperation (SSC) is defined as "a common endeavor of peoples and countries of the South, based on their common objectives and solidarity" (Yamoussoukro, 2008). It does not intent to replace the traditional North-South cooperation performed by the DAC members. Instead, it aims to add efforts on development cooperation by including developing partners. South-South Cooperation is not a novelty. For example, the Kuwait Fund for Arab Economic Development was set-up in 1961, with the Islamic Development Bank (IsDB). However, this kind of cooperation among developing countries has become more relevant since the failure of the WTO-Doha round in 2006, especially among the BRICS countries (European Parliament, 2012).

Different Southern actors define and perform assistance in distinct ways. It includes grants, loans, lines of credit, debt relief, studentships and technical training, provision of skilled professionals, humanitarian relief, among others. Some elements of South-South cooperation equate to the DAC ODA standards, but the majority of these cooperation are commercial in nature (Mawdsley, 2012). Consequently, we cannot directly compare south-south cooperation with the DAC traditional ODA.

One example of different approaches for developing cooperation is the usual blending of aid with commercial support, in ways that many traditional ODA agencies have eschewed. China is providing large non-concessional loans for infrastructure, natural resource development and industrial parks in poor countries; India provides sizable export credit lines; Brazil's Embrapa has spread the tropical soil management technology with which it transformed its agriculture to countries with similar environments (Kharas and Rogerson, 2012).

Korea has been recognized as an important actor in South-South cooperation. The country was the fifth largest Southern contributor in 2006 (ECOSOC, 2008: 11), performing assistance through technical cooperation grants, program grants, bilateral loans, and other kinds of assistance, mainly to Asian neighbor countries as is highlighted above. The Korean allocation to South-South Cooperation in 2006 was estimated at 10% of all Korean cooperation (ECOSOC, 2008:19). Especially worth mentioning is the notable contribution of a 100% debt relief to the Heavily Indebted Poor Countries-HIPC (ECOSOC, 2008:13).

Korea also seems to invest in triangular cooperation (ECOSOC, 2008), i.e. cooperation between one donor from the global North, one donor from the global South and one recipient country, aimed to provide assistance to this recipient country. Usually in this kind of cooperation, the donor from the global South assists with its particular expertise and experience in the area related to the cooperation program, financially supported by the donor from the global North. For example, at the High Level Event on South-South Cooperation and Capacity Development in March 2010, the Korean government shared experiences in implementing the Knowledge Sharing Program, which aims to assist capacity building efforts of developing countries (EDCF, 2010).

The participation in SSC and triangular cooperation seems to be a commitment of the South Korea government. As stated by the Ministry of Foreign Affairs and Trade, Korea aims to make "the best use of its unique development experience" and to "exert every effort to make meaningful contributions to the international community by playing a bridging role between developing and developed countries"[8]. The Korean government's view on its rule on South-

[8] See: <http://www.mofat.go.kr/ENG/policy/oda/index.jsp?menu=m_20_11>.

South cooperation is shared with some authors. For example, Jerve stated that "the Korean experience is relevant for shaping development policies as well as how to make best use of aid". The author also argued that "Korea can play a crucial role on bridging the gap between donor countries and developing partners by sharing their development experience with the help of aid" (Jerve, 2007:8). Also, the South Korean commitment with SSC was reinforced by joining the "Building Block Proposal on South-South and Triangular Cooperation", presented at the 4th High Level Forum on Aid Effectiveness in Busan, 2011. The outcome document of the 4th High Level Forum on Aid Effectiveness calls for the development community to deepen efforts to maximize the impact of this modality of aid, to strengthen its institutions and to scale-up knowledge sharing to adapt and learn from these experiences (HLF4, 2011).

Similar to the Republic of Korea, the EU and some of their member states such as Finland, France, Germany, Spain and Sweden have been closely involved as partner from the global North in triangular development cooperation (ECOSOC, 2008:14). The EU also support SSC and triangular cooperation, as stated by the European Commission in its *Agenda for Change* (2011). The EU has also joined to the Building Block Proposal at HLF4.

At this stage it is difficult to make any empirical assessment of South-South Cooperation and Triangular cooperation since there is no data available. Korea, as well as all other DAC members, report development assistance in terms of ODA flows to DAC. The DAC database organizes the assistance flows from all DAC members to all developing countries. However, this database does not report separately on the participation of the DAC members in South-South cooperation or triangular cooperation. Currently, there is no institution that coordinates, compiles and disseminates data related to South-South cooperation and triangular cooperation. This lack of data limits the assessment of such South-South and triangular initiatives.

Although the lack of data makes an assessment on SSC and triangular cooperation difficult, it could be argued that there are several opportunities for EU and South Korea collaboration in this context. Graph 20 shows the number of countries and sectors commonly assisted by Korea and the EU from 2006 to 2010, i.e., among all countries and sectors assisted by Korea and EU separately (see graph 18), graph 19 shows the subset of countries and sectors that are common for these two countries. These shared countries and sectors represent opportunities for collaboration.

The number of common countries/sectors have increased since 2006, representing from 10 to 16% of all countries/sectors assisted by the EU. For South Korea, these common countries/sectors represent 19 to 31% of all countries and sectors. For example, the 603 common sectors assisted by EU and Korea in

2010, represent 14% of the 3713 countries/sectors assisted by the EU and 19% of the 1977 countries/sectors assisted by Korea in this year. It seems that the trend is going to the opposite direction proposed in the guidelines for the division of labour, as discussed in the previous section. On the other hand, if one aims to promote triangular cooperation such overlap is inevitable and to a degree beneficial. This overlap also shows that there are real opportunities for triangular cooperation. For example, in 2010, both EU and Korea assisted Uganda and Kenya in agricultural development. If EU and Korea share information on the projects that each one is assisting in these countries, both EU and Korea could better coordinate their efforts and increase the aid effectiveness in these countries. Another example is that of Mozambique in 2010 where both EU and Korea have invested in agricultural development. Moreover, it creates potential opportunities with other new emerging donors such as Brazil, that have also invested in the agricultural sector in the Lusophone Africa (Vieira and Alden, 2011).

Graph 20: Common countries and sectors assisted by Korea and The European Union

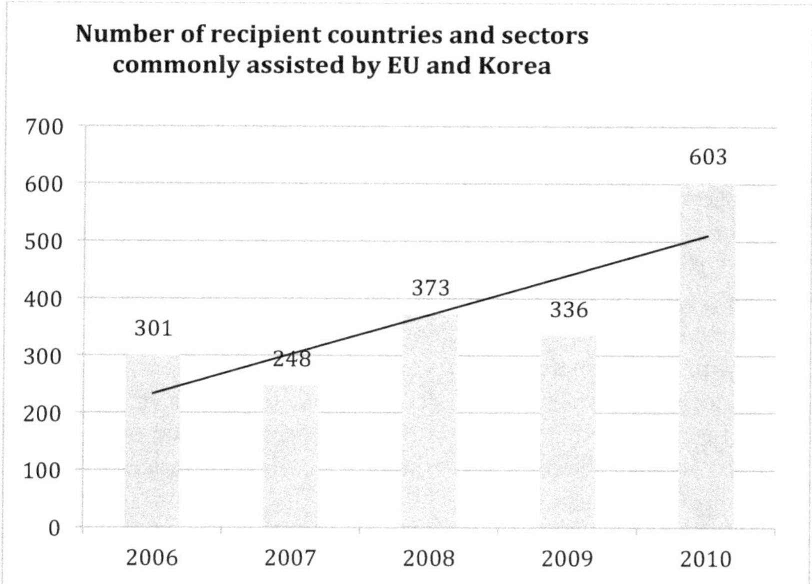

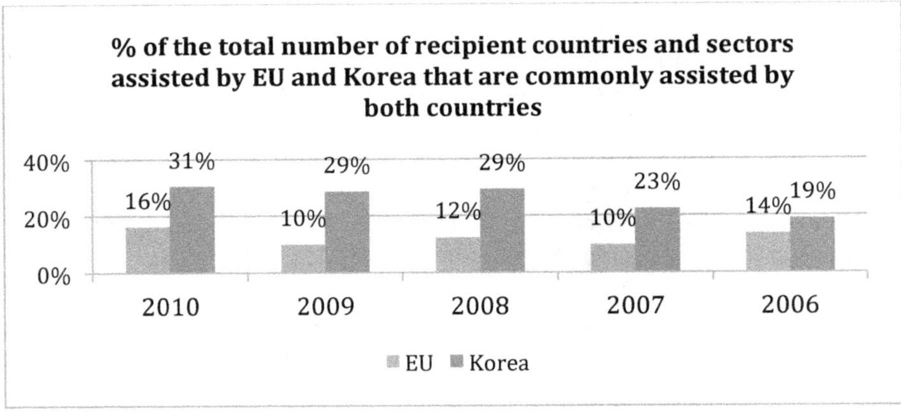

Source: DAC/OECD - Creditor Reporting System, 2012

4.2. EU-Korea Collaboration from a human rights perspective

Notwithstanding this potential for collaboration there is also a distinct and fundamental difference in approach between the two actors, most notably with regard to their position ont eh promotion of human rights. The EU's desire to "improve the tools of global governance" (European Commission, 2003) has led it to take a vested pursuit in becoming an active and leading actor in global economic development. The EU has had a role in development and development cooperation since the beginning of the European project. Over the years its role in development cooperation has steadily grown and its strategies have changed. Following the 2005 European Consensus on Development, EU development policy is required to improve the impact and effectiveness of global development assistance, progressing towards achieving the MDGs and the Paris and Accra Action Agenda targets. Article 21(2)(d) of the Treaty on the European Union (TEU) lists as one of the objectives of EU external action to "foster the sustainable economic, social and environmental development of developing countries, with the primary aim of eradicating poverty". The Treaty on the Functioning of the European Union (TFEU) stipulates that development cooperation is to be conducted in a framework of the principles and objectives of the EU's external action, which includes the promotion of democracy, the rule of law, and respect for human rights[9].

[9] Art. 208(1) TFEU states: 'Union policy in the field of development cooperation shall be conducted within the framework of the principles and objectives of the Union's external action. The Union's development cooperation policy and that of the Member States complement and reinforce each other.' Art. 21 TEU.

In recent years, the EU has made efforts to explicitly tie together development and human rights goals (Bartels, 2008:128) and develop a new agenda for development cooperation. The European Commission's (2011) *Agenda for Change* recognizes that "the objectives of development, democracy, human rights, good governance and security are intertwined" and the EU acknowledges that "sustainable development includes good governance, human rights and political, economic, social and environmental aspects"[10]. The Commission's communication 'Human Rights and Democracy at the Heart of EU External Action' underlines the need to develop a Human Rights Based Approach ('HRBA') to "ensure that human rights and democracy are reflected across the entire development cooperation process". (Commission, 2011:11) The development of a comprehensive "human rights based approach" for EU development policy was reiterated with the adoption of the EU Strategic Framework and Action Plan on Human Rights and Democracy ('EU Action Plan') by the EU's Foreign Affairs Council in 2012. These series of documents and policy actions put human rights central in the development cooperation policy of the EU. One can distinguish three distinct but interrelated policy strategies, adopted by the Commission to integrate human rights in development cooperation (D'Hollander et al., 2014). First, human rights have been integrated as part of the EU's policy on aid allocation. The EU applies 'negative' and 'positive' conditionalities whereby partner governments loose or gain access to development funding depending on their commitment to, and track record on, complying with human rights obligations and adhering to democratic governance. The rationale behind this strategy emphasizes the EU's financial 'leverage' to influence governance in partner countries. Second, the Commission promotes 'linkages' and projects which aim to support 'bottom-up' processes of citizens demanding human rights protection or democratic governance. (Lavenex and Schimmelfennig, 2011) This strategy of 'positive support' consists of 'enabling and empowering' actors, mainly civil society organizations ('CSOs'). This approach is also to a limited degree used by Korea. As the analysis above shows Korean development cooperation does invest, although only to a limited degree, in government-supporting and civil society targeted projects (see graph 13 above). More recently, a third approach towards integrating human rights 'horizontally' into all aspect of development planning has emerged on the agenda of the Commission. The concepts of 'mainstreaming human rights' and applying a HRBA aim to embed human rights issues and broader human rights based principles or

---

[10] Joint Statement by the Council and the Representatives of the governments of the Member States meeting within the Council, the European Parliament and the Commission on European Union Development Policy: 'The European Consensus' (2006/C 46/01), 2006, § 7.

standards in such areas of development cooperation as education, health care, agricultural development and food security, energy, infrastructure and water provision. The latter approach is a especially relevant from a collaboration perspective since it can be an enabling or constraining factor for collaboration. Enabling, if all actors align on the same approach. Constraining when actors take a different perspective (Marx et al., 2015).

Mainstreaming human rights and a HRBA are two policy concepts which aim for a systematic integration of human rights in development. This 'transversal integration' implies that human rights are accounted for in all sectors of development cooperation, including 'apolitical' service delivery or technical assistance programmes in agriculture, education, health services or infrastructure. These policy concepts require donors to develop internal measures for adjusting their policies to ensure greater alignment with human rights obligations, standards and principles. Besides specific measures or procedures, it is also about fostering an 'institutional culture' towards this end. (OECD/World bank, 2013:77; Marx et al., 2015) The EU Action Plan has signaled a commitment to the systematic integration of human rights in development policy, to be achieved through the development of a HRBA (Council of the European Union, 2012:10). While the concept of a HRBA is not new, the Commission had not formally adopted such a far-reaching approach. This approach is also adopted by several leading EU member states donors such as Sweden (OECD/World bank, 2013) A HRBA is often presented as a comprehensive 'vision' that places the fulfilment of political, civil, but also economic, social and cultural rights central. A HRBA redefines development in terms of 'rights-holders' and 'duty-bearers'[11]. Fostering processes of citizen-state accountability, within the limits set by the human rights framework, becomes a central preoccupation in development cooperation policy. While the concept of a HRBA has been endorsed by a range of development actors, there is little consensus on its direct operational implications. Rather than a set of concrete measures, a HRBA can be interpreted as a 'strategic' way of rethinking partnerships and prioritizing issues, often enhancing the 'political' dimensions of development cooperation (Hickey and Mitlin, 2014). The basic idea behind developing a HRBA policy is based on the general idea that human rights should be accounted for in each area of development cooperation, and in each phase of the development process. Most donors present a HRBA as an encompassing, holistic vision on development.

[11] See Statement on a Common Understanding of a Human Rights-Based Approach to Development Cooperation, Stamford Interagency Workshop on a Human Rights-Based approach in the Context of UN Reform, 2003.

The integration of a HRBA has been largely understood as working towards several human rights-based principles, including participation, empowerment, non-discrimination, transparency, accountability, and rule of law in the planning and programming of development cooperation interventions. This approach is absent in Korean development cooperation and might constitute a hurdle for further collaboration. In the quest of advancing this approach the EU is mainly looking for partner who align with this human-rights based vision to development cooperation, not only in their relation with implementing partner organizations such as UN agencies and NGOs, but also in relation to other donors. Particularly when engaging in multi-donor initiatives such as pooled funding in the context of a sector-wide approach, a degree of consensus among donors is needed to operationalize a HRBA. Disagreement on the application of a HRBA might hinder collaboration. From this perspective further collaboration between the EU and Korea might be more difficult. It is still to early to assess whether a HRBA will constitute hurdles for collaboration, but is one issue to follow up closely in the coming years.

Conclusion

In this chapter the development cooperation policies of the Republic of Korea were analyzed and compared to those of the European Union with the aim of identifying the differences and similarities between them. Such an analysis can contribute to a better understanding of the possibilities and limitations of further cooperation in the field of development cooperation. The chapter analyzed in depth the differences and similarities with regard to types of aid, focus areas and focus countries.

Development cooperation programming of both actors were analyze highlighting a significant degree of alignment. In this sense, opportunities for further collaboration between these actors are possible. In addition, Korea can offer unique experience to the EU. As a recipient country it made good use of foreign aid in order to promote economic and social development. Today, the Republic of Korea is figuring among the most developed countries in the world.

However the chapter also identified possible stumbling blocks for collaboration. Most notably, the turn towards a Human Rights Based Approach to development cooperation which is adopted by the EU but not Korea might constitute an impediment to cooperation. This is not to argue that Korea is opposed to human rights, but a HRBA to development cooperation does imply a very significant strategic and organizational shift in development co-operation policy which is promoted by the EU, but not by Korea.

Bibliography

AMSDEN, A. (2002) *The Rise of "The Rest". Challenges to the West from Late-Industrializing Economies.* Oxford: Oxford University Press.

BARTELS, L. (2008) The Trade and Development Policy of the European Union. In M. CREMONA (ed.), *Developments in EU External Relations Law.* Oxford Oxford University: Press.

CHUN, H.-M., MUNYI, E.-N., LEE, H. (2010) South Korea as an Emerging Donor: Challenges and Changes on its Entering OECD/DAC. *Journal of International Development*, 22: 788-802.

COUNCIL OF THE EUROPEAN UNION (2009) *Council conclusions on Policy Coherence for Development (PCD).* 2974th External Relations Council meeting, Brussels, 17 November. <http://ec.europa.eu/europeaid/where/asia/regional-cooperation/support-regional-integration/asem/documents/council_conclusions_ 17th_november_2009.pdf>.

D'HOLLANDER, D., MARX, A. and WOUTERS, J. (2014) Integrating Human Rights in EU Development Cooperation Policy: Achievements and Challenges. *European Yearbook of Human Rights*, 14: 255-268.

ECONOMIC DEVELOPMENT COOPERATION FUND (ECDF) (2010) *Annual Report. Korea, 2010.* <http://www.edcfkorea.go.kr/edcfeng/index.jsp>.

EVANS, P. (1995) *Embedded Autonomy.* Princeton: Princeton University Press.

EUROPEAN COMMISSION (2003) *Communication from the Commission to the Council and the European Parliament. The European Union and the United Nations: The choice of Multilateralism.* Brussels 10 September. COM (2003)526 Final.

EUROPEAN COMMISSION (2006) *The European Consensus on Development.* Official Journal of the European Union, 2006/C 46/01.

EUROPEAN COMMISSION (2011) *Increasing the impact of EU Development Policy: an Agenda for Change.* Brussels, 13 October. <http://eur-lex.europa.eu/LexUriServ/LexUriServ.do?uri=COM:2011:0637:FIN:EN:PDF>.

EUROPEAN PARLIAMENT (2012) *The Role of BRICS in the Developing World.* Directorate-General for External Policies of the Union. European Union, Brussels.

EUROPEAN COMMISSION (2007) *EU Code of Conduct on Division of labour in Development Policy.* Communication from the Commission to the Council and the European Parliament. Brussels, 28 February.

GHOSH, A., KHARAS, H. (2011) The Money Trail: Ranking Donor Transparency in Foreign Aid. *World Development.* 39(11): 1918-1929.

HACKENESCH, C. (2011*) European Good Governance Policies Meet China in Africa: Insights from Angola and Ethiopia*. European Development Co-operation to 2020 (EDC2020) consortium project. Available at: <www.edc2020.eu>.

HICKEY, S., MITLIN D. (2014) The Potential and Pitfall of Rights-based Approaches to Development. In S. HICKEY, D. MITLIN (eds), *Rights-based Approaches to Development; Exploring the Potential and Pitffals*. Sterling: Kumarian Press.

HLF4 – 4TH HIGH LEVEL FORUM ON AID EFFECTIVENESS (2011) South-south and triangular cooperation: unlocking the potential of horizontal partnerships for better development outcomes. 29 Nov.-1 Dec., Busan, Korea.

JERVE, A.M. (2007) *Asian Models for Aid: Is There a Non-Western Approach to Development Assistance?* Summary record of seminar held in Oslo, December 2006, Bergen: Chr. Michelsen Institute (CMI Report R 2007: 12). <http://www.cmi.no/publications/ publication/?2767=asian-models-for-aid>.

KHARAS H. (2007) The new reality of aid' Presented at Brookings Blum Roundtable. <http://www.brookings.edu/~/media/Files/rc/papers/2007/08aid_kharas/08aid_kharas.pdf>.

KHARAS, H., ROGERSON, A. (2012) *Horizon 2025: creative destruction in the aid industry*. Overseas Development Institute, July 2012.

KEOHANE, R.O., MACEDO, S., MORAVCSIK, A. (2009) Democracy-Enhancing Multilateralism. *International Organization*, 63, winter edition: 1-31.

KEUKELEIRE S., BRUYNINCKX H. (2011) The European Union, the BRIC's and the emerging new world order. In: C. HILL, & M. SMITH (eds), *International Relations and the European Union*. Oxford: Oxford University Press.

KIM, J.-Y. (2011) Foreign Aid and Economic Development: The Success Story of South Korea. *Pacific Focus*. 26(2): 260-286.

KIM, S.-Y. (2011) Bridging Troubled Worlds? An Analysis of the Ethical Case for South Korea Aid. *Journal of International Development*, 23: 802-822.

LAVANEX, S., SCHIMMELFENNIG F. (2011) EU democracy promotion in the neighbourhood: from leverage to governance? *Democratization*, 18(4): 885–909.

MARX, A., KITAOKA, K., MACGILLIVRAY, A. (2011) Private Sector Development, Knowledge Management and Networks. In UNIDO, *Networks for Prosperity. Achieving Millennium Development Goals through Knowledge Sharing*. Vienna: UNIDO.

MARX, A., MCINERNEY-LANKFORD, S., WOUTERS, J., D'HOLLANDER, D. (2015) Human Rights and Service Delivery: A Review of Current Policies, Practices and Challenges. *World Bank Legal Review*, vol. 6: 39-58.

MARX, A., SOARES J. (2013) South-Korea from recipient to DAC donor. Assessing Korea's Development Cooperation Policy. *International Development Policy*. 5(1):107-142.

MAWDSLEY, E. (2012) The Changing geographies of foreign aid and development cooperation: contributions from gift theory. *Transactions of the Institute of British Geographers*. 37(2): 256-272.

MILNER, H.V., TINGLEY, D.H. (2011) The Choice for Multilateralism: Foreign Aid and American Foreign Policy. APSA 2011 Annual Meeting Paper. Available at SSRN: <http://ssrn.com/abstract=1900147>.

MUNGCAL, I. (2012) For South Korea, aid to Uganda marks a trend. Devex. <http://www.devex.com/en/news/south-korea-and-its-ODA-spending-in-uganda/78856>.

OECD (2008) *Development co-operation of the republic of Korea: DAC* Special Review. OECD, Paris.

OECD (2011) DAC *Report on Multilateral Aid*. OECD, Paris.

OECD (2012) OECD Stats. (Database). <http://stats.oecd.org/Index.aspx>.

OECD (2012b) *European Union: Development Assistance* Committee (DAC) Peer Review 2012, OECD, Paris.

SLAUGHTER, A. (2004) *A New World Order: Government Networks and the Disaggregated State*. Princeton: Princeton University Press.

SLAUGHTER, A., ZARING, D. (2006) Networking goes international: An update. *Annual Review of Law and Social Science*. 2: 211-229.

THE REALITY OF AID (2008) *Reality of Aid 2008 country report: Republic of Korea*. <http://www.realityofaid.org/>.

UNITED NATIONS ECONOMIC AND SOCIAL COUNCIL (ECOSOC) (2008) *Trends in South-South and triangular development cooperation*. April. <http://www.un.org/en/ecosoc/newfunct/pdf/dcf%20bangkok%20meeting.pdf>.

WALZ, J., RAMACHANDRAN, V. (2010) *Brave New World: A Literature Review of Emerging Donors and the Changing Nature of Foreign Assistance*. Working paper 273, Center for Global Development, November.

UNIDO and LEUVEN CENTRE FOR GLOBAL GOVERNANCE STUDIES (2011) *Networks for Prosperity. Achieving Millennium Development Goals through Knowledge Sharing*. Vienna: UNIDO.

YAMOUSSOUKRO (2008) *Yamoussoukro Consensus on South-South Cooperation*. Twelfth Session of the Intergovernmental Follow-up and Cooperation Committee on Economic Cooperation among Developing Countries Yamoussoukro, Côte d'Ivoire, 10-13 June. <http://www.g77.org/ifcc12/Yamoussoukro_Consensus.pdf>.

Concluding remarks

A complex of effects and their consequences in the field of Asian and European official Development Assistance (ODA) and the development process

Thierry AMOUGOU

> *Foreign aid is a method by which United States maintains a position of influence and control around the world* (President John Kennedy to the Economic Club in 1961).

As far as these concluding remarks are concerned, the paramount challenge to overcome is to find and to say something new after such a enriched symposium which the topic has been turn in all directions by many eminent experts, lecturers and researchers. One can conclude a symposium in two manners. The first one, the simplest, is to repeat exactly what all the presentations have analyzed, discussed and found. The second one consists of a new development based on the symposium's presentations and discussions by trying to enlarge the topic with new questions. I will try to apply the second strategy. Thus these concluding remarks are mainly divided into four main parts:

1. Asian and European ODA are facing the same international conjuncture effect (similarities).

2. The cyclical effect of economic prosperity of capitalism (specificities).

3. Convergences by different instruments.

4. What about development, the main paradigm of development aid and a possible trilateral cooperation?

1. Asian and European ODA are facing the same international conjuncture effect

The international aid architecture has changed since the end of the cold war and the triumph of the neoliberal development approach. Which indicates that Asian and European ODA are facing the same international conjunctual effect whose principal components are:

1. The end of the cold war as a principal parameter entailing the dominant approach of ODA as a geopolitical instrument of European and Asian countries.

2. The extension of the international aid market with the arrival of former communist states in the aid field as an addition aid demand with the same level of aid supply.

3. The change in the idea of Sub-Saharan African countries being the first and prior destination of ODA.

4. The high level of political aid conditionality induced both in the supply and the demand side of aid by structural adjustment programs.

5. The great fears of the 21st century: HIV/AIDS, international terrorism, illegal immigration, unsustainable development, extreme poverty and social inequalities.

6. The Paris declaration of 2005: the shift from the "donorship model" to "ownership model".

7. The Busan Partnership for effective development cooperation.

8. The shift of many former south countries from the demand side of the international market of aid to the supply side: which is called nowadays emergent donors.

9. The multiplication of aid management's instruments.

10. The birth of several laws on international development cooperation (the Netherlands, Switzerland, Belgium...).

11. The arrival of private donors as the Foundation Bill and Melinda Gates.

2. The cyclical effect of economic prosperity of capitalism

Two aspects amongst others can highlight the principal specificity of Asian countries' model of aid.

The first one is that many Asian countries are nowadays emergent states characterized by the fact that they are embedding the new gravity center of the world capital accumulation when European countries are declining in capital accumulation. The consequence of this asymmetric economic situation is the fact that European countries do not have capital resources in order to stay more offensive in the international aid area: that is the cyclical effect of the economic prosperity of capitalism.

The second aspect includes different strategies. European countries are trying to develop poor countries with a vertical model of development cooperation. The logic of this vertical model is to induce indirect and long-term development effects by changing poor countries' institutions, structures and governance practices. That is why democracy and good governance are very important in the CAD conditions' access to European aid. The extension of the European cultural and political model of development by aid assistance in poor countries is then one of the CAD's main targets.

On the other hand, Asian countries are innovating with a strategy of horizontal development cooperation. That is to say, donors and recipients are not considered to have different status but to be at the same level as actors in cooperation. Thus, there is no conditionality imposed to underdeveloped countries as keys' access to Asian Aid development Assistance. So the aim here is not to extend the Asian cultural and political development model but to reach immediate goals in both sides by a direct development effect. In details one can pin up the following aspects that characterized the specificity of the Asian strategy of aid:

1. Political conditionality is very low: for instance, China wants nothing but the non-recognition of Taiwan and not to permit Japan to become a permanent member of the United Nations Security Council.

2. Economic and political conditions are put together in the European strategy of Aid supply conditions in order to promote democracy and human rights in poor countries. That is not systematically the situation in the Asian approaches and implementation of ODA.

3. There is no Asian global strategy, approaches of development and aid implementations as the European with CAD.

4. The increasing of Asian countries demand of raw materials permits them to diversify their Aid's package to poor countries.

5. Asian countries' economic prosperity is giving them a huge financial capacity to offer better conditions of cooperation to poor countries.

6. Many Asian countries like China do not have a colonial history with poor countries as European countries with African countries.

7. China for instance can do all what European countries are doing to monitor and improve their ODA; yet European countries do not have the financial ca-

pacity and the proper right to do what China is doing for instance in Africa by putting together aid and trade in the same contracts.

8. The financial capacity, the win/win and pragmatic aid strategy of China is a kind of a comparative advantage that this country approaches and implementations have on European one. So an eviction of the European strategy of ODA exists in many areas.

9. Aid evaluations are systematized in the European strategy of ODA but not in the Asian strategy of ODA.

3. Convergences by different instruments

Every Asian and European donor are looking forward to maximize the political, the ideological, the economical and the geopolitical impact of their own aid. How? by doing innovations on the design of aid. Thus one can talk about a design effect of aid with political, economic, geopolitical and ideological impact. The design of aid is using the following elements and relations to maximize its effects for the donor side:

1. History relations matter a lot on ODA.

2. The highlights of the official solidarity aspects of ODA are put forward.

3. The use of forums as political canals to discuss with the demand side of the international market of aid: China/Africa Forum and Europe/Africa Forum for instance.

4. The use of many skills as aid innovative instrument: budgetary aid, program aid, project aid, bilateral aid, multilateral aid and bilateral decentralized aid for the European Countries and hybrid contract (aid and trade for China), batter between raw materials and investment for China.

5. The promotion of liberty in the demand side of the international aid market by two different models of liberty: the European model is promoting liberty by the promotion of human rights and democracy when China is promoting liberty by refusing to promote democracy and human rights.

6. The promotion of aid efficiency by systematic evaluation for the European countries and by direct development effect by China.

7. The promotion of aid efficiency by diversification for China (states, firms, migrants, trade unions) but by specialization for Europe.

4. What about development, the main paradigm of development Aid and a possible trilateral cooperation?

A main problem that we cannot throw away while speaking of Official Development Assistance is to talk about development itself. In other words, it is not relevant to discuss about the Asian and the European strategies about Aid without a critical view of what development is all about?

In my opinion, to talk about aid efficiency is useless if poor countries are still strongly oriented in the dominant neoliberal model of development. Before the study of the efficiency of ODA, one must ask the following question: what can official development assistance do what in poor countries?

According to the symposium my strong impression is that we are not talking about aid for development but more about aid as a geopolitical, diplomatic and economic instrument for the donors' world hegemony strategy. That is not development but how to use the development demand to improve geopolitical and economical influences of donors.

Nowadays three paradigms are dominating the scientific research on development aid. The first model defended by Ignacy Sachs states that the developed world must augmented the level of aid development towards poor countries: The solution to reach a deep poor reduction is a paramount level of development aid. I think that Asian donors are largely closed of this model because they are in a positive conjuncture of capital accumulation.

The second model defended by William easterly and Dambisssa Moyo says that aid is a bad, fatal and a useless instrument for development: the solution to get many countries away for underdevelopment situation is to immediately stop aid: no European and Asian donor is following this model because the first aim of aid is not always the development of poor countries by that of donors strategic relations in a competitive world.

The third model defended by Esther Duflo and Bannerjee Abhijit tends to highlight the true, real and the main causes of extreme poverty in order to find the best instrument to struggle extreme poverty: several aspects of the European strategy are following this model inside Assistance Development Committee (CAD). The reason is that European countries are trying to be more efficient because they are facing a negative conjuncture in the cyclical trend of capitalist accumulation.

As far as trilateral cooperation is concerned, many trade-offs exist between the Asian approach and implementation and the European one. The Official Development Assistance cannot have a better development-effect in poor countries if there is no trilateral cooperation where one can put together the political conditionality of the European Strategy and the autonomy and pragmatism of the Asian Strategy: that is the challenge of our future if we want to unified aid development practices and politics supposing that we will not lose in flexibility if all the donors are applying the same strategy of official development assistance. But mains trade-off about possible trilateral aid cooperation are:

1. Evaluated strategy (transparency attitude in EU) versus non-evaluated strategy (state secret attitude).

2. Unified global strategy inside DAC versus fragmented strategy for Asian countries.

3. The link between one world strategy of ODA and flexibility.

4. More business model in Asia versus a more political model in Europe.

5. Aid with political conditions in Europe versus aid without political conditions or with low political conditions in Asia.

6. The link between ownership and political conditions.

7. The continuity of ODA as a sign of the failure of the development process in recipient countries since 1945.

Table of content

Recent evolution, persistent challenges and future direction of Taiwan's ODA and its comparison with European aid

Achevé d'imprimer par Corlet Numérique - 14110 Condé-sur-Noireau
N° d'Imprimeur : 129804 - Dépôt légal : juin 2016 - *Imprimé en France*

www.ingramcontent.com/pod-product-compliance
Lightning Source LLC
LaVergne TN
LVHW010939051026
849532LV00003B/1055
* 9 7 8 2 8 0 6 1 0 2 9 5 9 *